SHAKESPEARE'S

" —in the spicéd Indian air, by night,
Full often hath she gossip'd by my side.
And sat with me on Neptune's yellow sands."
II. i. 125-7.

A MIDSUMMER-NIGHT'S DREAM

EDITED BY

STANLEY WOOD, M.A.

(Editor of the Dinglewood Shakespeare Manuals)

London:

GEORGE GILL & SONS, LD.,

MINERVA HOUSE, PATERNOSTER SQUARE, E.C.4

First Edition, 1900.

*Twenty-three Editions and Impressions
to* 1935.

New Edition, 1937.

Reprinted December 1937.

Reprinted August 1938.

*Printed and Made in Great Britain by The Garden City Press Ltd.,
Letchworth, Herts.*

PREFACE.

THIS Edition of *A Midsummer Night's Dream* is intended to meet the requirements not only of candidates for all public examinations but also of all students who wish at the same time to gain a useful and lasting knowledge of the play and some training in the critical appreciation of the poet.

A distinctive feature of this, as of all the plays in the Oxford and Cambridge Edition, is the use of marginal notes separated from the text by a firm line. This means that, on the one hand the play can be read aloud in class without the reader's attention being distracted from the text, and on the other hand it can be read silently and with understanding by the student at a minimum expense of time in referring to explanatory notes.

Another feature which has earned the special approbation of teachers in the past is the very extensive use of quotations from the play in all the teaching parts of the book. This means that the student is not asked to take anything for granted ; statements are not made without their *raison d'être* being revealed. It also means that for purposes of revision these portions of the work can be studied apart from the text—a great saving of time.

In this revised edition of the play a few changes and additions have been made with the special idea of facilitating what is every teacher's aim, namely to assist young students to become lovers of Shakespeare rather than to be the storehouses of other people's critical knowledge. It has always been my endeavour to develop the student's individuality and power of critical selection.

To this end I have removed to one or other of the Appendices certain sections of the book which, in former editions, seemed to assume to themselves an undue importance by reason of their prominent position in the early pages of the book ; such sections, I mean, as might tend to overload the student with knowledge which could hardly be called educative and which would add but little to the genuine appreciation of the play.

The Examination Papers at the end have been revised and adapted to the improved style of question found in all the more recent examinations.

STANLEY WOOD.

CONTENTS

A MIDSUMMER-NIGHT'S DREAM

PART I. TYPES OF ENGLISH COMEDY.

A Midsummer Night's Dream is one of the earliest English comedies worthy of the name. It is interesting, therefore, to refer briefly to the origin of English comedy and its development by Shakespeare and his contemporaries. We shall see how vast a change was effected in this branch of the drama in a comparatively short time.

The earliest English plays, *miracle plays* or *miracles*, were connected with the church and were acted by the clergy as early as the 12th century. They were afterwards performed by trading companies of various towns, as Chester, Wakefield, Coventry, and York. Popular characters in these plays were Herod, and later, Hercules, types of the tyrant, as well as angels, demons, and souls. From about the reign of Henry VI. the miracle plays partly gave place to *Moralities*, which differed but little from the former class, but are of importance because it is in them that we first regularly see the Devil as a character with his attendant the *Vice*. The ordinary function of the Vice appears to have been to torment his master the Devil and this same Vice gradually developed into the Fool, who survived in the regular drama. The next step in advance towards Elizabethan comedy was made by John Heywood, who died in 1565, and whose *Interludes* were short farces, dealing with real men and women. The next influence that asserted itself was the "new learning" of Edward VI.'s reign. The earliest extant English comedy *Ralph Roister Doister*, written by Nicholas Udall in or about 1551, is an adaptation of Plautus. *Gammer Gurton's Needle*, a farce of a somewhat low order, was printed in 1575, and was the first English play acted at either university. After this the Italian drama began to exercise a strong influence upon English comedy and led to the introduction of characters and stories from classical mythology. Queen Elizabeth's liking for dramatic entertainments now led to the rapid progress of the drama. Of Shakespeare's immediate predecessors the following are the names of the more important. John Lyly (b. 1554) wrote his plays in prose and set the example of brisk and vigorous dialogue. Shakespeare was indebted to him, in respect both to subject and style in many of his plays. Next follow the "University Wits" Marlowe (1564-1593), Greene (1561-1592), Peele (1558-1598), Lodge (d. 1625), Nash (d. 1602), and Kyd. In the works of these dramatists we constantly see flashes which, as Mr. Saintsbury says, show *Hamlet* and *A Midsummer Night's Dream* in embryo. One of the peculiar features of the comedy of Shakespeare and some of his contemporaries is that, unlike the comedy of the Italian and Spanish Examples, it retained much of the mixed character of the Moralities and the Interludes. In the same play comedy and tragedy alternate as they do in real life. It was in consequence of this tradition that Shakespeare was able, without shocking the sense of propriety of his audience to introduce comic characters into such plays as *Hamlet*, *Othello*, and *King Lear*.

DESCRIPTION OF THE PLAY.

The play of *A Midsummer Night's Dream* is a sort of ideal dream and stands in a class by itself. Its very essence is irregularity and it follows no law but that of caprice. It most resembles a masque, but as we shall see it differs in important respects from a masque. Yet, in spite of its irregularities we may, by attentive study discover certain leading characteristics.

Harmonious blending of different elements. The play comprises four different histories :—that of Theseus and Hippolyta :—of the four Athenian lovers :—of the 'home-spun' actors :—and of the fairies. Here, indeed, are 'most dissimilar ingredients' which could not be blended without the aid of that magic which could not be copied. Shakespeare has invented the fairy machinery by means of which he has been able to blend together the apparently incongruous elements, the courtiers and the clowns. The complication of the plot, or plots, all or nearly all the actions of the characters, and the unravelling of the entanglements do not in *A Midsummer Night's Dream*, as they do in Shakespeare's other plays, proceed from the inner impulse of the actors, but all come from without. The fairies serve as motive forces for nearly all the other actors. Usurping the place of the classical god Cupid, they form the link of connection.

> "Upon the most superficial reading, we perceive that the actions in *A Midsummer Night's Dream*, still more than the characters themselves, are treated quite differently to those in other plays of Shakespeare. The great art of an underlying motive, his true magic wand, the poet has here quite laid aside. Instead of reasonable inducements, instead of natural impulses flowing from character and circumstance, caprice is master here. We meet with a double pair, who are entangled in strange mistakes, the motives to which we, however, seek for in vain in the nature of the actors themselves. . . . At first it is the warm season, the first night in May, the ghost-hour of the mystic powers, which heats the brain . . . then it is the power of Cupid who appears in the back-ground of the piece as a real character, who misleads the judgment and blinds the eyes, delighting in frivolous breach of faith. And last of all we see the lovers completely in the hand of the fairies, who ensnare their senses and bring them into that tumult of confusion, the unravelling of which, like the entanglement itself, is to come from without " (GERVINUS).

Another distinguishing feature of this play is the

Interfusion of the lyrical element. Lyric poetry, as the name implies (λύρα, lyre) is poetry originally intended to be accompanied by the lyre or by some other musical instrument. The term has come to signify any outburst in song which is composed under a strong impulse of emotion or inspiration. Shakespeare has not only given to *A Midsummer Night's Dream* a lyrical character, by interspersing songs here and there in the play, but, as Coleridge has said "the whole of *A Mid-*

summer Night's Dream is one continual specimen of the dramatized lyrical." To quote Verplanck—

" Its transitions are as rapid, and the images and scenes it presents to the imagination as unexpected and as remote from each other, as those of the boldest lyric; while it has also that highest perfection of the lyric art, the pervading unity of the poetic spirit—that continued glow of excited thought—which blends the whole rich and strange variety in one common effect of gay and dazzling brilliancy."

Not unconnected with this characteristic of the play is its

Dream-like character. We shall remark more fully upon this feature when we come to speak of the title of the play. For the present it is sufficient to point out that the play resembles a dream in its wonderful complications, its lawlessness, its ideality, and its disregard of the laws of time and place.

" Besides, the whole thing swarms with enchantment: all the sweet witchery of Shakespeare's sweet genius is concentrated in it, yet disposed with so subtle and cunning a hand, that we can as little grasp it as get away from it : its charms, like those of a summer evening, are such as we may see and feel, but cannot locate or define ; cannot say they are here, or they are there : the moment we yield ourselves up to them, they seem to be everywhere : the moment we go to master them, they seem to be nowhere " (HUDSON).

Another distinctive and important feature of the play is its

Resemblance to a Masque. In *A Midsummer Night's Dream* the masque " imperceptibly glides into comedy," but it still retains many of the distinctive features of the more showy form of entertainment. It resembles a masque in the following points :

1. In its general lyrical character, and in the special introduction of music and dances.
2. In the fact that in this play the delineation of character is a secondary object, and that there are no apparent motives for the action which is carried on by external causes.
3. In its adaptability for out-of-door representation.
4. In the predominance of classical and mythical names.
5. In the inclusion of the farcical interlude or anti-masque. The love-stories of Theseus and the Athenian youths form a kind of frame-work into which the anti-masque is inserted, the fairies corresponding to some extent with the choruses of dances of the regular Masque.
6. In the fact that the play has all the appearance of having been originally intended, like the masques, for a private entertainment, possibly to celebrate the marriage of some noble. On this point see the Notes on V. i. 93 and 420.

It differs from a Masque in the following respects :

1. It exhibits none of the profound classical learning which we associate with the regular masque as produced by Ben Jonson. Shakespeare has popularised the subject, and has borrowed from classical fable little more than a few names. The fairies themselves are creatures of mediæval fable.
2. The anti-masque is genuinely English. Its clowns are no " spirits, witches, Æthiopes, pigmies, turquets, nymphs," and the like, but common English tradesmen remarkable principally for their lack of imagination and their earnestness of purpose.

THE HUMOUR OF THE PLAY.

The comic element of the Play is, of course, to be found principally in those scenes in which Bottom and his fellow craftsmen display their happy imbecility, and these scenes are in themselves so irresistibly comic, that we can hardly feel surprise when we read that "The merry conceited .humours of Bottom the Weaver," were, at the period of the Restoration converted into a farce, and acted apart from the rest of the play. The incongruity between what the actors really are, and what they ought to be, or pretend to be, is the very essence of what is laughable; and Bottom's absolute unconsciousness of what others think of him, very much heightens the absurdity of the situation. But they very greatly erred who thought that in separating these comic scenes from their proper framework, they were extracting the best part of the humour of the play. Shakespeare hardly ever contents himself with what is merely comical; most often he carries his comedy to the verge of the serious, and mingles his mirth with beauty or pathos as in *A Midsummer Night's Dream*, and sometimes even with tragedy. This is the way of real life. Dr. Dowden reminds us that : " The traditions of the English drama had favoured the juxtaposition of the serious and comic; but it was reserved for Shakespeare to make each a part of the other; to interpenetrate tragedy with comedy, and comedy with tragic earnestness." It is when the comic characters, Bottom and his *confrères* pass into the serious parts of the drama that they really infect it with the element of humour. Nothing, for instance, could be more powerfully humorous than the scene in which Titania bids her fairies minister to the desires of Bottom. "Shakespeare's humour has enriched itself by coalescing with the fancy. The comic is here no longer purely comic; it is a mingled web, shot through with the beautiful."

"The clowns in the *Midsummer Night's Dream* are raised in the self-satisfaction and assurance of their actions above all disappointment in success, and are therefore insensible to the mischievous joy of others; with them nothing fails, neither their aims nor their humour . . . . the comic power of these characters survives all changes of taste; these types of folly and absurdity are completely dyed with the comic colours of nature, indelible for all ages " (GERVINUS).

CONCERNING THE TITLE.

In considering the fitness of the title which Shakespeare has chosen for his fairy comedy, we naturally ask ourselves two questions, viz. "Why is it called a Dream ? " and " Why is the dream associated with Midsummer Night ? " According to our ability or otherwise to answer satisfactorily . these two questions, we form our opinion of the fitness of the title.

The Play regarded as a Dream. Shakespeare has made it very evident by numerous passages in the play that he did not intend this comedy to be regarded from the same point of view as other plays, or to be judged by the laws that govern the drama of character and life. At the end of the play, in the lines which stand in the place and bear the character of an Epilogue, Puck asks his audience to think :

> *" That you have but slumber'd here*
> *While these visions did appear.*
> *And this weak and idle theme,*
> *No more yielding but a dream,*
> *Gentles do not reprehend "*   (V. i. 428).

The actions of the principal characters during the greater part of the play are performed whilst under the influence of illusion and enchantment, so that the actors themselves are no more masters and mistresses of their own thoughts, words, and conduct than if they were actually

> *" Begot of nothing but vain fantasy*
> *Which is as thin of substance as the air*
> *And more inconstant than the wind "*
> (*Rom. and Jul.,* IV. i.).

Titania, on being released from the spell that had been laid upon her, exclaims : " What visions have I seen! " (IV. i. 77). Lysander, Hermia, Helena and Demetrius relate their dreams to the Duke and Duchess, and Theseus regards them as " antique fables and fairy toys." The delicate and airy verse, the beautiful and tender imagery, the shadowy characterisation and the atmosphere of fairy-land all fit in admirably with the idea of a dream.

Bottom himself is solid and substantial enough, but even he has " had a most rare vision," a " dream past the wit of man to say what dream it was." As we have already remarked (p. ix.), one of the characteristic features of the comedy is that in it Shakespeare has given free play to his fancy and has not intended to convey any moral lesson, and though commentators often exert themselves to find the moral that points the tale, we ourselves are inclined to agree with Bottom when, on his awakening, he affirms that " man is but an ass, if he go about to expound this dream " (IV. i. 207).

"They (the fairies) are indeed a sort of personified dreams ; and so the Poet places them in a kindly or at least harmless relation to mortals as the bringers of dreams. Their very kingdom is located in the aromatic, flower-scented Indies, a land where mortals are supposed to live in a half-dreamy state. From thence they come, " following darkness," just as dreams naturally do ; or, as Oberon words it, " tripping after the night's shade, swifter than the wandering moon." . . . They love the dusk and the twilight, because this is the best dreaming time, whether the dreamer be asleep or awake. . . . It is a very noteworthy point that all their power or influence over the hearts and actions of mortals works through the medium of dreams, or of such fancies as are most allied to dreams. So that their whole inner character is fashioned in harmony with their external function " (HUDSON).

" I am convinced that Shakespeare availed himself of the title of this play in his own mind, and worked upon it as a dream throughout, but especially, and, perhaps, unpleasingly, in this broad determination of ungrateful treachery in Helena, so undisguisedly avowed to herself, and this too, after the witty cool philosophizing that precedes " (COLERIDGE on Helena's Speech, " I will go tell him of fair Hermia's flight," etc., I 1. 246).

Midsummer Night Associations.

We have seen that the play is appropriately called a Dream and now enquire, " Why, when the action of the play belongs to the end of April and the first of May, should it be associated in the title with Mid-summer Night" (June 24th or St. John the Baptist's Day). Two reasons suggest themselves in answer to our query.

1. It may have been specially written for performance on that day.
2. There may be in the play something specially connected with or recalling the traditionary observances of that day.

In view of our ignorance of the actual occasion (if any) for which the play was composed, and in the absence of definite information as to the date of the composition of the play we are unable to offer any argument in support of the first view except this ; that judging from its masque-like character it appears to have been written for some particular occasion and that (as is doubtless the fact in the case of *Twelfth Night* and *A Winter's Tale*, a tale " to beguile the dreary leisure of a long winter evening "), it may have derived its title from that occasion.

With respect to the second view we must take particular notice of two things (1) that many superstitious notions of a highly fanciful character were formally connected with St. John's Eve, and (2) that Shakespeare himself seems to allude to such superstitions in *Twelfth Night* when Olivia describes the strange behaviour of Malvolio as " very midsummer madness." Consequently, whatever may have been the circumstance that led Shakespeare to adopt his title for the play, we are justified in saying that the title chosen is an exceedingly appropriate one.

The " *Midsummer-Night's Dream* appears to have been so called because its exhibition was to take place on that night, for the *time of action* of the piece itself is the vigil of May-Day, as is that of the *Winter's Tale* the period of sheep-shearing. It is probable also, as Mr. Steevens has observed, that Shakespeare might have been influenced in his choice of the fanciful machinery of this play, by the recollection of the proverb attached to the season (the proverbial " midsummer madness ") . . . an adage founded on the common opinion, that the brain, being heated by the intensity of the sun's rays, was more susceptible of those flights of imagination which border on insanity than at any other period of the year " (DRAKE).

" Some of the superstitious notions connected with St. John's Eve are of a highly fanciful nature. The Irish believe that the souls of all people on this night leave their bodies, and wander to the place, by land or sea, where death shall finally separate them from the tenement of clay. . . In England, and perhaps in other countries also, it was believed that, if any one sat up fasting all night in the church porch, he would see the spirits of those who were to die in the parish during the ensuing twelvemonths come and knock at the church door, in the order and succession in which they were to die. . . . Young women likewise sought for what they called pieces of coal, but in reality, certain hard black, dead roots, often found under the living mugwort, designing to place these under their pillows, that they might dream of their lovers. . . . The observance of St. John's Day seems to have been, by a practical bull, confined mainly to the previous evening " (CHAMBERS' " Book of Days ").

ON CHARACTERISATION.

Shakespeare is distinguished from all his contemporaries (and from all subsequent dramatists) by his skill in depicting character. This excellence is not so apparent in *A Midsummer Night's Dream* as it is in his later plays, for, not only had he not yet developed his powers to their full extent, but he is prescribed by the nature of the play itself, its fantastical dream-like quality, in which the action is usually prompted from outside and does not so much proceed from the characters of the *dramatis personæ* as it does in his great tragedies and, to a less extent, in his later comedies.

Nevertheless, even in this early play Shakespeare has portrayed some unforgettable characters which are completely individual, while others, without being individualistic are always true to type. Sir John Squire has written, " Characters swarmed from Shakespeare's brain as (though mostly in the easier form of caricatures) they swarmed from Dickens's ; and he had an unparalleled power, by virtue of imagination, genius and craftsman's cunning, of making them comprehensible and memorable in a few sentences, of giving the mind the significant bones from which the whole skeleton could be automatically deduced."*

For the student of Shakespeare's plays the following simple rules will be found useful in his early attempts at indicating the nature of a character.

1. Take into account what is said of him (or her) by other characters in the play, at the same time having regard to the speaker whether he is friend or enemy or neutral.

2. Consider what the person says of himself, especially in soliloquy.

3. Watch him in action and draw conclusions.

4. Look out for contrasts. Characters in Shakespeare are often found in pairs and their contrast may be illuminating, e.g. Hermia and Helena.

5. Note carefully any descriptions of the person of the character.

6. Observe tricks of speech, remembering that Shakespeare's persons usually speak in character. The duke does not speak as does the carpenter, nor the fairy as the mortal. Everything that Bottom says contributes towards our knowledge of him.

7. Put yourself in the place of each character in the play, imagine his feelings, try to re-live his life, get to know him as you know (or think you know), yourself.

8. Do not think you must agree with everything that is said in the following pages on the characters. It is sometimes good to practise disagreement, and finding your reasons in the play.

* *Shakespeare as a Dramatist* by Sir John Squire. Cassell and Company.

THE CHARACTERS OF THE PLAY.

THESEUS.

Compared with King Henry the Fifth. Shakespeare's Theseus is really a romantic rather than a classical personage. As Duke of Athens he reminds us somewhat of Henry V., King of England. He appears to be Shakespeare's earlier conception of his ideal king. Like King Henry he is a great warrior and a ruler possessed of much dignity and majesty. He bears some resemblance to the English king also in the fact that his youth had been rather wild and dissolute (II. i. 76-81). But that was when he was still under the influence of the fairies, an influence which passed away before the period of his life presented in the play. Here we see him as

A Soldier and a Man of Action, who wooed his wife with his sword, and "won her love doing her injuries" (I. i. 16), and who in times of peace loved to hear the music of his hounds. His career has been one of conquest (V. i. 51, 93-100), his triumphs have been celebrated in set orations prepared by great scholars who have "shivered and looked pale" in the presence of so famous a soldier. But he, being a man of action rather than of words, who could appreciate any service done him "when simpleness and duty tender it," has a preference for "the modesty of fearful duty" rather than for

> "*The rattling tongue*
> *Of saucy and audacious eloquence*"　　　　　(V. i. 102).

A practical man of a high order of intelligence. His love for Hippolyta is no romantic passion like the loves of his young Athenian friends. Indeed, although he makes love at the beginning of the play in a dignified and stately fashion, yet we find him later comparing together "the lunatic, the lover and the poet," apparently without any idea of including himself in his description (V. i. 7-20). He is certainly not unimaginative, but he keeps his imagination well under control and therein differs from those who "are of imagination all compact." He cannot believe in the visions and dreams of the lovers in the forest, in "these antique fables, nor these fairy toys." His life has been too full of action and hard work to allow him to let his imagination run riot, but he has a very true idea of "the pleasures of the imagination." Unlike Hippolyta, to whom the Interlude is simply "the silliest stuff that ever I heard," he can find enjoyment in the honest attempts of imperfect actors. He can "piece out their imperfections with his thoughts." To him "the best in this kind are but shadows and the worst are no worse if imagination amend them."

He possesses a kindly and generous disposition, and shows a strong inclination to make everyone happy in his kingdom. He proclaims a fortnight's holiday on the occasion of his marriage. He endeavours to persuade Hermia to submit to her father's will, and though, being himself a ruler, he naturally upholds the Athenian law, yet we feel all the time that his sympathies are with the daughter rather than with the stern parent. When Demetrius expresses his determination to be true to his first love, the Duke unhesitatingly overrides the will of Egeus. During the Interlude he apologises for the imperfections of the actors, takes in very good part the amusing corrections of Bottom (V. i. 184-7 and 354-5), and sends away the players delighted with the assurance that it is "a fine tragedy, and very notably discharged."

It has often been said that in depicting the character of Theseus, Shakespeare has been at no pains to describe an Athenian monarch of a pagan age, but has really painted the picture of

A contemporary English hunting Squire. His great pleasure is to go

> "*Up to the mountain's top,*
> *And mark the musical confusion*
> *Of hounds and echo in conjunction*"   (IV. i. 110).

and he has chosen a wife who shares his own tastes. His pride is in his "flew'd and sanded" hounds, "bred out of the Spartan kind." And when he cannot be hunting he requires some other "sport" (V. i. 42, 90) with which "to ease the anguish of a torturing hour."

As a mythological personage Theseus is the national hero of the Ionians, as Hercules is of the Æolians. He has not unjustly been called the second Hercules with whom he has many features in common. He was the son of the Athenian king Ægeus (= wave-man), who himself is Poseidon (or Neptune) in another form. He is the mythical hero of a great number of adventures of which we need only allude here to such as seem to have some connection with the play.

In Crete he slew the Minotaur, and carried away Ariadne the daughter of Minos, king of Crete (see p. 111 and cf. II. i. 81, and IV. i. 113).

With Hercules as his comrade he fought against the Amazons on the occasion of an inroad made by them into Attica, and won the love of their queen Antiope, or Hippolyte, whom he wedded (cf. IV. i. 113).

At Thebes he helped Adrastus, king of Argos, to recover the bodies of those that were slain in battle before the city (cf. V. i. 51).

With the Lapithae he is said to have chastised the Centaurs, fighting in aid of the Thessalian Pirithous, the king of the Lapithæ (cf. V. i. 44). According to the later traditions he was accompanied on this expedition by his friend Hercules.

His death is reported to have happened as follows. During his absence from Athens the sovereignty was usurped by Menestheus, who was aided by the Dioscuri. Theseus withdrew to the island of Scyros, where he was at first hospitably received, but afterwards treacherously murdered by Lycomedes, the ruler of the island.

In Art. A representation of the conflict of Theseus with the invading army of the Amazons still exists on a large piece of frieze-work, which is now the property of the British Museum. Theseus may be recognized by his lion's skin and the club, which he is in the act of swinging against a mounted Amazon. He is usually represented as a beardless youth in his prime, and a perfect ideal of manly beauty.

"The central figure of the play is that of Theseus. There is no figure in the early drama of Shakespeare so magnificent. His are the large hands that have helped to shape the world. His utterance is the rich-toned speech of one who is master of events—who has never known a shrill or eager feeling. . . . . Theseus, a grand ideal figure, is to be studied as Shakespeare's conception of the heroic man of action in his hour of enjoyment and leisure. With a splendid capacity for enjoyment, gracious to all, ennobled by the glory, implied rather than explicit, of great foregone achievement, he stands as centre of the poem, giving their true proportions to the fairy tribe upon the one hand, and upon the other to the 'human mortals'" (DOWDEN).

HIPPOLYTA is for the most part a silent actor in the play. She takes her place with dignity as a soldier queen by the side of her soldier husband that is to be. She betrays no youthful longing for the rapid flight of time (I i. 7-11), nor does she often address her future lord in endearing terms We can hardly imagine her ever to have had a very close connection with the fairy world, although Titania speaks of her to Oberon as "your buskin'd mistress. and your warrior love." The remarks she makes during the performance of the Interlude—"This is the silliest stuff that ever I heard," "I am aweary of this moon; would he would change," "such a Pyramus," and "I hope she will be brief"—are hardly such as might tend to the encouragement of the actors—supposing them to be so commonplace as to require encouragement;—but this we may perhaps excuse in her, remembering that she has been until now a stranger to the civilisation of Athens.

EGEUS is the stern, unyielding parent who comes "full of vexation," with complaint against his child Hermia. On meeting with Lysander and Demetrius after the flight into the forest, the vehemence with which he urges his claims reminds us somewhat of Shylock by its intensity. "Enough, enough, my lord," he cries,

> "you have enough :
> I beg the law, the law upon his head"   (IV. i. 155).

He appears almost altogether devoid of human sympathies, and when the Duke overbears his will he silently and ungraciously submits to the wishes of his lord.

HERMIA—**her personal appearance.** She is described as "beau teous" (I. i. 104), "fair" (I. i. 117, 187, etc.), with "sphery eyne" (II. ii. 99), which are "blessed and attractive" (II. ii. 91), and a voice

> "More tuneable than lark to shepherd's ear
> When wheat is green, when hawthorn buds appear"   (I. i. 184)

Compared with Helena. There appears to have been little to choose between them in respect of beauty. They are "two lovely berries moulded on one stem " (III. ii. 211), and Helena is "through Athens" thought as fair as Hermia (I. i. 227). Hermia was dark (III. ii. 258, 265), Helena fair (III. ii. 298) ; Hermia was short (III. ii. 290, etc.), Helena tall (III. ii. 294, 298, etc.). See, however, p. xxxi. under Helena.

Her disposition in early life is hinted at more than once. Helena says :

> "She was a vixen, when she went to school ;
> And though she be but little she is fierce."   (III. ii. 326).

But although hasty of temper, 'shrewish' as she is called, she was a true and maidenly lover, and had been a dear friend to Helena all her life.

> "We, Hermia, like two artificial gods,
> Have with our needles created both one flower,
> Both on one sampler, sitting on one cushion,
> Both warbling of one song, both in one key,
> As if our hands, our sides, voices, and minds
> Had been incorporate"   (III. ii. 203).

She cannot fairly be judged by the language of which she makes use when all her friends are under the influence of " Cupid's flower " and she herself is in distress, smarting under the pain of the apparently unnatural faithlessness of the two persons who had hitherto been all the world to her. Her violent language at this crisis must be regarded only as the exaggeration of

Her natural strong will.   This is evident in the earlier part of the play when she expresses her determination to enter a nunnery, or even to die, rather than submit to the "unwished yoke" of one whom she felt she could not love.   " So will I grow," she says;

> " So live, so die, my lord,
> Ere I will yield my virgin patent up
> Unto his lordship to whose unwished yoke
> My soul consents not to give sovereignty "   (I. i. 79).

We may be sure that not a little pressure had been brought to bear upon her by her father in order that he might turn her from what he pleases to call her "stubborn harshness." It was she, be it remembered, who, notwithstanding the warmth of her nature, suggested to Lysander,

> " Then let us teach our trial patience,
> Because it is a customary cross "   (I. i. 152).

HELENA.   The character of Helena is no more distinctly drawn by the poet than that of Hermia, and bears so many points of resemblance to that of the friend of her youth that many commentators have even gone so far as to say that no distinction can be made between them, except in so far as their outward appearance is concerned.   But a closer study of the play will, we think, reveal in Helena

A more timid and gentler disposition.   She compares herself with a spaniel (II. i. 204), and spaniel-like she "devoutly dotes, dotes in idolatry" upon the "spotted and inconstant" Demetrius.   She seems to lack faith in herself; although reputed throughout Athens to be as beautiful as Hermia, yet she would give the world, she says, " Demetrius being bated," to possess the charms of Hermia.   She longs for *her* voice, *her* eye, *her* "favour."   She fears to be left alone in the dark (II. ii. 86), bemoans her own "insufficiency" (II. ii. 128), deplores Lysander's lack of "true gentleness" (II. ii. 132), casts herself for protection upon the mercy of others, and appeals to Demetrius' and Lysander's sense of courtesy and manliness (III. ii. 151-2, etc.).   She reproaches Hermia with having "no modesty, no maiden shame, no touch of bashfulness" (III. ii. 287), and bitterly laments that she should "tear impatient answers from her gentle tongue" (III. ii. 288).   Finally, she fears the physical violence threatened by Hermia, and begs the rivals for her love to "let her not hurt me."   "I was never curst" (shrewish), she says:

> " I have no gift at all in shrewishness;
> I am a right maid for my cowardice:
> Let her not strike me "   (III. ii. 302),

and she runs away from the contest to which she feels she is not equal.

The betrayal of her friend.   Her faithlessness toward Hermia does not seem to have been a plot thought out with any intention of doing an

B

injury to her former playfellow, but rather a sudden, impulsive action, intended only to bring herself once more in contact with Demetrius

> " *To have his sight thither and back again* "   (I. i. 251).

"The characters of Hermia and Helena are beautifully drawn and finely contrasted, and in much of the dialogue which occurs between them, the chords of love and pity are touched with the poet's wonted skill. In their interview in the wood the contrariety of their dispositions is completely developed; Hermia is represented as

> —' *keen and shrewd :*
> *—a vixen when she went to school,*
> *And, though but little, fierce,'*

and in her difference with her friend, threatens to scratch her eyes out with her nails, while Helena, meek, humble and retired, sues for protection, and endeavours in the most gentle manner to deprecate her wrath. . . . And in an earlier part of this scene, where Helena first suspects that her friend had conspired with Demetrius and Lysander to mock and deride her, nothing can more exquisitely paint her affectionate temper, and the heartfelt pangs of severing friendship, than the following lines, most touching in their appeal, an echo from the very bosom of nature itself :—

> ' *Injurious Hermia ! most ungrateful maid !—*
> . . . .
> *Though I alone do feel the injury,* ' "   (III. ii. 195-219).
> (DRAKE).

LYSANDER, the lover of Hermia, is spoken of as " a worthy gentleman," of high rank and good fortune. Before the play opens he has impressed his image firmly upon Hermia's fancy and being secure in the possession of her love, he treats his future father-in-law with some scorn (I. i. 93–5).

He must not be thought faithless because, owing to Puck's blunder he came under the influence of " Cupid's flower " and suddenly transferred his affections to Helena.

DEMETRIUS differs from Lysander in character only in one important respect. He was inconstant and sinned through faithlessness to his betrothed Helena. The supernatural power of the fairies was needed in order to restore him to his " natural taste," and then, having returned to his first love he remembers his breach of faith only as youthful playfulness (IV. i. 165-177).

The two pairs of lovers.

"In the two pairs of lovers there are hardly any lines deep and firm enough to be rightly called characteristic. Their doings, even more than those of the other humane persons, are marked by the dream-like freakishness and whimsicality which distinguish the piece. Perhaps the two ladies are slightly discriminated as individuals, in that Hermia, besides her brevity of person, is the more tart in temper, and the more pert and shrewish of speech, while Helena is of a rather milder and softer disposition, with less of confidence in herself. So too in the case of Demetrius and Lysander the lines of individuality are exceedingly faint ; the former being perhaps a shade the more caustic and spiteful, and the latter somewhat the more open and candid " (HUDSON).

TITANIA and **OBERON** are described with sufficient fulness on pp. xxi.-xxiii., where we have pointed out the characteristics which are common to all the fairies, of whom the king and queen may be taken as representative types.

PUCK.

The Origin and Use of the Name.

Puck, pug and *pouke*, are all appellations for a fiend. *Puki,* demon, is Icelandic and Gothic. M.E. *puca,* W. *pwca.* The name appears as *Pug* in Ben Johnson's play *The Devil is an Ass,* and as *Puck-hairy* in the *Sad Shepherd* of the same author. It is *Puckle* in Reginald Scot's *Discovery of Witchcraft,* and the name re-appears in the modern *pixy,* or in Cornwall *pisky,* a fairy. In *Piers Plowman,* Golding's translation of Ovid's *Metamorphoses* and in Spenser's *Epithalamium* we read about "the pouke." It is worthy of note that although "Puck" is generally used in our play as a proper name, it occurs also as a generic name for a sprite in V. i. 434, where Robin calls himself "an honest Puck," and in 438 of the same scene where he says:—

> "*We will make amends ere long ;*
> *Else the Puck a liar call.*"

The Robin Goodfellow of tradition.
Shakespeare has, in his delineation of Puck, departed but little from the familiar conception of the character and attributes of the spirit of Scandinavian origin. He has divested the character of most of the malignant characteristics which were popularly associated with this mischievous elf, and he has infused into it a poetic and picturesque element which is the product of his own imagination. Many of his attributes are referred to by Reginald Scot in his *Discoverie of Witchcraft* (1584) from which we quote the following:—

"The Virunculi terrei are such as was *Robin good fellowe,* that would supplie the office of servants, specialle of maids; as to make a fier in the morning, sweepe the house, grind mustard and malt, drawe water, etc." (p. 521, quoted from DRAKE).

Speaking of the *Incubus,* he adds:—"In deede your grandams maides were wont to set a boll of milke before him and his cousine *Robin good fellow,* for grinding of malt or mustard, and sweeping the house at midnight: and you have also heard that he would chafe exceedingly, if the maid or goodwife of the house, having compassion on his nakednesse, laid anie clothes for him, beesides his messe of white bread and milke, which was his standing fee. For in that case he saith: What have we here? Hemten, hamten, here will I never more tread nor stampen" (p. 85 do.).

"It may be also remarked, that the idea of fixing "an ass's nowl" on Bottom's head is most probably taken from Scot, who gives us a very curious receipt for this singular metamorphosis."

IN THE PLAY.

His duties and power.
To the fairy whom he first meets in the forest he appears as a "lob (clown) of spirits " (II. i. 16), Oberon's jester (II. i. 44). He acts throughout the play as the prime minister of Oberon, whom he addresses as "my lord" (II. i. 269), "captain of our fairy band" (III. ii. 110), "my fairy lord" (III. ii. 380), and "fairy king" (IV. i. 94). He possesses the power of changing his shape at will, transforming himself at different times into a "filly foal" (II. i. 47), "a roasted crab" (II. i. 49), a "three-foot stool" (II. i. 53), and he can counterfeit noises and people's voices (III. i. 110, 362).

> "*Sometime a horse I'll be, sometime a hound,*
> *A hog, a headless bear, sometimes a fire ;*
> *And neigh, and bark, and grunt, and roar, and burn,*
> *Like horse, hound, hog, bear, fire, at every turn*" (III. ii. 108).

He can move with extraordinary swiftness (II. i. 176, etc.), but he did not possess the same powers of vision as were possessed by the superior spirit, his master (II. i. 156).

His love of Mischief is the most prominent feature of his character. He is a "shrewd and knavish sprite," that frights maidens, misleads night-wanderers, beguiles fat and bean-fed horses, and plays pranks on old women (II. i. 33-53) often making the whole company

> " hold their hips and laugh
> And waxen in their mirth and neeze and swear."

Seeing the "hard-handed men of Athens" move so far away from their natural sphere of action as to take upon themselves the rôle of actors, his mischievous instinct very soon declares itself. He fixes the ass's head on the thickest skull of that "barren sort," and then frightening his companions almost out of their senses, he leaves them scattered in a state of "distracted fear."

> " And left sweet Pyramus translated there :
> When in that moment, so it came to pass,
> Titania waked, and straightway loved an ass"   (III. ii. 32)

Far from repenting of the blunders he commits in his master's service he even glories in them and takes a keen delight in the embarrassing and perplexing situations brought about by his own clumsiness.

> " Then will two at once woo one :
> That must needs be sport alone ;
> And those things do best please me
> That befall preposterously"   (III. ii. 118),

and again

> " And so far am I glad it so did sort
> And this their jangling I esteem a sport"   (III. ii. 354).

Not even is love sacred to him, and a lover in distress is a "fond pageant." He moralises upon such a spectacle,

> " Lord, what fools these mortals be ! "   (III. ii. 115).

He takes pleasure in leading Lysander and Demetrius astray, mocking them, scoffing and taunting first one, then the other with lack of courage (III. ii. 360, etc.).

His more pleasing qualities are only occasionally exhibited. He is evidently a favourite with his master who calls him " my gentle Puck " (II. i. 149, IV. i. 64) and "good Robin " (IV. i. 47), and who frequently welcomes him back from his aerial wanderings (II. i. 248, IV. i. 47); whilst for " those that Hobgoblin call him and sweet Puck " (II. i. 40), he does their work and "they shall have good luck." He has a feeling of pity for beauty in distress, addressing Hermia asleep as "pretty soul " (II. ii. 76). His concluding speech is couched in a modest strain which does not altogether fit his character. He claims to be "an honest Puck " (V. i. 434) and asks for the indulgence of the audience in case he has offended any.

BOTTOM.

Bottom takes his name from one of the implements of his trade, a "bottom" in weaving being either a ball of thread or the block on which it was wound. He is one of the most distinctly drawn characters of the play. For **self-assurance, audacity and conceit** he has no equal From the very commencement, although Quince was nominally the stage-manager, Bottom takes upon himself the whole management of the play. His self-confidence is such that he would have liked to act all the parts himself from the greatest to the least. His abilities are frankly recognised by his fellow-actors, who defer to his opinion on all points. They acknowledge that there is "not a man in all Athens able to discharge Pyramus, but he" and that "he hath simply the best wit of any handi-craft man in Athens." Nothing daunts him. He is not in the least awed by the imposing audience of courtiers in the Duke's palace. Twice he boldly contradicts the Duke when he thought he showed an imperfect understanding of the progress of the piece. Whatever failings he may have had, we may feel sure his blunders did not proceed from any nervousness on his part. Furthermore he is—

A practical man, full of resource. He organises the rehearsal. He suggests difficulties and objections apparently that he may show how easily he can sweep them away by his devices. He accommodates himself readily to his novel position amongst the fairies and he is not slow to find suitable occupation for the spirits that are told off to minister to his wants. Even his dream he proposes to turn to practical account : "I will get Peter Quince to write a ballad of this dream. . . . I will sing it in the latter end of the play before the Duke" (IV. i. 215). Between his awaking from his vision and his entrance in Quince's house (*i.e.* between IV. i. and IV. ii.) he has made good use of his time. He has learnt that "the Duke hath dined" and that the play has been presented for approval.

As seen by other characters. Bottom looked upon himself as a man of genius with a special gift for acting of the highest order, and this view of himself he imposed upon his fellow tradesmen. But he was not universally regarded in this light. Puck speaks of him as one of a crew of swaggering "hempen home-spuns," and even calls him "the shallowest thick-skin of that barren sort" (III. ii. 13). To the king of the fairies he is nothing less than a "hateful fool" (IV. i. 50). Puck, on taking off the ass's head bids him, "Now, when thou wakest, with thine own fool's eyes peep" (IV. i. 85). In the opinions of the courtiers he cuts a sorry figure. Hippolyta even pities the man. Theseus regards him as "an ass" and his wonderful performance as a "palpable-gross play" (V. i. 370).

"And then Bottom! Who but the most skilful artist could have given us such a character? Of him Malone says, 'Shakespeare would naturally copy those manners first with which he was first acquainted. The ambition of a theatrical candidate for applause he has happily ridiculed in Bottom the weaver.' A theatrical candidate for applause! Why, Bottom the weaver is the representative of the whole human race. His confidence in his own power is equally profound, whether he exclaims, 'Let me play the lion too;' or whether he sings alone, 'that they shall hear I am not afraid'; or whether, conscious that he is surrounded with spirits, he cries out, with his voice of authority, 'Where's Peaseblossom?' In every situation Bottom is the same—the same personification of that self-love which the simple cannot conceal, and the wise can with difficulty suppress" (KNIGHT).

"Bottom is incomparably a finer efflorescence of the absurd than any preceding character of Shakespeare's invention. How lean and impoverished his fellows, the Athenian craftsmen, confess themselves in presence of the many-sided genius of Nick Bottom! Rarely is a great artist appreciated in the degree that Bottom is—' He hath simply the best wit of any handicraft man in Athens; yea, and the best person too; and he is a very paramour for a sweet voice.' With what a magnificent multiplicity of gifts he is endowed! How vast has the bounty of nature been to him! The self-doubtful Snug hesitates to undertake the moderate duties assigned to the lion. Bottom, though his chief humour is for a tyrant, knows not how to suppress his almost equal gift for playing a lady. How, without a pang can he deprive the world, through devotion to 'the Ercles vein' of the monstrous little voice in which he can utter 'Thisne, Thisne—Ah, Pyramus, my lover dear; thy Thisby dear and lady dear!' And as to the part assigned to the too bashful Snug—that Bottom can undertake in either of two styles, or in both, so that the Duke must say, 'Let him roar again, let him roar again,' or the ladies may be soothed by the 'aggravated voice' in which he will 'roar you as gently as any sucking dove.' But from these dreams of universal ambition he is recalled by Quince to his most appropriate impersonation:—'You can play no part but Pyramus, for Pyramus is a sweet-faced man ; a proper man as one shall see in a summer's day; a most lovely, gentleman-like man; therefore you must needs play Pyramus'" (DOWDEN).

QUINCE, SNUG, FLUTE and STARVELING are not specially characterised in the play. They are subordinate characters, amusing from their ignorance and for the respect—almost reverence—they pay to Bottom. Quince may perhaps lay claim to a larger share of education than the rest, whilst Flute is the boldest of them and Snug the most diffident. Starveling, the tailor, keeps the peace, and objects to the lion and the drawn sword. With a few words about their respective names we may dismiss them without further comment. Quince, the carpenter, is so called from the tree of that name, M.F. *coignasse*, "the greatest kind of quince." F. *coing*, a quince. Gk. κυδώνιον μῆλον, a quince, *lit.* a Cydonian apple (Cydonia, one of the chief cities of Crete). The musical name Flute naturally belongs to the bellows-mender (bellows = the pipes of an organ). Starveling carries a reference to the traditional leanness and pinched appearance formerly associated with the members of his craft. Snug is in prov. E. *snug*, tidy, Icel. *snöggr*, and may bear reference to the trimming and planing of planks which would naturally fall to the part of Snug the Joiner.

ABSTRACT OF THE PLAY.

I. i. The curtain rises to disclose the palace of Theseus, Duke of Athens, who is about to marry Hippolyta, Queen of the Amazons. To them enter Egeus with his daughter Hermia, and two suitors for her hand, Lysander and Demetrius. Egeus complains that his daughter refuses to marry Demetrius whom he has chosen to be her husband. and claims the ancient privilege of Athens to dispose of her as he pleases. Theseus tries gentle persuasion with the lady, who inquires what must be her fate if she declines to wed Demetrius. The answer is that she must die or go into a convent. She is given a few days, until "the next new moon," in which to consider. The Duke departs with his train, and Lysander being left alone with Hermia appoints a trysting-place for the morrow night. Helena enters and is told about the intended flight of the lovers.

I. ii. A company of Athenian artisans are assembled in the house of Quince, a carpenter, to discuss a play on the subject of Pyramus and Thisbe, which they hope to act before the Duke and Duchess on the occasion of their wedding. They arrange the parts, Bottom, a self-satisfied weaver with a very exalted opinion of his own abilities, taking the rôle of the hero and assuming the direction of affairs generally.

II. i. Puck (or Robin Goodfellow) and a fairy meet in a wood near Athens. Here also Oberon, the king of the fairies, meets Titania his queen, from whom he has been separated for some time owing to a difference they have had about a little changeling boy, who has been brought up by Titania and whom Oberon wants to join his train of knights. Titania refuses to give up the boy and goes away to avoid further quarrelling. Oberon determines to punish her and sends Puck, his chief minister, to find a flower called love-in-idleness, the juice of which when dropped upon sleeping eyelids, will make either man or woman dote upon the next living object seen. As Puck vanishes on his errand Demetrius enters followed by Helena, who seeks in vain to win again his love or even his endurance of her company, for they had formerly been betrothed and Demetrius has proved unfaithful. Oberon, who is invisible to mortals, sees how cruelly Demetrius treats his former lover, and determines to make him kinder to Helena. After their departure and on Puck's returning with the flower, Oberon sends him after Demetrius and bids him anoint his eyes at such a time that the next person he sees may be Helena.

II. ii. Titania enters another part of the wood and bids her fairies sing her to sleep. Oberon comes in and squeezes the flower on her eyelids and leaves her there asleep. Lysander and

Hermia who have lost their way in the wood, now come to the same spot and being weary lie down and sleep. Puck, coming upon the scene, and seeing an Athenian lying asleep near a lady, mistaking Lysander for Demetrius, anoints his eyes with the juice of the flower. Then into the same part of the wood come Demetrius with Helena closely following him. Helena perceives Lysander asleep and wakens him. He, being affected by the magic juice, at once falls passionately in love with Helena and follows her. Hermia awakens to find herself alone and goes in search of Lysander.

III. i.   The rustic actors meet in this same eventful part of the wood to rehearse their play. Puck comes in, bent on mischief, and when, in the course of the rehearsal, Bottom retires from sight for a moment, he fixes on him an ass's head. When Bottom returns, thus disguised, the rest of the actors run away terrified. Bottom, all unconscious of the cause of their sudden flight remains and sings. The noise of his voice wakens Titania, who was still lying asleep and under the influence of Cupid's flower. The pretty, dainty, fairy queen falls in love with the ugly, rough and coarse Bottom with the ass's head fixed on his shoulders.

III. ii.   Puck tells Oberon how Titania " with a monster is in love," and that he has anointed the eyes of the Athenian, as ordered. Demetrius and Hermia then approach and she, thinking that Demetrius must have murdered her lover Lysander reproaches him bitterly. When she goes away Demetrius lies down and sleeps. Oberon, seeing the mistake that Puck has made sends him away to bring Helena in order that she may be the first person seen by Demetrius when he awakens after having his eyes anointed. Lysander and Helena enter, he declaring, and she protesting against, his love. Demetrius wakes and loves Helena. She, unable, of course, to understand such changes, thinks the two men are mocking her. Hermia comes in and the game of cross purposes continues. Demetrius and Lysander quarrel about Helena, with whom Hermia is furious. The two men go out to fight. Oberon, to end the trouble for all, dispatches Puck to the rescue, charging him to render the night dark with fog and lead the rivals astray from one another. This he does, and when the two pairs of lovers again lie down to sleep in one part of the wood and not very far from each other, he again anoints Lysander's eyes, but this time not with Cupid's flower, as before, but with " Dian's bud," which has the property of removing all error from the mind of the person anointed. So when they awake they will love each other in pairs as they ought to do.

IV. i.   Titania is sitting with Nick Bottom on a flowery bank, surrounded by her pretty little fairies who wait on Bottom and obey his absurd directions. When they two sleep, Oberon orders Puck to release the fairy queen from her enchantment, and remove the ass's head.

Theseus, Hippolyta, and Egeus enter to the sound of horns and are surprised to find the two pairs of lovers lying asleep in the same part of the wood. When all are awake, and Demetrius has declared his love for Helena, the Duke tells Egeus that the two couples shall be joined together in the temple at the same time as himself and Hippolyta. All go away together to Athens. Bottom awakes and finds himself alone. He thinks he has been dreaming a wonderful dream.

IV. ii. The actors are at a loss to know what to do without Bottom, whom they cannot find. No other man, in all Athens, they say, could play the part of Pyramus. Fortunately he enters, and bids them make haste and go to the Duke's Palace.

V. i. In the Palace of Theseus, Philostrate, the master of the revels, offers the duke his choice of several forms of entertainment. Theseus chooses to see the play of Pyramus and Thisbe, which is to be both " merry and tragical." The play begins, and Quince enters as Prologue with a flourish of trumpets. The other actors perform their parts indifferently in this most ridiculous of plays. The noble audience criticise good-naturedly, being amused at the blunders and absurd pantomime of the actors. The tragedy ends with the death of the principal players, and is followed by a Bergomask or rustic dance. The audience retires to rest, and Puck and all the fairies come in to bless the house and the wedded couples " to all prosperity."

A MIDSUMMER-NIGHT'S DREAM.

Dramatis Personæ.

THESEUS, *Duke of Athens.*

EGEUS, *Father to Hermia.*

LYSANDER, } *in love with Hermia.*
DEMETRIUS,

PHILOSTRATE, *Master of the Revels to Theseus.*

QUINCE, *a Carpenter.*

SNUG, *a Joiner.*

BOTTOM, *a Weaver.*

FLUTE, *a Bellows-mender.*

SNOUT, *a Tinker.*

STARVELING, *a Tailor.*

HIPPOLYTA, *Queen of the Amazons, betrothed to Theseus.*

HERMIA, *daughter to Egeus, in love with Lysander.*

HELENA, *in love with Demetrius.*

OBERON, *King of the Fairies.*

TITANIA, *Queen of the Fairies.*

PUCK, *or Robin Goodfellow.*

PEASEBLOSSOM,
COBWEB,   } *Fairies.*
MOTH,
MUSTARD-SEED,

Other Fairies attending their King and Queen.

Attendants on Theseus and Hippolyta.

SCENE: *Athens and a Wood near it.*

ACT I.

SCENE I.—*Athens. A Room in the Palace of*
THESEUS.

Enter THESEUS, HIPPOLYTA, PHILOSTRATE. *and Attendants.*

The. Now, fair Hippolyta, our nuptial hour
Draws on *apace*[a] ; four happy days bring in
Another moon : but, O, methinks, how slow
This old moon wanes ! she *lingers*[b] my desires,
Like to a step-dame, or a [1]*dowager*,
Long *withering*[c] out a young man's revenue.

  Hip. Four days will quickly steep themselves in
    night ;
Four nights will quickly dream away the time ;
And then the moon, like to a silver bow
New-bent in heaven, shall behold the night   10
Of our *solemnities*.[d]

  The.   Go, Philostrate,
Stir up the Athenian youth to merriments ;
Awake the *pert*[e] and nimble spirit of mirth :
Turn melancholy forth to funerals,
The pale companion is not for our pomp.

                 [*Exit* PHILOSTRATE.
Hippolyta, I [2]*woo'd thee with my sword*,
And won thy love doing thee injuries ;
But I will wed thee in another key,
With pomp, with triumph, and with revelling.

Enter EGEUS, HERMIA, LYSANDER, *and* DEMETRIUS.

  Ege. Happy be Theseus, our renownéd duke !   20
  The. Thanks, good *Egeus*[f] : what's the news with
    thee ?
  Ege. Full of vexation come I, with complaint
Against my child, my daughter Hermia.
Stand forth, Demetrius. My noble lord,
This man hath my consent to marry her.

[a] *rapidly*

[b] *delays the ful filment of*

[c] *causing to wither away or dwindle*

[d] *wedding celebration*

[e] *lively*

[f] *trisyllable*

---

[1] A dowager is a widow with a jointure, *i.e.* one to whom the 'young man
has to pay a yearly revenue during his life-time.

[2] Theseus, according to tradition, defeated the Amazons and carried off their
queen Hippolyta.

Stand forth, Lysander: and, my gracious duke,
This man hath *bewitch'd*[a] the *bosom*[b] of my child :
Thou, thou, Lysander, thou hast given her rhymes,
And interchanged love-tokens with my child.
Thou hast by moonlight at her window sung,   30
With feigning voice, verses of feigning love ;
And *stolen the impression of her fantasy*[c]
With bracelets of thy hair, rings, *gawds,*[d] *conceits,*[e]
Knacks,[f] trifles, nosegays, sweetmeats, *messengers*
[1]*Of strong prevailment in unharden'd youth ;*
With cunning hast thou *filch'd*[g] my daughter's heart,
Turn'd her obedience, which is due to me,
To stubborn harshness : and, my gracious duke,
Be it so[h] she will not here before your grace
Consent to marry with Demetrius,   40
I beg [2]*the ancient privilege of Athens,*
As she is mine, I may dispose of her :
Which shall be either to this gentleman
Or to her death, according to our law
Immediately provided[i] in that case.
      The. What say you, Hermia? be *advised,*[k] fair
            maid :
To you your father should be as a god ;
One that composed your beauties ; yea, and one
To whom you are but as a form in wax,
By him imprinted, and within his power   50
[3]*To leave the figure or disfigure it.*
Demetrius is a worthy gentleman.
      Her. So is Lysander.
      The.   In himself he is ;
But in this *kind,*[l] *wanting*[m] your father's *voice,*[n]
The other must be held the worthier.
      Her. I would my father look'd but with my eyes !
      The. Rather your eyes must with his judgment
            look.

a *pronounce as
   two syllables*
b *heart*

c *stealthily im-
   printed thy
   image upon
   her heart*
d *ornaments*
e *presents fanci-
   fully devised*
f *knick-knacks*
g *stolen*
h *if it so be that*

i *specially pro-
   vided to meet*
k *cautious*

l *respect*
m *lacking*
n *approval*

[1] *I.e.* by means of which, impressionable youth is strongly influenced.

[2] A law of Solon's gave to parents absolute power of life and death over their
children.

[3] *I.e.* to leave you with your life or deprive you of it.

Her. I do entreat your grace to pardon me.
I know not by what power I am made bold,
Nor how it may *concern*[a] my modesty,   60
In such a presence here, to plead my thoughts;
But I beseech your grace that I may know
The worst that may befall me in this case,
If I refuse to wed Demetrius.

The. Either to die *the death*,[b] or to abjure
For ever the society of men.
Therefore, fair Hermia, question your desires,
Know of your youth, examine well your blood,
Whether, if you yield not to your father's choice,
You can endure [1]*the livery of a nun*[c];   70
For aye to be in shady cloister *mew'd*,[d]
To live a barren sister all your life,
Chanting faint hymns to the cold fruitless moon.
Thrice blessèd they that master so their blood,
[2]*To undergo such maiden pilgrimage*;
But earthlier happy is the rose [3]*distill'd*
Than that which, withering on the virgin thorn,
Grows, lives, and dies in single blessedness.

Her. So will I grow, so live, so die, my lord,
Ere I will *yield my virgin patent up*   80
Unto his lordship[e] whose unwishéd yoke
My soul consents not to give *sovereignty*.[f]

The. Take time to pause; and by the next new
          moon,—
The *sealing-day*[g] betwixt my love and me,
For everlasting bond of fellowship,—
Upon that day, either prepare to die
For disobedience to your father's will,
Or else to wed Demetrius, as he would;
Or on *Diana's*[h] altar to protest
For aye, austerity and single life.   90

a *becomes*

b *death by judicial sentence*

c *to take the veil*

d *shut up*

e *give myself up to the power of him*

f *sovereign power*

g i.e. *day on which our contract is to be completed*

h *the maiden goddess, identified with the moon cf. l.* 83

---

[1] The mention of 'nun,' 'sister,' 'cloister,' is an anachronism.

[2] *I.e.* That they can endure to pass through life without the blessing of marriage. Shakespeare frequently uses the word 'pilgrimage' for time spent irksomely.

[3] The idea is that the rose which is plucked in order to be distilled into scent (*i.e.* the woman who marries) leads a happier life in this world than the rose that is left to fade away on the stalk (the unmarried woman).

Dem. Relent, sweet Hermia : and, Lysander,
    yield
Thy *crazéd title*[a] to my certain right.   *a weak claim*
    Lys. You have her father's love, Demetrius ;
Let me have Hermia's : do you marry him.
    Ege. Scornful Lysander ! true, he hath my love,
And what is mine my love shall render him ;
And she is mine, and all my right of her
I do estate unto Demetrius.
    Lys. I am, my lord, as well *derived*[b] as he,   *b born*
As *well possess'd*[c] ; my love is more than his ;   100   *c richly endowed*
My fortunes every way *as fairly rank'd*,
If not with vantage, as[d] Demetrius' ;   *d rank as high if not higher than*
And, which is more than all these boasts can be,
I am beloved of beauteous Hermia.
Why should not I then prosecute my right ?
Demetrius, I'll *avouch*[e] it to his head,   *e maintain*
Made love to Nedar's daughter, Helena,
And won her *soul*[f] ; and she, sweet lady, dotes,   *f heart*
Devoutly dotes, *dotes in idolatry*,
Upon[g] this *spotted*[h] and inconstant man.   110   *g idolises*
    h polluted
    The. I must confess, that I have heard so much,
And with Demetrius thought to have spoke thereof ;
But, being over-full of *self-affairs*,[i]   *i matters relating to myself*
My mind did lose it.—But, Demetrius, come ;
And come, Egeus : you shall go with me,
I have some private *schooling*[k] for you both.   *k announcements*
For you, fair Hermia, look you arm yourself
To fit your fancies to your father's will,
Or else the law of Athens yields you up,
Which by no means we may *extenuate*,[l]   120   *l lessen the severity of*
To death, or to a vow of single life.
Come, my Hippolyta : what cheer, my love ?
Demetrius and Egeus, go along :
I must employ you in some business
Against our nuptial, and confer with you
Of something *nearly that*[m] concerns yourselves.   *m that nearly*
    Ege. With *duty and desire*[n] we follow you.   *n dutifully and eagerly*
        [*Exeunt all but* LYSANDER *and* HERMIA.
    Lys. How now, my love ? Why is your cheek so
    pale ?

How chance the roses there do fade so fast?

Her. *Belike*[a] for want of rain, which I could well
Beteem[b] them from the tempest of mine eyes. 131

Lys. Ay me! for aught that I could ever read,
Could ever hear by tale or history,
The course of true love never did run smooth ;
But, either it was different in blood,—

Her. O *cross !*[c] too high to be *enthrall'd*[d] to low !

Lys. Or else *misgraffèd*[e] in respect of years,—

Her. O spite ! too old to be engaged to young !

Lys. Or else it *stood upon*[f] the choice of friends,—

Her. O hell ! to choose love by another's eyes ! 140

Lys. Or, if there were a *sympathy*[g] in choice,
War, death, or sickness did lay siege to it,
Making it *momentary*[h] as a sound,
Swift as a shadow, short as any dream,
Brief as the lightning in the *collied*[i] night,
That, in a *spleen*,[k] unfolds both heaven and earth,
And ere a man hath power to say,—" Behold ! "
The jaws of darkness do devour it up :
So quick bright things come to *confusion.*[l]

Her. If then true lovers have been *ever*[m]crossed, 150
It stands as an *edict in*[n] destiny :
Then let us *teach our trial patience,*[o]
Because it is a customary cross
As *due*[p] to love as thoughts, and dreams, and sighs,
Wishes, and tears, poor *fancy's*[q] followers.

Lys. A good *persuasion*[r] ; therefore, hear me,
Hermia
I have a widow aunt, a *dowager*[s]
Of great revenue, and she hath no child :
From Athens is her house remote seven leagues ;
And she *respects*[t] me as her only son. 160
There, gentle Hermia, *may*[u] I marry thee ;
And to that place the sharp Athenian law
Cannot pursue us. If thou lovest me, then,
Steal forth thy father's house to-morrow night,
And in the wood, a *league*[v] without the town,
Where I did meet thee once with Helena.

a	*probably*
b	*bestow upon*
c	*perversity of fortune*
d	*bound*
e	*ill-matched*
f	*rested on*
g	*happy fitness*
h	*as short-lived*
i	*black*
k	*sudden outburst or flash*
l	*four syllables*
m	*invariably*
n	*irrevocable law of*
o	*learn patiently to endure our trial*
p	*natural*
q	*love's*
r	*belief*
s	*see l. 5*
t	*regards*
u	*can*
v	*cf. I. ii. 102*

To ¹*do observance to a morn of May*,
There will I stay for thee.
    Her.   My good Lysander!
I swear to thee, by *Cupid's*ᵃ strongest bow;
By his *best arrow*ᵇ with the golden head;   170
By the *simplicity*ᶜ of Venus' doves,
By that which knitteth souls and prospers loves;
And by that fire which burn'd the ²*Carthage queen*,ᵈ
When the ²*false Troyan*ᵉ under sail was seen;
By all the vows that ever men have broke,
In number more than ever women spoke;
In that same place thou hast appointed me,
To-morrow truly will I meet with thee.
    Lys. Keep promise, love.—Look, here comes
        Helena.

Enter HELENA.

    Her. God speed, fair Helena! Whither away? 180
    Hel. Call you me fair? that *fair*ᶠ again unsay.
Demetrius loves your *fair*ᵍ: O happy fair!
Your eyes are *lode-stars*,ʰ and your tongue's sweet air
More *tuneable*ⁱ than lark to shepherd's ear
When wheat is green, when hawthorn buds appear.
Sickness is catching: O, were *favour*ᵏ so,
Yours would I catch, fair Hermia, ere I go;
My ear should catch your voice, my eye my eye,
My tongue should catch your tongue's sweet melody.
Were the world mine, Demetrius being *bated*,ˡ   190
The rest I'ld give to be to you *translated*.ᵐ
O, teach me how you look, and with what art
You *sway the motion of*ⁿ Demetrius' heart.
    Her. I frown upon him, yet he loves me still.
    Hel. O, that your frowns would teach my smiles
        such skill!
    Her. I give him curses, yet he gives me love.
    Hel. O, that my prayers could such affection move!

Marginal glosses:
a *the god of love*
b i.e. *with which he would inspire the strongest love*
c *guilelessness*
d *Dido*
e *Æneas*
f sc. *word*
g *beauty*
h *guiding-stars*
i *tuneful*
k *features*
l *excepted*
m *transformed*
n *control at your will*

¹ Celebrate the customary rites of May day. (See Supplementary Notes.)
² Vergil (Æneid iv. 584, etc.) tells how Æneas in his voyage from Troy to Latium landed at Carthage, where the queen Dido fell in love with him. When he sailed away to seek the new home the gods had promised him, Dido in despair destroyed herself on a funeral pile. (See also Æneid v 1 7.)

Her. The more I hate, the more he follows me.

Hel. The more I love, the more he hateth me.

Her. His folly, Helena, is no fault of mine.   200

Hel. None, but your beauty : would that fault were mine !

Her. Take comfort : he no more shall see my face ;
Lysander and myself will fly this place.
¹*Before the time I did Lysander see,*
Seemed Athens as a paradise to me :
O, then, what graces in my love do dwell,
That he hath turn'd a heaven unto a hell !

Lys. Helen, to you our minds we will unfold :
To-morrow night,ᵃ when *Phœbe*ᵇ doth behold
Her silver visage in the watery glass,   210
Decking with *liquid pearl*ᶜ the bladed grass,
A time that lovers' flights doth *still*ᵈ conceal,
Through Athens' gates have we devised to steal.

Her. And in the wood, where often you and I
Upon *faint*ᵉ primrose-beds were wont to lie,
Emptying our bosoms of their *counsel*ᶠ sweet,
There my Lysander and myself shall meet ;
And thence, from Athens turn away our eyes,
To seek new friends and *stranger companies.*ᵍ
Farewell, sweet playfellow : pray thou for us,   220
And good luck grant thee thy Demetrius !
Keep word, Lysander : *we must starve our sight*
*From lovers' food,*ʰ till morrow deep midnight.

Lys. I will, my Hermia. [*Exit* HERM.] Helena, adieu :
As you on him, Demetrius dote on you !   [*Exit.*

Hel. How happy some *o'er other some*ⁱ can be !
Through Athens I am thought as fair as she ;
But what of that ? Demetrius thinks not so ;
He will not know what all but he do know ;
And as he errs, doting on Hermia's eyes,   230
So I, *admiring of*ᵏ his qualities.
Things base and vile, *holding no quantity,*ˡ

ᵃ *cf. line 2*
ᵇ *the moon*
ᶜ *dew-drops*
ᵈ *constantly*

ᵉ *pale*
ᶠ *inmost thoughts*

ᵍ *less familiar associates*

ʰ *i.e. we must not see each other*

ⁱ *as compared with others*

ᵏ *admiring*
ˡ *bearing no proportion (to what they are rated at)*

¹Athens, which was a Paradise to me before I saw Lysander, has become a hell to me now that, having seen and loved him, I am prohibited from meeting him. Such are the excellencies (which you s envy) that reside in my love !

Love can transpose to form and dignity :
Love looks not with the eyes, but with the mind,
And therefore is wing'd Cupid painted blind :
Nor hath Love's mind of any judgment taste ;
Wings and no eyes, *figure*[a] *unheedy*[b] haste :
And therefore is Love said to be a child,
Because in choice he is so oft *beguiled*.[c]
As waggish boys in game themselves forswear,   240
So the boy Love is perjured everywhere ;
For ere Demetrius look'd on Hermia's *eyne*,[d]
He hailed down oaths that he was *only mine*[e] ;
And when this hail some heat from Hermia felt,
So he dissolved, and showers of oaths did melt.
I will go tell him of fair Hermia's flight :
Then to the wood will he to-morrow night
Pursue her ; and for this intelligence
If I have thanks, [1]*it is a dear expense* :
But herein mean I to enrich *my pain*,[f]   250
To have his sight thither and back again.   [*Exit.*

a *denote*
b *rash*

c *cheated*

d *eyes*
e *mine alone*

f *the pain it causes me to bring them together*

SCENE II.—*Athens.   A Room in* QUINCE'S *House.*

Enter QUINCE, SNUG, BOTTOM, FLUTE, SNOUT, *and*
STARVELING.

Quin. Is all our company here ?

Bot. You *were best to*[g] call them *generally*,[h] man by man, according to the *scrip*.[i]

Quin. Here is the scroll of every man's name, which is thought fit, through all Athens, to play in our *interlude*[k] before the duke and the duchess on his wedding-day at night.

Bot. First, good Peter Quince, say what the play treats on ; then read the names of the actors ; and so *grow to a*[l] point.   10

g *had better*
h *Bottom's mistake for severally, i.e. one by one*
i *scroll or roll (list of actors)*
k *play.   See Gl*

l *come to the*

---

[1] It will be a high charge to make him, *i.e.* more than I expect to get from him.

Quin. Marry, our play is, The most lamentable comedy and most cruel death of Pyramus and Thisby.

Bot. A very good piece of work, I assure you, and a merry. Now, good Peter Quince, call forth your actors by the scroll. Masters, spread yourselves.

Quin. Answer, as I call you. Nick Bottom, the weaver.

Bot. Ready. Name what part I am for, and proceed.   20

Quin. You, Nick Bottom, are set down for Pyramus.

Bot. What is Pyramus? a lover, or a ¹*tyrant* ?

Quin. A lover, that kills himself most *gallant*ᵃ for love.   **a** *gallantly*

Bot. That will *ask*ᵇ some tears in the true per-   **b** *demand*
forming of it: if I do it, let the audience look to
their eyes; I will move storms, I will *condole* ᶜ in   **c** *lament*
some measure. *To the rest*ᵈ : yet my chief humour   **d** *sc. Proceed*
is for a tyrant: I could play *Ercles*ᵉ rarely, or a   **e** *Hercules*
part to tear a cat in, to make all split.   31

       The *raging rocks*ᶠ   **f** *Note the*
       And *shivering shocks*ᶠ   *alliteration*
       Shall break the locks
        Of prison gates ;
       And *Phibbus' car*ᵍ   **g** *Phoebus' car,*
       Shall shine from far,   *the sun*
       And make and mar
        The foolish Fates.

This was lofty ! Now name the rest of the players.
—This is Ercles' vein, a tyrant's vein; a lover is
more condoling.   42

Quin. Francis Flute, the bellows-mender.

Flu. Here, Peter Quince.

---

¹ The *tyrant* was a common character in the earlier Mystery-plays. In *Hamlet* III. ii., Shakespeare refers to such a character as Bottom would like to represent: "O, it offends me to the soul to hear a robustious periwig-pated fellow tear a passion to tatters, to very rags. . . I would have such a fellow whipped for o'erdoing Termagant; it out-herods Herod." Herod and Hercules were typical tyrants in these early plays.

Quin. You must take Thisby on you.

Flu. What is Thisbe? a *wandering knight?* [a]   a *knight-errant*

Quin. It is the lady that Pyramus must love.

Flu. Nay, faith, let me not [1]*play a woman;* I have a beard coming.

Quin. That's *all one.*[b]   You shall play it in a   b *does not matter*
mask, and you may speak as *small*[c] as you will.   51   c *shrill*

Bot. An I may hide my face, let me play Thisby too. I'll speak in a monstrous little voice: "Thisne, Thisne;" "Ah, Pyramus, my lover dear! thy Thisby dear, and lady dear!"

Quin. No, no; you must play Pyramus; and, Flute, you Thisby.

Bot. Well, proceed.

Quin. Robin Starveling, the tailor.

Star. Here, Peter Quince.   60

Quin. Robin Starveling, you must play Thisby's mother. Tom Snout, the tinker.

Snout. Here, Peter Quince.

Quin. You, Pyramus' father; myself, Thisby's   d *with actors to*
father. Snug, the joiner, you the lion's part: and,   *fit the parts*
I hope, here is a play *fitted.*[d]

Snug. Have you the lion's part written? pray you, if it be, give it me, for I am slow of study.

Quin. You may do it extempore, for it is nothing but roaring.   70

Bot. Let me play the lion too: I will roar, that I will do any man's heart good to hear me; I will roar, that I will make the duke say, "Let him roar again, let him roar again."

Quin. *An*[e] you should do it too terribly, you   e *If*
would *fright*[f] the duchess and the ladies, that they   f *frighten*
would shriek; and that were enough to hang us all.

All. That would hang us, every mother's son.

---

[1] In Shakespeare's time ladies' parts were played by boys or young men. Cf. *Hamlet* II. ii.: "What, my young lady and mistress! By'r lady, your ladyship is nearer to heaven than when I saw you last, by the altitude of a chopine (high shoe). Pray God, your voice . . . . be not cracked"

Bot. I grant you, friends, if that you should fright the ladies out of their wits, they would have no more discretion but to hang us: but I will *aggravate*[a] my voice so, that I will roar *you*[b] as gently as any sucking dove; I will roar *you*[c] an[d] 'twere any nightingale.   84

Quin. You can play no part but Pyramus; for Pyramus is a sweet-faced man; a *proper*[e] man, as one shall see in a summer's day; a most lovely, gentleman-like man: therefore, you must needs play Pyramus.

Bot. Well, I will undertake it. What beard were I best to play it in?   91

Quin. Why, what you will.

Bot. I will *discharge it*[f] in either your straw-colour beard, your *orange-tawny*[g] beard, your *purple-in-grain*[h] beard, or your *French-crown-colour*[i] beard, your perfect yellow.

Quin. Some of your French *crowns*[k] have no hair at all, and then you will play bare-faced. But, masters, here are your parts: and I am to entreat you, request you, and desire you, to *con*[l] them by to-morrow night, and meet me in the palace wood, a *mile*[m] without the town, by moonlight: there will we rehearse, for if we meet in the city, we shall be *dogged with*[n] company, and our *devices*[o] known. In the meantime I will draw a *bill*[p] of properties, such as our play wants. I pray you, fail me not.   106

Bot. We will meet; and there we may rehearse more *obscenely*[q] and courageously. Take pains; be perfect; adieu.

Quin. At the duke's oak we meet.   110

Bot. Enough; *hold, or cut bowstrings.*[r]

[*Exeunt.*

---

a *perhaps he means 'attenuate,' make thin*
b *see p. 97*
c *see p. 97*
d *as if*

e *handsome*

f *play the part*
g *dark orange (like tanned leather)*
h *scarlet-dyed*
i *yellow*
k *a pun on crown*

l *learn*

m *it is a league in I. i. 165.*

n *following too closely by*
o *plans*
p *list*

q *obscurely, secretly*

r *keep your appointment or throw up the game.*
See Notes

HERMIA.

ACT II.

SCENE I.—*A Wood near Athens.*

Enter, from opposite sides, a Fairy and PUCK.

Puck. How now, spirit, whither wander you?
Fai. Over hill, over dale,
   Thorough[a] bush, *thorough*[a] brier,
Over park, over *pale*,[b]
   Thorough[a] flood, *thorough*[a] fire,
I do wander everywhere,
Swifter than the *moon's*[c] [1]*sphere ;*
And I serve the fairy queen,
To *dew*[d] her *orbs*[e] upon the green :
The cowslips tall her *pensioners*[f] be ;   10
In their [2]*gold coats* spots you see,
Those be rubies, *fairy favours,*[g]
In those freckles live their *savours*[h] *;*
I must go seek some dew-drops here,

[a] *through*
[b] *a space en-
closed by rails*

[c] *dissyllable*

[d] *be-dew, moisten*
[e] *fairy-rings*
[f] *body-guard*
[g] *tokens of love
from the
fairies*
[h] *perfume*

---

[1] The 'sphere' is the orbit in which a star moves, and which in Shakespeare's time was generally thought to move also.
[2] The 'gold coats' and the 'rubies' contain an allusion to the splendour of the uniform of the Elizabethan body-guard

And hang a pearl in every cowslip's ear.
Farewell, thou *lob of*[a] spirits; I'll be gone:
Our queen and all her elves come here *anon.*[b]

    Puck. The king doth keep his revels here to-
night:
Take heed the queen come not within his sight;
For Oberon is *passing fell*[c] and *wrath,*[d]   20
Because that *she*[e] as her attendant hath
A lovely boy, stolen from an [1]*Indian* king,
She never had so sweet a *changeling*[f],
And jealous Oberon would have the child
Knight of his train, to *trace*[g] the forests wild;
But she perforce withholds the lovéd boy,
Crowns him with flowers, and makes him all her
    joy:
And now they never meet in grove or green,
By fountain clear or spangled starlight *sheen,*[h]
But they do *square,*[i] *that*[k] all their elves, for fear,   30
Creep into acorn cups and hide them there.

    Fai. Either I mistake your shape and *making*[l]
    quite,
Or else you are that *shrewd*[m] and knavish sprite
Call'd [2]*Robin Goodfellow.* Are not you he
That frights the maidens of the *villagery*[n];
Skim milk, and sometimes labour in the *quern,*[o]
And bootless make the breathless housewife churn;
And sometime make the drink to bear no *barm :*[p]
Mislead[q] night-wanderers, laughing at their *harm*[r] *?*
Those that Hobgoblin call you, and sweet Puck,   40
You do their work, and they shall have good luck:
Are not you he?

    Puck.   Thou speak'st aright;
I am that merry wanderer of the night.
I jest to Oberon, and make him smile,

Side glosses:

a *clown among*
b *shortly*
c *exceedingly fierce*
d *wroth*
e *subject of "hath stolen"*
f *stolen child*
g *range over*
h *brightness*
i *quarrel*
k *so that*
l *external appearance*
m *mischievous*
n *villages*
o *hand-mill for grinding corn*
p *yeast*
q *lead astray*
r *misfortune*

---

[1] Notice that the fairies are associated with India, which in Shakespeare's
time included all the islands of the Archipelago. (See p. 117.)

[2] Robin Good-fellow, Puck and Hob-goblin were only different for the same
mischievous sprite. Burton, in his "Anatomy of Melancholy," refers to some of
his peculiar functions: "A bigger kind there is of them (fairies), called with us
Hobgoblins, and *Robin Good-fellows,* that would in these superstitious times,
grind corn for a mess of milk, cut wood, or do any manner of drudgery work."

When I a fat and bean-fed horse *beguile*[a]
Neighing in likeness of a *filly foal*[b] ;
And sometime lurk I in a *gossip's bowl,*[c]
In very likeness of a roasted crab,
And when she drinks, against her lips I bob,   50
And on her wither'd [1]*dewlap* pour the ale.
The wisest *aunt,*[d] telling the saddest tale,
Sometime for three-foot stool mistaketh me,
Then slip I from her bum, down topples she,
And [2]*'tailor'* cries, and falls into a cough,
And then *the whole quire*[e] hold their hips and laugh
And *waxen*[f] in their mirth and *neeze*[g] and swear
A merrier hour was never *wasted*[h] there.
But, room, fairy ! here comes Oberon.

    Fai. And here my mistress. Would that he were gone !   60

Enter, from one side, OBERON *with his Train, and from the other* TITANIA *with hers.*

    Obe. Ill met by moonlight, proud Titania.
    Tita. What, jealous Oberon ! Fairies, skip hence :
I have forsworn his bed and company.
    Obe. Tarry, rash wanton.   Am not I thy lord ?
    Tita. Then I must be thy lady : but I know
When thou hast stolen away from fairy land
And in the shape of *Corin*[i] sat all day,
Playing on [3]*pipes of corn* and *versing love*[k]
To amorous *Phillida.*[l]   Why art thou here,
Come from the farthest *steppe*[m] of India,   70
But that, forsooth, the *bouncing*[n] Amazon,
Your *buskin'd*[o] mistress and your warrior love,

---

a	*deceive*
b	*young mare*
c	*christening-cup. See Note, p. 77.*
d	*old woman*
e	*all in chorus*
f	*grow boisterous*
g	*sneeze*
h	*spent*
i	*a typical name for a shepherd*
k	*making love songs*
l	*a shepherdess*
m	*steep. See l. 22*
n	*mannish*
o	*booted*

---

[1] The 'dewlap' is the loose flesh hanging from the throat ; properly applied only to cattle.   In IV. i., Theseus' hounds are spoken of as being "dew-lapp'd like Thessalian bulls."

[2] Referring to the custom of crying tailor at a sudden fall backwards. Johnson remarks : "He that slips beside his chair, falls as a tailor squats upon his board."   (See also the Notes.)

[3] 'Pipes of corn' are oaten straws which shepherds converted into musical wind instruments

To Theseus must be wedded? and you come
To give their bed joy and prosperity.

    Obe. How canst thou thus, for shame, Titania,
Glance at[a] my *credit*[b] with Hippolyta,
Knowing I know thy love to Theseus?
Didst thou not lead him through the glimmering
      night
From [1]*Perigenia*, whom he ravishéd?
And make him with fair [1]*Ægle* break his faith,   80
With [1]*Ariadne*, and [1]*Antiopa?*

    Tita. These are the *forgeries of*[c] jealousy:
And never, since the *middle summer's spring*,[d]
Met we on hill, in dale, forest, or mead,
By *pavéd fountain*,[e] or by rushy brook,
Or *in the beachéd margent*[f] of the sea,
To dance our *ringlets*[g] to the whistling wind,
But with thy brawls thou hast disturb'd our sport,
Therefore the winds, *piping*[h] to us in vain,
As in revenge, have suck'd up from the sea   90
Contagious[i] fogs, which, falling in the land,
Hath every *pelting*[k] river made so proud,
That they have overborne their *continents;*[l]
The ox hath therefore stretch'd his yoke in vain,
The ploughman *lost his sweat*,[m] and the green corn
Hath rotted *ere his youth attain'd a beard*[n]:
The fold stands empty in the drownéd field,
And crows are fatted with the *murrion*[o] flock;
The [2]*nine men's morris* is filled up with mud;
And the quaint *mazes*[p] in the *wanton green*[q]   100
For lack of tread are undistinguishable:
[3]*The human mortals want their winter here,*

a *call in question*
b *influence*

c *false tales invented by*
d *beginning of mid-summer*
e *pebbly stream*
f *on the margin formed by the beach*
g *small fairy rings*
h *whistling*
i *noxious, pestilential*
k *paltry*
l *banks*
m *wasted his efforts*
n *i.e. before it ripened, his = its*
o *murrain*
p *tracks. See Notes*
q *luxuriant grass*

---

[1] Perigenia, Ægle, Ariadne, Antiopa are names taken from North's "Plutarch's Life of Theseus."

[2] The 'nine men's morris' was a kind of out-door draughts, for which a series of squares were cut out on the green turf. The confusion of seasons described in this speech is generally supposed to refer to the extraordinarily bad weather that prevailed in 1593 and 1594, and consequently affords an indication as to the date of the play.

[3] The meaning seems to be: 'Not only have our quarrels resulted in spoiling the summer season for human beings all around us, but they have not even the consolations that winter brings with it.'

No night is now with hymn or carol blest,
Therefore[a] the moon, *the governess of floods,*[b]
Pale in her anger, washes all the air,
That rheumatic diseases do abound:
And *thorough*[c] this *distemperature*[d] we see
The seasons alter: hoary-headed frosts
Fall in the fresh lap of the crimson rose;
And on old Hiems' *thin and icy*[e] crown   110
An odorous chaplet of sweet summer buds
Is, as in mockery, set.   The spring, the summer,
The *childing*[f] autumn, angry winter, change
Their wonted *liveries*[g]; and *the mazéd world,*[h]
By their *increase,*[i] now knows not which is which.
And this same progeny of evils comes
From our *debate,*[k] from our dissension;
We are their parents and *original.*[l]

Obe. Do you amend it, then; it *lies in you.*[m]
Why should Titania *cross*[n] her Oberon?   120
I do but beg a little changeling boy,
To be my *henchman.*[o]

Tita.   Set your heart at rest,
The fairy land buys not the child of me.
His mother *was a votaress*[p] of my order:
And, in the *spicéd*[q] Indian air, by night,
Full often hath she gossip'd by my side,
And sat with me on Neptune's yellow sands,
Marking the *embarkéd traders*[r] on the *flood*[s];
When we have laugh'd to see the sails conceive
And grow big-bellied with the wanton wind;   130
Which she, with pretty and with swimming *gait*[t]
Following,—her womb then rich with my young
          squire—
Would imitate, and sail upon the land
To fetch me trifles, and return again,
As from a voyage, rich with merchandise.
But she, being mortal, of that boy did die;
And for her sake do I rear up her boy,
And for her sake I will not part with him.

Obe. How long within this wood intend you
          stay[u]?
Tita. Perchance, till after Theseus' wedding-day.

a i.e. *because of
    our quarrels*
b *that rules the
    tides*
c *through*
d *strife between
    us*

e i.e. *thinly
    covered with
    white hair*

f *fertile*
g *appearance*
h *confused
    humanity*
i *products*
k *quarrel*
l *originators*
m *rests with you*
n *thwart*

o *page*

p *had taken the
    vow*
q *fragrant*

r *trading ships
    embarked*
s *sea*
t *action*

u sc. *to*

* See p. 109 on which this passage is paraphrased

If you will patiently dance in our round,
And see our moonlight revels, go with us;
If not, shun me, and I will *spare*[a] your haunts.

    Obe. Give me that boy, and I will go with thee.

    Tita. Not for thy fairy kingdom. Fairies, away!
We shall *chide downright*,[b] if I longer stay.

             [*Exit* TITANIA, *with her Train.*

    Obe. Well, go thy way: thou *shalt not*[c] from this grove
Till I torment thee for this injury.
My gentle Puck, come hither: thou rememberest
Since[d] once I sat upon a promontory,   150
And heard a [1]*mermaid on a dolphin's back*
Uttering such *dulcet*[e] and harmonious *breath*,[f]
That the rude sea grew *civil*[g] at her song,
And certain stars shot madly from their *spheres*,[h]
To hear the sea-maid's music,

    Puck.   ·   I remember.

    Obe. That very time I saw, but thou couldst not,
Flying between the cold moon and the earth,
Cupid *all arm'd*; a *certain*[k] aim he took
At a fair *vestal*[l] thronéd by the west,
And loosed his love-shaft smartly from his bow 160
As it should pierce a hundred thousand hearts:
But I *might*[m] see young Cupid's fiery shaft
Quench'd[n] in the chaste beams of the watery moon,
And the imperial votaress passed on,
In maiden meditation, *fancy-free*.[o]
Yet mark'd I where the bolt of Cupid fell:
It fell upon a little [2]*western flower*,
Before milk-white, now purple with love's wound,
And maidens call it love-in-idleness.
Fetch me that flower: the herb I show'd thee once: 170

Marginal glosses
a *avoid*
b *quarrel violently*
c sc. *go*
d *when*
e *sweet*
f *sounds*
g *calm, smooth*
h *orbits. See l. 7*
i *fully equipped*
k *deliberate*
l i.e. Q. *Elizabeth, vowed to maidenhood*
m *was able to*
n *lose its fire*
o *unaffected by love's shafts*

---

[1] Possibly the 'mermaid' symbolises Mary Queen of Scots, and the 'dolphin' the Dauphin of France, and Shakespeare may have had in his mind the festivities which were held at Kenilworth, in 1575, when the Earl of Leicester entertained Queen Elizabeth. The 'fair vestal thronéd by the west,' of line 159 and the 'imperial votaress,' of line 164, certainly refer to the virgin queen.

[2] The 'western flower' is the pansy, that flourishes in the West.

The juice of it, on sleeping eyelids laid,
Will make or man or woman madly dote
Upon the next live creature that it sees.
Fetch me this herb ; and be thou here again
Ere the *leviathan*[a] can swim a league.

   Puck. I'll *put a girdle round about*[b] the earth
In forty minutes.   *[Exit.*

   Obe.   Having once this juice,
I'll watch Titania when she is asleep,
And drop the liquor of it in her eyes.
The next thing then she waking looks upon,   180
Be it on lion, bear, or wolf, or bull,
On meddling monkey, or on busy ape,
She shall pursue it with the *soul of*[c] love :
And ere I take this charm from off her sight,
As I can take it with another herb,
I'll make her render up her page to me.
But who comes here ?   I am invisible ;
And I will overhear their *conference.*[d]

     Enter DEMETRIUS, HELENA *following him.*

   Dem. I love thee not, therefore pursue me not.
Where is Lysander and fair Hermia ?   190
The one I'll slay, the other slayeth me.
Thou told'st me, they were stolen unto this wood ;
And here am I, and *wood*[e] within this wood
Because I cannot meet my Hermia.
Hence, get thee gone, and follow me no more.

   Hel. You draw me, you hard-hearted *adamant*[f];
[1]*But yet you draw not iron,*[g] *though my heart
Is true as steel :* leave you your power to draw,
And I shall have no power to follow you.

   Dem. Do I *entice*[h] you ? do I speak you fair ? 200
Or, rather, do I not in plainest truth
Tell you, I do not, *nor*[i] I can*not*[i] love you ?

   Hel. And even for that do I love you the more.
I am your spaniel ; and, Demetrius,

Glosses (right margin):

a *whale*
b *encircle, travel round*
c *most intense, cf. our 'soul of honour'*
d *conversation*
e *mad*
f *lodestone*
g *You draw not one whose heart is iron*
h *exert myself to attract*
i *double negative used for emphasis*

---

[1] A pun on the two meanings of iron; (1) a metal, (2) hard-hearted. ' Though ' is Lettsom's emendation for the ' for ' of the quartos and folios. If the reading ' for ' is retained we must suppose that Shakespeare imagined that the lodestone which attracted *iron* did not also attract *steel.*

The more you beat me, I will fawn on you :
Use me but as your spaniel, spurn me, strike me,
Neglect me, lose me; only give me leave,
Unworthy as I am, to follow you.
What *worser*[a] place can I beg in your love,—
And yet a place *of high respect with*[b] me,—   210
Than to be uséd as you use your dog?

    Dem. Tempt not too much the hatred of my spirit,
For I am sick when I do look on thee.

    Hel. And I am sick when I look not on you.

    Dem. You do *impeach*[c] your modesty too much
To leave[d] the city, and *commit*[e] yourself
Into the hands of one that loves you not ;
To trust the opportunity of night
And the ill *counsel*[f] of a desert place
With the rich worth of your virginity.   220

    Hel. Your virtue [1]*is my privilege*[g] : for that
It is not night when I do see your face,
Therefore I think I am not in the night ;
Nor doth this wood lack worlds of company,
For you, *in my respect,*[h] are all the world,
Then how can it be said I am alone,
When all the world is here to look on me ?

    Dem. I'll run from thee and hide me in the *brakes*[i]
And leave thee to the mercy of wild beasts.

    Hel. The wildest hath not such a heart as you. 230
Run when you will, the story shall be changed,
[2]*Apollo flies, and Daphne holds the chase ;*
The dove pursues the griffin ; the mild hind
Makes speed to catch the tiger. *Bootless*[k] speed,
When cowardice pursues, and valour flies !

    Dem. I will not stay thy *questions*[l] : let me go ;
Or, if thou follow me, do not believe

a *more humble*
b *valued highly*

c *expose to reproach*
d *in leaving*
e *committing*

f *suggestions*

g *affords me protection*

h *to me, in my eyes*

i *thickets*

k *purposeless*

arguments

---

  [1] Or, taking 'virtue' in the sense of 'excellence,' the meaning of this and the following lines may be : 'Your surpassing merits, in my eyes, enable me to do with safety that which others might not do ; since when you are in my sight I am in the light of day.'

  [2] Daphne was a beautiful nymph of whom Apollo became enamoured. She fled from him, and, as she was on the point of being overtaken, prayed to the gods for aid and was changed into a laurel-tree ($\delta\acute{\alpha}\phi\nu\eta$), which became in consequence the favourite tree of Apollo.

But I shall[a] do thee mischief in the wood.

  Hel. Ay, in the temple, in the town, the field,
You do me mischief.   Fie, Demetrius !   240
Your wrongs do set[b] a scandal on my sex.
We cannot fight for love, as men may do ;
We should be woo'd, and were not made to woo.
I'll follow thee, and make a heaven of hell,

                                   [*Exit* DEMETRIUS.

To die *upon*[c] the hand I love so well.   [*Exit.*

  Obe. Fare thee well, nymph : ere he do leave this
      grove,
Thou shalt fly him, and he shall seek thy love.

                Re-enter PUCK.

Hast thou the flower there ?   Welcome, wanderer.
  Puck. Ay, there it is.
  Obe.   I pray thee, give it me.
I know a bank where the wild thyme *blows*,[d]   250
Where oxlips and the nodding violet grows ;
Quite *over-canopied*[e] with *luscious woodbine*,[f]
With sweet musk-roses, and with *eglantine*[g] :
There sleeps Titania, sometime of the night,
Lull'd in these flowers with dances and delight ;
And there the snake *throws*[h] her *enamell'd*[i] skin,
Weed[k] wide enough to wrap a fairy in :
And with the juice of this I'll *streak*[l] her eyes,
And make her full of hateful *fantasies*,[m]
Take thou some of it, and seek through this grove.
A sweet *Athenian lady*[n] is in love   261
With a *disdainful youth*[o] : anoint his eyes ;
But do it, when the next thing he espies
May be the lady.   Thou shalt know the man
By the Athenian garments he hath on.
Effect it with some care, that he may prove
More fond on[p] her than she upon her love.
And look thou meet me ere the first cock crow
  Puck. Fear not, my lord, your servant shall do so.

                             [*Exeunt.*

Marginal notes:

a *that I shall not*

b *the injuries
   you do me are*

c *by*

d *flowers, bloom*

e *overspread*
f *fragrant honey-
   suckle*
g *sweet-brier*

h *casts*
i *glossy and
   variegated*
k *garment*
l *overspread*
m *fancies*

n i.e. *Helena*

o i.e. *Demetrius*

p *to dote more
   upon*

SCENE II.—*Another part of the Wood.*

Enter TITANIA, *with her Train.*

Tita. Come, now a *roundel*[a] and a fairy song;
Then, for the third part of a minute, hence;
Some, to kill *cankers*[b] in the musk-rose buds;
Some, war with *rere-mice*[c] for their leathern wings
To make my small elves coats; and some, keep back
The clamorous owl that nightly hoots and wonders
At our quaint spirits. Sing me now asleep;
Then to your *offices*,[d] and let me rest.

The Fairies sing :—

You spotted snakes with *double*[e] tongue,
   Thorny hedge-hogs, be not seen;   10
[1]*Newts and blind-worms*, do no wrong,
   Come not near our fairy queen.
Philomel,[f] with melody
   Sing in our sweet *lullaby*[g];
Lulla, lulla, lullaby; lulla, lulla, lullaby :
   Never harm,
   Nor spell nor charm,
Come our lovely lady nigh;
So, good night, with lullaby.
Weaving [1]*spiders*, come not here;   20
   Hence, you long-legg'd spinners, hence!
Beetles black, approach not near;
   Worm nor snail, do no offence.
Philomel, with melody, &c.

A Fairy. Hence, away! now all is well.
   One, aloof, stand sentinel.

        [*Exeunt Fairies.* TITANIA *sleeps.*

Enter OBERON, *and squeezes the flower on*
        TITANIA'S *eyelids.*

Obe. What thou seest, when thou dost wake,
  Do it for thy *true-love take*[h];

Margin notes:

a *a round dance (in a fairy ring)*
b *worms or flies that prey on blossoms*
c *bats*
d *duties*
e *forked*
f *the nightingale. See Clas. Names*
g *a song to send to sleep*
h *take it to be etc.*

---

[1] It was popularly believed in Shakespeare's time that newts, blind-worms (or slow-worms), and spiders were venomous.

Love, and *languish*[a] for his sake :
Be it *ounce*,[b] or cat, or bear,   30
Pard,[c] or boar with bristled hair,
In thy eye that shall appear
When thou wakest, it is thy dear :
Wake when some vile thing is near.   [*Exit.*

    Enter LYSANDER *and* HERMIA.

Lys. Fair love, you faint with wandering in the
    wood ;
And, to speak *troth*,[d] I have forgot our way :
We'll rest us, Hermia, if you think it good,
And tarry for the comfort of the day.

  Her. Be it so, Lysander : find you out a bed ;
For I upon this bank will rest my head.   40

  Lys. One turf shall serve as pillow for us both ;
One heart, one bed, two bosoms, and one *troth*.[e]

  Her. Nay, good Lysander ; for my sake, my dear,
Lie further off yet, do not lie so near.

  Lys. O, *take the sense, sweet, of my innocence*[f] !
[1]*Love takes the meaning in love's conference.*
I mean, that my heart unto yours is knit,
So that but one heart we can make of it :
Two bosoms interchainéd with an *oath*[g] ;
So then, two bosoms and a single *troth*.[h]   50
Then by your side no bed-room me deny,
For, *lying*[i] so, Hermia, I do not *lie*.[i]

  Her. Lysander riddles very prettily :
Now much *beshrew*[k] my manners and my pride,
If Hermia meant to say Lysander lied.
But, gentle friend, for love and courtesy
Lie further off ; in *human*[l] modesty,
Such separation as may well be said
Becomes a virtuous bachelor and a maid,
So far be distant ; and good night, sweet friend : 60
Thy love ne'er alter till thy sweet life end !

  Lys. Amen, amen, to that fair prayer, say I ;
And [2]*then end life when I end loyalty* !

---

[a] *pine away (for love)*
[b] *an animal between a panther and a cat*
[c] *panther*
[d] *the truth*
[e] *fidelity, faith*
[f] *understand my innocent meaning rightly*
[g] *pledge of fidelity*
[h] *fidelity*
[i] *pun on 'lie'*
[k] *a plague upon*
[l] *humane, worthy of a man*

---

[1] True lovers understand each other without words ; or, Love supplies the true meaning when lovers converse.
[2] May I die if I cease to be loyal

D

Here is my bed : sleep give thee all his rest !

Her. *With half that wish the wisher's eyes be*
    pressed^a !   [*They sleep.*

            Enter PUCK.

Puck. Through the forest have I gone,
    But Athenian found I none,
    On whose eyes I might *approve*^b
    This flower's force in stirring love.
    Night and silence ! Who is here?   70
    Weeds^c of Athens he doth wear :
    This is he, my master said,
    Despiséd the Athenian maid ;
    And here the maiden, sleeping sound
    On the *dank*^d and dirty ground.
    Pretty soul ! she durst not lie
    Near this lack-love, this kill-courtesy.
    Churl,^e upon thy eyes I throw
    All the power this charm doth *owe.*^f
    When thou wakest, let love forbid   80
    Sleep *his seat*^g on thy eyelid :
    So awake when I am gone ;
    For I must now to Oberon.   [*Exit.*

   Enter DEMETRIUS *and* HELENA, *running.*

Hel. Stay, though thou kill me, sweet Demetrius.

Dem. I charge thee, hence, and do not haunt me
    thus.

Hel. O, wilt thou *darkling*^h leave me? do not so.

Dem. Stay, on thy peril : I alone will go.   [*Exit.*

Hel. O, I am out of breath in this *fond chase*ⁱ !
The more my prayer, the lesser is *my grace.*^k
Happy is Hermia, wheresoe'er she lies ;   90
For she hath blesséd and attractive eyes.
How came her eyes so bright?   Not with salt tears :
If so, my eyes are oftener wash'd than hers.
No, no, I am as ugly as a bear ;
For beasts, that meet me, run away for fear :
Therefore no marvel though Demetrius
Do, *as a monster, fly my presence*^l thus.
What wicked and dissembling glass of mine
Made me compare with Hermia's *sphery eyne*^m?

---

a i.e. *May sleep give thee half his rest*

b *prove*

c *garments*

d *damp*

e *Unyielding boor*

f *own, possess*

g *to settle ; his = its*

h *in the dark*

i *mad pursuit*

k *the favour I find*

l *flies from me as from a monster*

m *eyes bright as stars*

But who is here?   Lysander! on the ground!   100
Dead? or asleep?   I see no blood, no wound.
Lysander, if you live, good sir, awake.

   Lys. [*Awaking.*] And run through fire I will for
     thy sweet sake.
Transparent Helena! Nature shows art,
That through thy bosom makes me see thy heart.
Where is Demetrius?   O, how fit a word
Is that vile name to perish on my sword!

   Hel. Do not say so, Lysander; say not so.
What though he love your Hermia? Lord, what
     though?
Yet Hermia still loves you: then be content.   110

   Lys. Content with Hermia!   No; I do repent
The tedious minutes I with her have spent.
Not Hermia, but Helena I love:
Who will not change a raven for a dove?
The will of man is by his reason sway'd,
And reason says you are the worthier maid.
Things growing are not ripe until their season,
So I, being young, till now ripe not to reason;
And [1]*touching now the point of human skill*,
Reason *becomes the marshal to*[a] my will,   120
And leads me to your eyes; *where I o'erlook*[b]
Love's stories written in love's richest book.

   Hel. Wherefore was I to this keen mockery born?
When at your hands did I deserve this scorn?
Is't not enough, is't not enough, young man,
That I did never, no, *nor never*[c] can,
Deserve a sweet look from Demetrius' eye,
But you must *flout*[d] my insufficiency?
Good *troth*,[e] you do me wrong, good *sooth*,[e] you do,
In such disdainful manner me to woo.   130
But fare you well: perforce I must confess
I thought you lord of more true gentleness.
O, that a lady *of*[f] one man refused
Should *of*[f] another therefore be abused!   [*Exit.*

a *guides*
b *wherein I see*

c *double negative*

d *jeer at*
e *truth*

f *by*

---

[1] Now that I have reached the highest point of wisdom (skill) attainable by mortals (human).

Lys. She sees not Hermia. Hermia, sleep thou
    there :
And never mayst thou come Lysander near !
For, as *a surfeit*[a] of the sweetest things
The deepest loathing to the stomach brings ;
Or, as the *heresies*[b] that men *do leave*[c]
Are hated most *of*[d] those they did deceive ;   140
So thou, [1]*my surfeit and my heresy*,
Of[d] all be hated, but the most *of*[d] me.
And, all my powers, address your love and might
To honour Helen, and to be her knight.   [*Exit*.

    Her. [*Awaking*.] Help me, Lysander, help me ! do
    thy best,
To pluck this crawling serpent[e] from my breast !
Ay me, for pity ! what a dream was here !
Lysander, look how I do quake with fear.
Methought a serpent ate my heart away,
And you sat smiling at his *cruel prey*.[f]   150
Lysander ! what, removed ? Lysander ! lord !
What, out of hearing ? gone ? no sound, no word ?
Alack ! where are you ? speak, *an if*[g] you hear ;
Speak, *of all loves*[h] ! I swoon almost with fear.
No ? then I well perceive you are not nigh :
Either death, or you, I'll find immediately.   [*Exit*.

a *excess*

b *wrong beliefs*
c *abandon*
d *by*

e *Hermia is still
under the in-
fluence of her
dream*

f *cruelly preying
upon me*

g *if*
h *by all the
powers of love*

---

[1] Ot whom I have had more than enough, and in whom I erringly believed.

ACT III.

Scene I.—*The Wood.* Titania *lying asleep.*

Enter Quince, Snug, Bottom, Flute, Snout, *and*
Starveling.

Bot. Are we all met?

Quin. *Pat, pat*^a; and here's a marvellous con-
venient place for our rehearsal. This green plot
shall be our stage, this hawthorn-*brake*^b our *tiring-
house*^c; and we will do it in action, as we will do it
before the duke.

Bot. Peter Quince,—

Quin. What sayest thou, [1]*bully*^d Bottom?

Bot. There are things in this comedy of Pyramus
and Thisby, that will never please. First, Pyramus
must draw a sword to kill himself, which the ladies
cannot abide. How answer you that? 12

Snout. By'r *lakin,*^e a *parlous*^f fear.

a *to a nicety,
  exactly*

b *thicket*

c *dressing-room*

d *comrade*

e *lady-kin =
  little lady =
  the Virgin
  Mary*

f *perilous*

---

[1] 'Bully' is a term of admiring familiarity addressed by his comrades to a
dashing, swaggering fellow. The oldest sense in English is 'dear one.' 'lover.'
(Cf. Ger. *buhle.* a lover.)

Star. I believe, we must leave the killing out, *when all is done.*[a]

Bot. Not a whit : I have a device to make all well. Write me a prologue ; and let the prologue seem to say, we will do no harm with our swords, and that Pyramus is not killed indeed ; and, for the more better assurance, tell them that I, Pyramus, am not Pyramus, but Bottom, the weaver. This will put them out of fear.   22

Quin. Well, we will have such a prologue, and it shall be written in *eight and six.*[b]

Bot. No, make it two more : let it be written in eight and eight.

Snout. Will not the ladies be afeard of the lion ?

Star. I fear it, *I promise you.*[c]

Bot. Masters, you ought to consider with your-selves : to bring in,—God shield us !—a lion among ladies, is a most dreadful thing ; for there is not a more fearful *wild-fowl*[d] than *your*[e] lion living ; and we ought to look to it.   33

Snout. Therefore another prologue must tell he is not a lion.

Bot. Nay, you must name his name, and half his face must be seen through the lion's neck ; and he himself must speak through, saying thus, or to the same *defect,*[f]—' Ladies,' or, ' Fair ladies ;—I would wish you,'—or, ' I would request you,'—or, ' I would entreat you,—not to fear, not to tremble : *my life*[g] for yours. If you think I come hither as a lion, it were *pity of my life*[h] : no, I am no such thing ; I am a man as other men are :'—and there, indeed, let him name his name, and tell them plainly he is Snug, the joiner.   46

Quin. Well, it shall be so. But there *is*[i] two hard things :—that is, to bring the moonlight into a chamber : for, you know, Pyramus and Thisby meet by moonlight.   50

Snug. Doth the moon shine that night we play our play ?

Bot. A calendar, a calendar ! look in the *almanac*[k] ; find out moonshine, find out moonshine.

a *after all*

b *alternate lines of eight and six syllables*

c *let me tell you*

d *this is Bottom's wit*
e *see p. 97*

f *effect*

g *I stake, etc.*

h *as much as my life is worth*

i *are*

k *an anachronism*

Quin. Yes, *it doth shine that night.*[a]

Bot. Why, then you may leave a casement of the great chamber-de-window, where we play, open ; and the moon may shine in at the casement.

Quin. Ay ; or else one must come in with a bush of thorns and a lanthorn, and say, he comes to *disfigure,*[b] or to *present,*[c] the person of Moonshine. Then, there is another thing : we must have a wall in the great chamber ; for Pyramus and Thisby, says *the story,*[d] did talk through the chink of a wall.   64

Snug. You can never bring in a wall. What say you, Bottom ?

Bot. Some man or other must present Wall ; and let him have some plaster, or some loam, or some *rough-cast*[e] about him, to signify wall ; and let him hold his fingers thus, and through that cranny shall Pyramus and Thisby whisper.   71

Quin. If that may be, then all is well. Come, sit down, every mother's son, and rehearse your parts. Pyramus, you begin. When you have spoken your speech, enter into that *brake*[f] : and so every one according to his cue.

Enter Puck *behind.*

Puck. What [1]*hempen home-spuns*[g] have we swaggering here,
So near the cradle of the fairy queen ?
What, a play *toward*[h] ? I'll be an auditor ;
An actor too, perhaps, if I see cause.   80

Quin. Speak, Pyramus. Thisby, stand forth.

Bot. Thisby, the flowers of *odious*[i] savours sweet,

Quin. *Odours, odours.*[i]

Bot. . . . . . *Odours*[i] savours sweet :
[2]*So hath thy breath,*[k] my dearest Thisby, dear.

a *the new moon would not afford any light*

b *figure*
c *represent*

d *see p. 84*

e *fluid mortar mixed with gravel*

f *thicket*

g *coarse-mannered fellows*

h *in preparation*

i *for 'odorous'*

k *sc. odorous savours*

---

[1] Puck naturally contrasts the rude Athenian swains with the 'fairy grace of Titania. They are to her as coarse hemp is to the flowers and gossamer threads that form the cradle of the fairy queen.

[2] Perhaps a line is omitted between Bottom's first and second lines, or perhaps 'of' in the first line is a mistake for 'have.' But we must not look to find much sense in any of Bottom's utterances. His verses are purposely incorrect and absurd

But, hark, a voice! stay thou but here awhile,
And by and by I will to thee appear.   [*Exit.*

   Puck. A stranger Pyramus than e'er played
here!   [*Exit.*

   Flu. Must I speak now?

   Quin. Ay, marry, must you; for you must understand, he goes but to see a noise that he heard, and
is to come again.   92

   Flu. Most radiant Pyramus, most lily-white of
hue,

Of colour like the red rose on triumphant brier,
Most *brisky juvenal*,[a] and *eke*[b] most lovely [1]*Jew*,

    As true as truest horse, that yet would never tire,

I'll meet thee, Pyramus, at Ninny's tomb.

> a *brisk juvenile
> or lively youth*
> b *likewise*

   Quin. 'Ninus' tomb,' man. Why, you must not
speak that yet; that you answer to Pyramus. You
speak all your part at once, cues and all. Pyramus,
enter: your cue is past; it is 'never tire.'   101

   Flu. O,—As true as truest horse, that yet would
never tire.

Re-enter PUCK, *and* BOTTOM, *with an ass's head.*

   Bot. *If I were fair, Thisby*,[c] *I were only thine.*

   Quin. O monstrous! O strange! we are haunted.
Pray, masters! fly, masters! help!

> c *for* 'If I were
> fair Thisbe'

[*Exeunt* QUINCE, SNUG, FLUTE, SNOUT, *and*
                   STARVELING.

   Puck. I'll follow you, I'll lead you about a round,
Through bog, through bush, through brake,
    through brier:
Sometime a horse I'll be, sometime a hound,
   A hog, a headless bear, sometime a *fire*[d];
And neigh, and bark, and grunt, and roar, and burn,
Like horse, hound, hog, bear, fire, at every turn.
                      [*Exit.*

> d *i.e. the Will-
> of-the-wisp*

---

[1] That 'Jew' rhymes with 'hue' is sufficient justification for its use here, in
the play in which "There is not one word apt, one player fitted." If further
explanation seem to be necessary, it may be taken as Bottom's mistake for 'juel'
the M.E. form of 'jewel.'

Bot. [1]*Why do they run away?* this is a knavery of them to make me afeard. 113

Re-enter SNOUT.

Snout. O Bottom! thou art changed! what do I see on thee?

Bot. What do you see? [1]*you see an ass-head of your own, do you?* [*Exit* SNOUT.

Re-enter QUINCE.

Quin. Bless thee, Bottom! bless thee! thou art translated.[a] [*Exit.*

Bot. I see their knavery. This is to make an ass of me; to fright me, if they could. But I will not stir from this place, do what they can. I will walk up and down here, and I will sing, that they shall hear I am not afraid. [*Sings.*

> The *ousel*[b]-cock, so black of hue, 125
>   With *orange-tawny*[c] bill;
> The *throstle*[d] with his note so true,
>   The wren with *little quill*[e];—

Tita. [*Awaking.*] What angel wakes me from my flowery bed?

Bot. [*Sings.*] The finch, the sparrow, and the lark;
> The *plain-song cuckoo*[f] gray, 131
> Whose note full many a man doth mark,
>   And dares not answer, nay;—

for, indeed, who would *set*[g] his wit to so foolish a bird? who would give a bird the lie, though he [2]*cry 'cuckoo'* never so?

Tita. I pray thee, gentle mortal, sing again:
Mine ear is much enamour'd of thy note;
So is mine eye enthrallèd to thy shape;
And *thy fair virtue's force*,[h] perforce, doth move me,
On the first view, to say, to swear, I love thee. 141

Bot. Methinks, mistress, you should have little reason for that: and yet, to say the truth, reason

a for 'transformed'

b *blackbird*

c *cf.* I. ii. 94
d *song-thrush*
e *shrill note*

f *cuckoo with its simple note*

g *oppose*

h *the force of thy fair virtue (beauty)*

---

[1] Bottom is of course unconscious of the change in his appearance.
[2] There is a pun intended here. To cry 'cuckoo' or 'cuckold' to a married man was an insult, suggesting as it did, that his wife was unfaithful to him.

and love keep little company together now-a-days:
the more the pity, that some honest neighbours will
not make them friends. Nay, I can ¹*gleek* ᵃ upon   ᵃ *scoff, jest*
occasion.

Tita. Thou art as wise as thou art beautiful.

Bot. Not so, neither; but if I had wit enough to
get out of this wood, I have enough to serve mine
own turn.   151

Tita. Out of this wood do not desire to go:
Thou shalt remain here, whether thou wilt or no.
I am a spirit of no common rate:
The summer *still*ᵇ doth *tend*ᶜ upon my *state*ᵈ ;   ᵇ *constantly*
And I do love thee: therefore, go with me ;   ᶜ *wait*
I'll give thee fairies to attend on thee ;   ᵈ *court*
And they shall fetch thee jewels from the deep,
And sing while thou on presséd flowers dost sleep :
And I will *purge* thy mortal grossness so,   160   ᵉ *purify*
That thou shalt like an airy spirit go.—
Peaseblossom ! Cobweb! Moth! and Mustardseed !

Enter PEASEBLOSSOM, COBWEB, MOTH, *and*
MUSTARDSEED.

Peas. Ready.

Cob.   And I.

Moth.   And I.

All.   Where shall we go ?

Tita. Be kind and courteous to this gentleman ;
Hop in his walks, and gambol in his eyes ;
Feed him with *apricocks*,ᶠ and *dewberries*,ᵍ   ᶠ *apricots*
With purple grapes, green figs, and mulberries   ᵍ *fruit resem-*
The honey-bags steal from the humble-bees,   *bling dwarf*
And for night-tapers crop their waxen thighs,   *blackberries*
And light them at the fiery ²*glow-worm's eyes*, 170
To *have*ʰ my love to bed, and to arise ;   ʰ *see*
And pluck the wings from painted butterflies,
To fan the moonbeams from his sleeping eyes.
Nod to him, elves, and do him *courtesies*.ⁱ   ⁱ *acts of kind-*
                                                          ness

---

¹ Bottom can hardly believe yet that Titania is really in love with him, but
with his usual self-conceit he very soon accustoms himself to his new rôle.

² The phosphorescent light of the glow-worm is situated in its tail. But,
here and elsewhere (*cf.* II. ii. 11) Shakespeare writes as a poet, not as a scientist.

Peas. Hail, mortal!

Cob. Hail!

Moth. Hail!

Mus. Hail!

Bot. I *cry*[a] your worship's *mercy*,[a] heartily: I beseech your worship's name.   180

Cob. Cobweb.

Bot. I shall desire you of more acquaintance, good Master Cobweb. If I cut my finger, I shall make *bold*[b] with you. Your name, honest gentleman?

Peas. Peaseblossom.

Bot. I pray you, commend me to Mistress *Squash*,[c] your mother, and to Master *Peascod*,[d] your father. Good Master Peaseblossom, I shall desire you of more acquaintance too. Your name, I beseech you, sir?   190

Mus. Mustardseed.

Bot. Good Master Mustardseed, I know your patience well: that same cowardly, giant-like ox-beef hath devoured many a gentleman of your house. I promise you, your kindred hath made my eyes water ere now. I desire your more acquaintance, good Master Mustardseed.

Tita. Come, wait upon him; lead him to my bower.
The moon, methinks, looks with a watery eye;
And when she weeps, weeps every little flower,   200
Lamenting some *enforcéd*[e] chastity.
Tie up my love's tongue, bring him silently. [*Exeunt.*

SCENE II.   *Another part of the Wood.*

Enter OBERON.

Obe. I wonder, if Titania be awaked;
Then, what it was that next came in her eye,
Which she must dote on in[f] extremity.

Enter PUCK.

Here comes my messenger. How now, mad spirit?
What *night-rule*[g] now about this haunted grove?

Puck. My mistress with a monster is in love.
Near to her close and *consecrated*[h] bower,

a *beg pardon*

b *free*

c *an unripe pod of pease*
d *the pod, or husk, containing the peas*

e *violated*

f *to*

g *order of the night; nightly diversion*
h *sacred*

While she was in her dull and sleeping hour,
A crew of *patches*,^a rude *mechanicals*,^b
That work for bread upon Athenian stalls,   10
Were met together to rehearse a play,
Intended for great Theseus' nuptial day.
The shallowest thick-skin of that *barren sort*,^c
Who Pyramus *presented*^d in their sport,
Forsook his scene, and entered in a brake,
When I did him at this advantage take;
An ass's *nole*^e I fixéd on his head:
Anon, his Thisbe must be answeréd,
And forth my *mimic*^f comes. When they him spy,
As wild geese that the creeping *fowler*^g eye,   20
Or *russet-pated choughs*,^h many in *sort*,ⁱ
Rising and cawing at the gun's report,
Sever themselves,^k and madly sweep the sky,
So, at his sight, away his fellows fly,
And, at our stamp, here o'er and o'er one falls;
He^l murder cries, and help from Athens calls.
Their sense thus weak, lost with their fears thus
          strong,
Made senseless things begin *to do them wrong*^m;
For briers and thorns at their apparel snatch;
Some, sleeves, some, hats, ¹*from yielders all things
          catch*.   30
I led them on in this distracted fear,
And left sweet Pyramus translated there:
When in that moment, so it came to pass,
Titania waked, and straightway loved an ass.
   Obe. This falls out better than I could devise.
But hast thou yet *latch'd*ⁿ the Athenian's eyes
With the love-juice, as I did bid thee do?
   Puck. I took him sleeping,—that is finished too—
And the Athenian woman by his side,
That, when he waked, of force she must be eyed. 40

          Enter DEMETRIUS *and* HERMIA.

   Obe. Stand close; this is the same Athenian.
   Puck. This is the woman; but not this the man.

Glossary (right margin):

a *clownish fellows*
b *artisans*
c *empty-handed crew*
d cf. III. i. 61
e *head*
f *actor*
g *sportsman*
h *gray-headed jackdaws*
i *company*
k *separate*
l *another*
m *injure them*
n *caught or entrapped, but see Glossary*

---

¹ *I.e.* the briers and thorns catch everything that will yield.

Dem. O, why rebuke you him that loves you so?
Lay *breath*[a] so bitter on your bitter foe.

    Her. Now I but chide ; but I *should*[b] use thee worse,
For thou, I fear, hast given me cause to curse.
If thou hast slain Lysander in his sleep,
Being o'er shoes in blood, *plunge in the deep,*[c]
And kill me too.
The sun was not so true unto the day   50
As he to me. Would he have stolen away
From sleeping Hermia ? I'll believe as soon
This whole earth may be bored, and that the moon
May through the centre creep, and so displease
[1]*Her brother's noontide with the Antipodes.*
It cannot be but thou hast murder'd him ;
So should a murderer look, so *dead,*[d] so grim.

    Dem. So should the murder'd look, and so should I,
Pierced through the heart with your stern cruelty ;
Yet you, the murderer, look as bright, as clear,   60
As yonder *Venus*[e] in her glimmering sphere.

    Her. *What's this to*[f] my Lysander ? where is he ?
Ah, good Demetrius, wilt thou give him me ?

    Dem. I had rather give his carcass to my hounds.

    Her. Out, dog ! out, cur ! thou drivest me past
        the bounds
Of maiden's patience. Hast thou slain him then ?
Henceforth be never number'd among men !
O, once tell true, tell true, even for my sake !
Durst thou have look'd upon him, being awake,
And hast thou kill'd him sleeping ? O *brave touch*[g] !
Could not a *worm,*[h] an adder, do so much ?   71
An adder did it ; for with *doubler tongue*[i]
Than thine, thou serpent, never adder stung.

    Dem. You *spend*[k] your passion *on a misprised
    mood*[l] :
I am not guilty of Lysander's blood ;
Nor is he dead, for aught that I can tell.

    Her. I pray thee, tell me then, that he is well.

    Dem. *An if*[m] I could, what should I get therefore ?

---

a *language*
b *ought to*

c *immerse thy-
self altogether
(in blood)*

d *death-like,
pallid, or per-
haps deadly*

e i.e. *the planet
Venus*
f sc. *do with*

g *test of bravery
(Schmidt) or
brave stroke*

h *serpent*
i *more treachery*
k *waste*

l *in anger due to
a mistake*

m *If*

---

[1] Selene (Luna). the Moon. was. in classical mythology. the twin-sister of
Helios (Sol), the Sun. (See also p 80.)

Her. A privilege never to see me more.
And from thy hated presence part I so ;   80
See me no more, whether he be dead or no. [*Exit.*

   Dem. There is no following her in this fierce
     vein[a] :

         a *temper, dis-
           position*

Here, therefore, for a while I will remain.
So [1]*sorrow's heaviness doth heavier grow*
For debt that bankrupt sleep doth sorrow owe ;
Which now in some slight measure it will pay,
If for *his tender*[b] here I make some stay.

         b *its(sleep's) offer*

        [*Lies down and sleeps.*

   Obe. What hast thou done? thou hast mistaken
    quite,
And laid the love-juice on some true-love's sight :
Of thy *misprision*[c] must perforce ensue   90
Some true-love *turn'd,*[d] and not a false turn'd true.

         c *mistake*
         d *sc. false*

   Puck. [2]*Then fate o'er-rules,*[e] *that, one man holding*
    troth,
A million fail, confounding oath on oath.

         e *prevails*

   Obe. About the wood go swifter than the wind,
And Helena of Athens look thou find :
All *fancy*[f]-sick she is, and pale of *cheer*[g]
With sighs of love, that costs the fresh blood dear.
By some *illusion*[h] see thou bring her here :
I'll charm his eyes against she do appear.

        *love
        countenance*

        h *trick played
          upon her
          vision*

   Puck. I go, I go ; look how I go,   100
Swifter than arrow from the [3]*Tartar's bow.* [*Exit.*

   Obe. Flower of this purple die,
     Hit with *Cupid's archery,*[i]
     Sink in apple of his eye !
     When his love he doth espy,
     Let her shine as gloriously
     As *the Venus*[k] of the sky.
     When thou wakest, if she be by,
     Beg of her for remedy.

        i *cf. II. i.* 158-169

        k *cf. line* 61

---

[1] (The oppression of) sorrow becomes more oppressive by reason of its debt (which it cannot pay) to sleep.

[2] Puck means, 'Then they are only acting in accordance with the decree of fate, which ordains that for every man that is true in love a million are false, breaking one oath after another.'

[3] The natives of Tartary were famous for their skill in archery.

Re-enter PUCK.

Puck. Captain of our fairy band, 110
  Helena is here at hand ;
  And the youth, mistook by me,
  Pleading for a *lover's fee.*[a]
  Shall we their *fond pageant*[b] see ?
  Lord, what fools these mortals be !
Obe. Stand aside : the noise they make
  Will cause Demetrius to awake.
Puck. Then will two at once woo one ;
  That must needs be sport alone ;
  And those things do best please me 120
  That befall *preposterously.*[c]

[a] *payment in kisses*
[b] *exhibition of folly*

[c] *contrarily*

Enter LYSANDER *and* HELENA.

Lys. Why should you think that I should woo in
  scorn ?
Scorn and derision never come in tears :
Look, when I vow, I weep ; and vows so born,
  In their nativity all truth appears.
How can these things in me seem scorn to you,
Bearing the badge of faith to prove them true ?
Hel. You do advance your cunning more and
  more.
[1]*When truth kills truth, O devilish-holy fray !*
These vows are Hermia's : will you give her o'er ? 130
  Weigh oath with oath, and *you will nothing
    weigh*[d] :
Your vows, to her and me, put in two scales,
Will even weigh, and both as light as tales.
Lys. I had no judgment, when to her I swore.
Hel. Nor none, in my mind, now you give her
  o'er.
Lys. Demetrius loves her, and he loves not you.
Dem. [*Awaking.*] O Helen, goddess, nymph,
  perfect, divine !

[d] *neither will turn the scales*

[1] When one truth (your present vow to me) kills another truth (your former
vow to Hermia) then must there be a conflict at the same time wicked and holy
(wicked because truth has been slain, holy because truth has prevailed). A
specimen of Shakespeare's earlier manner ; so also the extravagant language of
lines 137-144.

To what, my love, shall I compare thine *eyne*[a] ?
Crystal is muddy.   O, how ripe in show
Thy lips, those kissing cherries, tempting grow !   140
[1]*That pure congealéd white, high Taurus' snow,*
Fann'd with the eastern wind, turns to a crow,
When thou hold'st up thy hand.   O, let me kiss
This princess of pure white, this *seal of bliss*[b] !

Hel.   O spite ! O hell ! I see, you all are bent
To set against me for your merriment :
If you were civil and knew *courtesy*[c]
You would not do me thus much injury.
Can you not hate me, as I know you do,
But you must *join in souls*[d] to mock me too ?   150
If you were men, as men you are in show,
You would not use a gentle lady so ;
To vow, and swear, and *superpraise*[e] my *parts*.[f]
When I am sure you hate me with your hearts.
You both are rivals, and love Hermia ;
And now both rivals, to mock Helena :
A *trim*[g] exploit, a manly enterprise,
To conjure tears up in a poor maid's eyes
With your derision ! none of noble sort
Would so offend a virgin, and extort   160
A poor *soul's*[h] patience, all to make you sport.

Lys.   You are unkind, Demetrius , be not so ;
For you love Hermia ; this you know I know :
And here, with all good will, with all my heart,
In Hermia's love I yield you up my part ;
And yours of Helena to me bequeath,
Whom I do love, and will do till my death.

Hel.   Never did mockers waste more idle breath.

Dem.   Lysander, keep thy Hermia ; I will *none*[i] :
If e'er I loved her, all that love is gone.   170
My heart [2]*to her but as guest-wise sojourn'd,*
And now to Helen is it home return'd,
There to remain.

Lys.   . Helen, it is not so.

---

[a] *eyes*

[b] *i.e. the hand whose clasp seals a contract*
[c] *·good breeding*

[d] *cf. our 'put your heads together'*

[e] *praise to excess*
[f] *qualities*

[g] *pretty, clever, used ironically*

[h] *creature's*

[i] *sc. of her*

---

[1] *I.e.* The purest, whitest snow is black in comparison with thy hand
[2] In respect to her was but a temporary visitor.

Dem. *Disparage not*[a] the faith thou dost not know,
Lest to thy peril thou *aby*[b] it dear.
Look, where thy love comes ; yonder is thy dear.

        Enter HERMIA.

Her. Dark night, that from the eye *his*[c] function
    takes,
The ear more quick of *apprehension*[d] makes ;
Wherein[e] it doth impair the seeing sense,
It pays the hearing double recompense.   180
Thou art not by mine eye, Lysander, found ;
Mine ear, I thank it, brought me to thy sound.
But why unkindly didst thou leave me so ?
  Lys. Why should he stay, whom love doth press
    to go ?
  Her. What love could press Lysander from my
    side ?
  Lys. Lysander's love, that would not let him
    bide,
Fair Helena, who more engilds the night
Than all yon fiery *oes*[f] and eyes of light.
Why seek'st thou me ? could not this make thee
    know,
The hate I bear thee made me leave thee so ?   190
  Her. You speak not as you think : it cannot be.
  Hel. Lo, she is one of this confederacy !
Now I perceive they have conjoin'd all three,
To fashion this false sport *in spite of*[g] me.
Injurious[h] Hermia ! most ungrateful maid !
Have you conspired, have you with these contrived
To *bait*[i] me with this foul derision ?
Is all the counsel that we two have shared,
The sisters' vows, the hours that we have spent,
When we have chid the hasty-footed time   200
For parting us,—O, is all forgot ?
All school-days' friendship, childhood innocence ?
We, Hermia, like two *artificial gods*,[k]
Have with our *needles*[l] created both one flower,
Both on one sampler, sitting on one cushion,
Both warbling of one song, both in one key,
As if our hands, our sides, voices, and minds,

[a] *speak not slightingly of*
[b] *pay for*
[c] *its*
[d] *perception*
[e] *insomuch as*
[f] *circles, 'fiery oes and eyes' = the stars*
[g] *to spite*
[h] *unjust*
[i] *set upon, harass (like dogs)*
[k] *creators of works of art*
[l] *pronounce as one syllable*

E

Had *been incorporate.*[a]   So we grew together,
Like to a double cherry, seeming *parted,*[b]
But yet *an union in partition*[c] ;   210
Two lovely berries moulded on one stem ;
So, with two seeming bodies, but one heart ;
[1]*Two of the first, like coats in heraldry,*
Due but to one, and crownèd with one crest.
And will you *rent*[d] our ancient love asunder,
To join[e] with men in scorning your poor friend ?
It is not friendly, 'tis not maidenly :
Our sex, as well as I, may chide you for it,
Though I alone do feel the injury.

   Her. I am amazèd at your passionate words. 220
I scorn you not : it seems that you scorn me.

   Hel. Have you not set Lysander, as in scorn,
To follow me, and praise my eyes and face ?
And made your other love, Demetrius,
Who even *but now*[f] did spurn me with his foot,
To call me goddess, nymph, divine, and rare,
Precious, celestial ?   Wherefore speaks he this
To her he hates ? and wherefore doth Lysander
Deny your love, so rich within his soul,
And tender me, forsooth, affection,   230
But by your setting on, by your consent ?
What though I be not so *in grace*[g] as you,
So *hung upon*[h] with love, so fortunate ;
But miserable most *to love*[i] unloved ?
This you should pity rather than despise.

   Her. I understand not what you mean by this.

   Hel. Ay, do, perséver, counterfeit sad looks,
Make mouths upon me when I turn my back ;
Wink at each other ; *hold*[k] the sweet jest *up*[k] .
This sport, well carried, shall be chronicled.   240
If you have any pity, grace, or manners,
You would no* make me such an *argument.*[l]
But, fare ye well : 'tis partly my own fault ;

---

a *belonged to one body*
b *divided*
c *united though divided*
d *rend*
e *by joining*
f *see II.i.189 298*
g *favoured*
h *clung to*
i *in that I love*
k i.e. ' *keep it up* '
l *subject for ridicule*

---

[1] *I.e.* the same quartering appearing twice (' two of the first ') upon one shield,
but belonging only to one person (' due but to one '), and crowned with only one
crest, the crest of the bearer. Thus Hermia and Helena possessed two bodies,
but only one heart.

Which death or absence soon shall remedy.

Lys. Stay, gentle Helena ; hear my excuse :
My love, my life, my soul, fair Helena !

Hel.   O excellent !

Her.   Sweet, do not scorn her so.

Dem. If she cannot entreat, I can compel.

Lys. Thou canst compel no more than she entreat :
Thy threats have no more strength than her weak
        prayers.   250
Helen, I love thee ; by my life, I do :
I swear by *that*[a] which I will lose for thee,   a i.e. *my life*
To prove him false that says I love thee not.

Dem. I say, I love thee more than he can do.

Lys. If thou say so, withdraw, and prove it too.

Dem. Quick, come !

Her. Lysander, whereto tends all this ?

Lys. Away, you ¹*Ethiope*[b] !   b *Ethiopian*

Dem. ²*No, no ; he'll* . . .   c *be furious*
Seem to break loose, *take on,*[c] as you would follow, 260
But yet come not : You are a *tame*[d] man, go !   d *spiritless*

Lys. Hang off, thou *cat*, thou *burr*[e] ! vile thing, let   e *Herm. clings*
    loose,   *fast to Lys.*
Or I will shake thee from me like a serpent !

Her. Why are you grown so rude ? what change is
        this ?
Sweet love,—

Lys.   Thy love ! Out, tawny Tartar, out !
Out, loathéd medicine ! hated potion, hence !

Her. Do you not jest ?

Hel.   Yes, sooth ; and so do you.

Lys. Demetrius, I will keep my word with thee.

Dem. I would I had your bond ; for I perceive   f i.e. *Hermia*
A *weak bond*[f] holds you ; I'll not trust your word. 270   *Note the pun*
        on 'bond'

Lys. What, should I hurt her, strike her, kill her
        dead ?
Although I hate her, I'll not harm her so.

---

¹ Hermia was dark-complexioned, and to be dark was in the Elizabethan age
regarded as a taint or defect. (*Cf.* line 265 below and V. i. 11.)

² This passage is thus explained by Mr. Wright : 'Demetrius first addresses
Hermia, and then breaks off abruptly to taunt Lysander with not showing much
eagerness to meet him '

Her. What can you do me greater harm than hate ?
Hate me! wherefore ? O me! *what news*,[a] my love !
Am not I Hermia ? Are not you Lysander ?
I am as fair now as I was *erewhile*.[b]
Since night[c] you loved me ; yet, since night you left
    me :
Why, then you left me,—O, the gods forbid !—
In earnest, shall I say ?
    Lys.   Ay, by my life ;
And never did desire to see thee more.   280
Therefore, be out of hope, of question, of doubt ;
Be certain nothing truer ; 'tis no jest
That I do hate thee, and love Helena.
    Her. O me! you *juggler*[d] ! you [1]*canker-blossom* !
You thief of love ! what have you come by night,
And stolen my love's heart from him ?
    Hel.   Fine, i' faith !
Have you no modesty, no maiden shame,
No *touch*[e] of bashfulness ? What, will you *tear*
Impatient answers[f] from my gentle tongue ?
Fie, fie ! you *counterfeit*,[g] you *puppet*,[h] you !   290
    Her. Puppet ! why so ? ay, that way goes the
    game.
Now I perceive that she hath made *compare*[i]
Between our statures ; she hath urged her height ;
And with her *personage*,[k] her tall *personage*,[k]
Her height, forsooth, she hath prevail'd with him.
And are you grown so high in his esteem,
Because I am so dwarfish, and so low ?
How low am I, thou [2]*painted maypole ?* speak :
How low am I ? I am not yet so low
But that my nails can reach unto thine eyes.   300
    Hel. I pray you, though you mock me, gentlemen,
Let her not hurt me : I was never *curst*[l] :
I have no gift at all in *shrewishness*[m] ;
I am a *right*[n] maid for my cowardice :

a *what is the matter*
b *a short time ago*
c *i.e. so lately as this night*

d *impostor*

e *sense*
f *cf. l. 160*
g *false friend*
h *doll*

i *comparison*

k *stature*

shrewish, cf. ll. 325 and 343
m *quarrelsomeness*
n *thorough*

---

[1] *I.e.* blossom-eating canker; you worm preying upon the heart (love) of Lysander. (*Cf.* II. ii. 3.)

[2] In 'painted maypole' there is an allusion both to Helena's height and her pink-and-white complexion. Maypoles were often painted with stripes of red and white.

Let her not strike me. You perhaps may think,
Because she is something lower than myself,
That I can match her.

   Her.   Lower! hark, again.

   Hel. Good Hermia, do not be so bitter with me.
I *evermore*[a] did love you, Hermia,   a *always*
Did ever keep your counsels, never wrong'd you; 310
Save that, in love unto Demetrius,
I told him of your *stealth*[b] unto this wood.   b *stealing*
He followed you; *for*[c] love, I follow'd him,   c *out of*
But he hath chid me hence, and threaten'd me
To strike me, spurn me, nay, to kill me too:
And now, so you will let me quiet go,
To Athens will I bear my folly back,
And follow you no further: let me go: d *silly*
You see how *simple*[d] and how *fond*[e] I am.   e *foolish*

   Her. Why, get you gone: who is't that hinders
      you?   320

   Hel. A foolish heart, that I leave here behind.

   Her. What, with Lysander?

   Hel.   With Demetrius.

   Lys. Be not afraid; she shall not harm thee,
      Helena.

   Dem. No, sir, she shall not, though you take her
      part.

   Hel. O, when she's angry, she is keen and
      shrewd[f]!   f *shrewish*
She was a vixen, when she went to school;
And, though she be but little, she is fierce.

   Her. 'Little' again! nothing but 'low' and
      'little'!
Why will you suffer her to *flout*[g] me thus?   g *scoff at*
Let me come to her.

   Lys.   Get you gone, you dwarf; 330
You *minimus*,[h] of [i]*hindering knot-grass* made; h *smallest of*
You bead, you acorn.   *creatures*

   Dem.   You are too *officious*[i]   i *forward*

---

   [i] 'Knot-grass' is a well-known grass, having numerous knots in its stem, anciently supposed, if taken in an infusion, to have the power of stopping the growth of any animal.

In her behalf that scorns your services.
Let her alone ; speak not of Helena ;
Take not her part ; for if thou dost intend
Never*a* so little show of love to her,
Thou shalt *aby*b it.

  Lys.   Now she holds me not ;
Now follow, if thou darest, to try whose right,
Of thine or mine, is *most*c in Helena.

  Dem. Follow ! nay, I'll go with thee, *cheek by
jole.*d   340
      [*Exeunt* LYSANDER *and* DEMETRIUS.

  Her. You, mistress, all this *coil*e is 'long of you.
Nay, go not back.

  Hel.   I will not trust you, I,
Nor longer stay in your *curst*f company.
Your hands than mine are quicker for a fray ;
My legs are longer though, to run away. [*Exit.*

  Her. I am *amazed,*g and know not what to say.
      [*Exit.*

  Obe. This is thy negligence : *still*h thou mistakest,
Or else committ'st thy knaveries wilfully.

  Puck. Believe me, king of *shadows,*i I mistook.
Did not you tell me, I should know the man 350
By the Athenian garments he had on ?
And so far blameless proves my enterprise,
That I have 'nointed an Athenian's eyes :
And so far am I glad it so did *sort,*k
As this their *jangling*l I esteem a sport.

  Obe. Thou see'st, these lovers seek a place to
fight :
Hie therefore, Robin, overcast the night ;
The starry *welkin*m cover thou *anon*n
With drooping fog, as black as *Acheron*o ;
And lead these *testy*p rivals so astray, 360
*As*q one come not within another's way.
Like to Lysander sometime frame thy tongue,
Then stir Demetrius up with bitter *wrong*r ;
And sometime rail thou like Demetrius ;
And from each other look thou lead them thus,
Till o'er their brows death-*counterfeiting*s sleep

a *ever*
b *pay for*

c *strongest*

d *side by side*

e *trouble, con-
fusion*

f *cf. 325 and 302*

g *dumb-founded*

h *constantly*

i *spirits*

k *happen*
l *noisy quar-
relling*

m *sky*
n *forthwith*
o *seeClas.Names*
p *hot-headed*
q *that*

r *insult*

s *resembling*

With leaden legs and batty wings[a] doth creep:
Then crush this herb into Lysander's eye;
Whose liquor[b] hath this *virtuous*[c] property,
To take from thence all error *with his might,*[d]   370
And make his eyeballs roll with *wonted*[e] sight.
When they next wake, all this derision
Shall seem a dream and fruitless vision;
And back to Athens shall the lovers wend,
[1] *With league whose date till death shall never end.*
Whiles I in this affair do thee employ,
I'll to my queen, and beg her Indian boy;
And then I will her charméd eye release
From monster's view, and all things shall be peace.

> **Puck.** My fairy lord, this must be done with
> haste,   380
For *night's swift dragons*[f] cut the clouds full fast,
And yonder shines *Aurora's harbinger,*[g]
At whose approach, ghosts, wandering here and
there,
Troop home to churchyards; *damnéd*[h] spirits all,
That in crossways and floods have burial,[i]
Already to their wormy beds are gone;
For fear lest day should look their *shames*[k] upon,
They wilfully themselves exile from light
And must for aye consort with black-brow'd night.

> **Obe.** But we are spirits *of another sort.*[l]   390
I with *the morning's love*[m] have oft made sport;
And, like a forester, the groves may tread,
Even till the eastern gate, all fiery-red,
Opening on *Neptune*[n] with fair blesséd beams,
Turns into yellow gold his salt green streams.
But, notwithstanding, haste; make no delay:
We may effect this business yet ere day.   *[Exit.*

> **Puck.** Up and down, up and down,
>   I will lead them up and down:
>   I am fear'd in field and town;   400
>   Goblin, lead them up and down.
Here comes one.

[a] *i.e. bringing heaviness and darkness*
[b] *the juice of which*
[c] *beneficial*
[d] *by its power*
[e] *customary*

[f] *Night's chariot drawn by dragons*
[g] *the morning star*
[h] *i.e. condemned to wander*
[i] *i.e. suicides see p. 81*
[k] *the evidence of their crimes*

[l] *cf. III. i. 154*
[m] *Cephalus, see Notes*

[n] *the sea cf. II. i. 127*

---

[1] *I.e. Their mutual love shall continue till death.*

Re-enter LYSANDER.

Lys. Where art thou, proud Demetrius? speak
    thou now.

Puck. Here, villain! *drawn*ᵃ and ready. Where
    art thou?

ᵃ with my sword
drawn

Lys. I will be with thee straight.

Puck.   Follow me then
To *plainer*ᵇ ground.

ᵇ more even

        [*Exit* LYSANDER, *as following the voice.*

Re-enter DEMETRIUS.

Dem.   Lysander! speak again.
Thou runaway, thou coward, art thou fled?
Speak! In some bush? Where dost thou hide
    thy head?

Puck. Thou coward, art thou bragging to the
    stars,
Telling the bushes that thou look'st for wars, 410
And wilt not come? Come, *recreant*ᶜ; come, thou
    child;

ᶜ coward

I'll whip thee with a rod. He is defiled,
That draws a sword on thee.

Dem.   Yea; art thou there?

Puck. Follow my voice: we'll *try no manhood*ᵈ
    here.   [*Exeunt.*

ᵈ not fight, or
not test each
other's courage

Re-enter LYSANDER.

Lys. He goes before me, and still dares me on;
When I come where he calls, then he is gone.
The villain is much lighter-heel'd than I:
I follow'd fast, but faster he did fly;
*That*ᵉ fallen am I in dark uneven way,

ᵉ So that

And here will rest me. [*Lies down.*] Come, thou
    gentle day!   420
For if but once thou show me thy grey light,
I'll find Demetrius, and revenge this spite. [*Sleeps.*

Re-enter PUCK *and* DEMETRIUS.

Puck. Ho, ho, ho! Coward, why comest thou
    not?

Dem. *Abide*[a] me, if thou darest; for well I *wot*,[b]
Thou runn'st before me, *shifting every place*,[c]
And darest not stand, nor look me in the face.
Where art thou now?

Puck.   Come hither: I am here.

Dem. Nay, then, thou mock'st me   Thou shalt
      buy[d] this dear,
If ever I thy face by daylight see:
Now, go thy way.   Faintness constraineth me   430
To *measure out my length*[e] on this cold bed.
By day's approach look to be visited.
                              [*Lies down and sleeps.*

            Re-enter HELENA.

Hel. O weary night, O long and tedious night,
  Abate[f] thy hours! [1]*shine comforts from the east*,
That I may back to Athens, by daylight,
  From these that my poor company detest.
And *sleep*[g] that sometimes shuts up sorrow's eye,
Steal me awhile from mine own company.   [*Sleeps.*

Puck. Yet but *three*[h] ? Come one more;
            Two of both kinds makes up four.   440
            Here she *comes*,[h] *curst*[i] and sad.
            Cupid is a knavish lad,
            Thus to make poor females mad.

            Re-enter HERMIA.

Her. Never so weary, never so in woe,
  Bedabbled[k] with the dew, and torn with briers:
I can no further crawl, no further go:
  My legs can keep no pace with my desires.
Here will I rest me till the break of day.
Heaven shield Lysander if they mean a fray!
                              [*Lies down and sleeps.*

Puck.   On the ground   450
            Sleep sound:
            I'll apply
            To your eye,
          Gentle lover, remedy.
          [*Squeezing the juice on* LYSANDER'S *eye.*

a *wait for*
b *know*
c *changing from one place to another*

d *pay for*

e *lie down*

f *shorten*

g i. e. *may sleep, etc.*

h *dissyllable*

i *see l.* 343

k *wet*

---

[1] May sunrise bring its cheering influence.

When thou wakest,
Thou takest
True delight
In the sight
Of thy former lady's eye :
And the country proverb known,   460
That every man should take his own,
In your waking shall be shown :
    [1]*Jack shall have Jill ;*
    Nought shall go ill ;
The man shall have his mare again,
    And all shall be well.   [*Exit* PUCK.

[1] Jack and Jill were familiar representatives of the two sexes in low life. *Cf.* "A good Jack makes a good Jill" (*Ray's Proverbs*). 'The man shall have his mare again' was another familiar country proverb, denoting that everything would end up well.

ACT IV.

SCENE I.—*The same.*   DEMETRIUS, HELENA,
   LYSANDER, *and* HERMIA, *lying asleep.*

Enter TITANIA *and* BOTTOM, PEASEBLOSSOM, COB-
  WEB, MOTH, MUSTARDSEED, *and other Fairies
   attending ;* OBERON *behind unseen.*

Tita. Come, sit thee down upon this flowery
    bed,
While I thy *amiable*[a] cheeks do *coy*,[b]
And stick musk-roses in thy sleek smooth head,
And kiss thy fair large ears, my gentle joy.
  Bot. Where's Peaseblossom ?
  Peas. Ready.
  Bot. Scratch my head, Peaseblossom.   Where's
Mounsieur[c] Cobweb ?
  Cob. Ready.
  Bot. Mounsieur Cobweb, good mounsieur, get
your weapons in your hand, and kill me a red-
hipped humble-bee, on the top of a thistle ; and, good
mounsieur, bring me the honey-bag.   Do not fret

a *lovable*
b *caress*

c *Bottom's pro-
nunciation of
Monsieur*

yourself too much in the action, mounsieur; and, good mounsieur, have a care the honey-bag break not; I would be loath to have you *over flown*[a] with a honey-bag, signior. Where's Mounsieur Mustardseed? 17

Must. Ready.

Bot. Give me your *neaf*,[b] Mounsieur Mustardseed. Pray you, *leave your courtesy*,[c] good mounsieur. 20

Must. What's your will?

Bot. Nothing, good mounsieur, but to help *Cavaler*[d] *Cobweb*[1] to scratch. I must to the barber's, mounsieur; for, methinks, I am marvellous hairy about the face, and I am such a tender ass, if my hair do but tickle me, I must scratch.

Tita. What, wilt thou hear some music, my sweet love?

Bot. I have a reasonable good ear in music. Let's have the *tongs*[e] and the bones.

Tita. Or, say, sweet love, what thou desirest to eat. 30

Bot. Truly a peck of provender; I could munch your good dry oats. Methinks, I have a great desire to a *bottle*[f] of hay; good hay, sweet hay hath no *fellow*.[g]

Tita. I have a venturous fairy that shall seek The squirrel's hoard, and fetch thee new nuts.

Bot. I had rather have a handful or two of dried peas. But, I pray you, let none of your people stir me: I have an *exposition*[h] of sleep come upon me. 40

Tita. Sleep thou, and I will wind thee in my arms.

Fairies, be gone, and be *all ways*[i] away.

[*Exeunt Fairies.*

[2]*So doth the woodbine the sweet honey-suckle*

---

a *drowned*

b *fist*

c *use no unnecessary ceremony*

d *Cavalero*

e *an instrument played with a key*

f *a small bundle*

g *equal*

h *for 'disposition '*

i *in all directions*

---

[1] This should be Peaseblossom, as Cobweb's duties have already been assigned him. See line 10.

[2] Commentators are generally in doubt as to the meaning of this passage. Shakespeare elsewhere uses 'woodbine' and 'honeysuckle' as different names for the same plant, and the simplest explanation appears to be that Titania entwines Bottom, as the tendrils of the honeysuckle twine around the stronger branch. Some editors take 'woodbine' to refer to the convolvulus.

Gently entwist ; the ¹*female ivy so*
*Enrings*ᵃ the barky fingers of the elm.   ᵃ *encircles*
O, how I love thee ! how I dote on thee !
                              [*They sleep.*

            Enter PUCK.

  Obe. [*Advancing.*] Welcome, good Robin.   See'st
        thou this sweet sight?
Her *dotage*ᵇ now I do begin to pity :   ᵇ *love folly*
For, meeting her of late behind the wood,
Seeking sweet *favours*ᶜ for this hateful fool,   50   ᶜ *gifts, such as*
I did upbraid her, and fall out with her ;   *flowers. Cf.*
For she his hairy temples then had rounded   *II. i. 12*
With coronet of fresh and fragrant flowers ;
And that same dew, which sometime on the buds
*Was wont to swell*ᵈ like round and *orient*ᵉ pearls,   ᵈ *used to gather*
Stood now within the pretty flowerets' eyes,   *and grow*
Like tears that did their own disgrace bewail.   ᵉ *shining*
When I had at my pleasure taunted her,
And she in mild terms begg'd my patience,
I then did ask of her her changeling child ;   60
Which *straight*ᶠ she gave me, and her fairy sent   ᶠ *at once*
To bear him to my bower in fairy land.
And now I have the boy, I will undo
This hateful imperfection of her eyes :
And, gentle Puck, take this transforméd scalp
From off the head of this Athenian swain ;
That, he awaking when the other do,
*May*ᵍ all to Athens back again repair,   ᵍ *sc. they*
And think no more of this night's accidents,
But as the fierce vexation of a dream.   70
But first I will release the fairy queen.
            [*Touching her eyes with a herb.*
        Be, as thou wast wont to be ;
        See, as thou wast wont to see :
        ²*Dian's bud* o'er *Cupid's flower*ʰ   ʰ *the heart's-ease*
        Hath such force and blessed power.   *or pansy. See*
                                                        II. i. 169

---

¹ The ivy is called ' female ' because it requires support, and (like the vine) is
sometimes said to be married to the tree that sustains it.
² Usually thought to be the *Agnus castus*, which was supposed to possess the
property of keeping men and women chaste.

Now, my Titania wake you, my sweet queen!

Tita. My Oberon! what visions have I seen!
Methought, I was enamour'd of an ass.

Obe. There lies your love.

Tita. How came these things to pass?
O, how mine eyes do loathe his visage now!   80

Obe. Silence awhile. Robin, take off this head.
Titania, music call, and strike more dead
Than common sleep of *all these five*[a] the sense.

Tita. Music, ho, music, such as charmeth sleep!
                              [*Music, still.*[b]

Puck. Now, when thou wakest, with thine own
              fool's eyes peep.

Obe. Sound, music! Come, my queen, take
              hands with me,
And *rock*[c] the ground whereon these sleepers be.
Now thou and I are *new*[d] in amity,
And will to-morrow midnight *solemnly*[e]
Dance in Duke Theseus' house triumphantly,   90
And bless it to all fair prosperity.
There shall the pairs of faithful lovers be
Wedded, with Theseus, all in jollity.

Puck. Fairy king, attend, and mark:
              I do hear the morning lark.

Obe. Then, my queen, in silence sad,
              Trip we after the *night's*[f] shade;
              We the globe can compass soon,[g]
              Swifter than the wandering moon.

Tita. Come, my lord, and in our flight   100
              Tell me how it came this night,
              That I sleeping here was found
              With these mortals on the ground.

              [*Exeunt. Horns winded*[h] *within.*

Enter THESEUS, HIPPOLYTA, EGEUS, *and Train.*

The. Go, one of you, find out the *forester*[i];
For now our *observation is perform'd*;
And since we *have the vaward*[k] of the day,

---

[a] i.e. *the four lovers and Bottom*
[b] *softly*
[c] i.e. *as one rocks a cradle*
[d] *again*
[e] *with pomp and ceremony*
[f] *dissyllable*
[g] *cf. II. i.176*
[h] *sounded*
[i] *master of the hounds*
[k] *are in the fore part*

---

[1] We have done our 'observance to a morn of May,'—celebrated the customary rites. (*Cf.* I. i., 167, and l. 134 of this Scene, and see Note on p. 74.)

My love shall hear the music of my hounds.
Uncouple^a in the western valley; let them go:
Despatch, I say, and had the forester.
We will, fair queen, up to the mountain's top,   110
And mark the musical confusion
Of hounds and echo in conjunction.

   Hip.   I was with Hercules and Cadmus once,
When, in a wood of Crete, they *bay'd*^b the bear
With hounds of Sparta: never did I hear
Such gallant *chiding*^c; for, besides the groves,
The skies, the *fountains*,^d every region near
Seem'd all one mutual cry.   I never heard
So musical a discord, such sweet thunder.

   The.   My hounds are bred out of the Spartan kind,
¹*So flew'd, so sanded;* and their heads are hung   121
With ears that sweep away the morning dew;
Crook-knee'd, and *dew-lapp'd*^e like Thessalian bulls;
Slow in pursuit, but ²*match'd in mouth like bells,*
Each under each.   A *cry more tuneable*^f
Was never holla'd to, nor cheer'd with horn,
In Crete, in Sparta, nor in Thessaly:
Judge, when you hear.   But, soft! what nymphs
     are these?

   Ege.   My lord, this is my daughter here asleep;
And this, Lysander; this Demetrius is;   130
This Helena, old Nedar's Helena:
I wonder of^g their being here together.

   The.   No doubt, they rose up early, to observe
The rite of May, and, hearing our *intent*,^h
Came here in grace of our *solemnity*.ⁱ
But speak, Egeus, is not this the day
That Hermia should give answer of her choice?

   Ege.   It is, my lord.
   The.   Go, bid the huntsmen wake them with their
     horns.

---

a *unleash the hounds*

b *drove to bay*

c *noise (of barking). Cf. II. i. 146*

d *streams, cf. II. i. 85*

e *with loose flesh hanging from their throats, cf. II. i. 51*

f *more musical pack of hounds*

g *at*

h *intention*

i *wedding festivities*

---

¹ They have the same large hanging chaps (or flews), and are of the same sandy colour.

² Barking in unison like a chime of bells, some higher, some lower (each under each).

[*Horns, and shout within.* LYSANDER, HERMIA,
  DEMETRIUS, *and* HELENA, *wake and start up.*

The. Good morrow, friends. St. Valentine is past;
[1] *Begin these wood-birds but to couple now ?*　　141
Lys. Pardon, my lord.
The.　　　　　　I pray you all, stand up.
I know you two are rival enemies :
How comes this gentle concord in the world,
That hatred is so far from jealousy,
To sleep by hate, and fear no enmity ?
　Lys. My lord, I shall reply *amazedly*,ᵃ　　　　ᵃ *confusedly*
Half *sleep*,ᵇ half waking : but as yet, I swear,　ᵇ *sleeping*
I cannot truly say how I came here ;
But, as I think—for truly would I speak,　　150
And now I do bethink me, so it is,—
I came with Hermia hither : our intent
Was to be gone from Athens, *where we might*ᶜ,　ᶜ *whithersoever*
*Without*ᵈ the peril of the Athenian law.　　　　*we could*
　Ege. Enough, enough, my lord ; you *have*ᵉ enough :　ᵈ *away from*
I beg the law, the law, upon his head.　　　ᵉ *have heard*
They would have stolen away, they would, Demetrius,
Thereby to have *defeated*ᶠ you and me ;　　ᶠ *cheated*
You, of your wife, and me, of my consent,
Of my consent, that she should be your wife.　160
　Dem. My lord, fair Helen told me of their *stealth*,ᵍ　ᵍ *stealing away*
Of this their purpose hither to this wood ;
And I in fury hither followed them,
Fair Helena *in fancy*ʰ following me.　　　ʰ *as we say 'out*
But, my good lord, I *wot*ⁱ not by what power—　*of love'*
But by some power it is—my love to Hermia,　ⁱ *know*
Melted as doth the snow, seems to me now
As the remembrance of an idle *gawd*ᵏ　　ᵏ *toy, cf. I. i. 3*5
Which in my childhood I did dote upon ;
And all the *faith, the virtue*ˡ of my heart,　170　ˡ *true love, the*
The object and the pleasure of mine eye,　　*very substance*
Is only Helena.　To her, my lord,
Was I betroth'd ere I saw Hermia :

---

[1] Birds were popularly supposed to choose their mates on St. Valentine's
day, February 14th. The mention of this Saint's day by Theseus is, of course,
an anachronism.

But, like in sickness, did I loathe this food ;
But, as in health *come*^a to my natural taste,   ^a *being restored*
Now do I wish it, love it, long for it,
And will for evermore be true to it.

   The. Fair lovers, you are fortunately met :
Of this discourse we more will hear anon.
Egeus, I will *overbear*^b your will,   180   ^b *overrule*
For in the temple, by and by, with us,
These couples shall eternally be knit.
And, for the morning now is something worn,
Our purposed hunting shall be set aside.
Away, with us, to Athens !   *Three and three,*^c   ^c *being three*
We'll hold a feast *in great solemnity.*^d   *couples*
Come, Hippolyta.   ^d *with great fes-*
     [*Exeunt* THESEUS, HIPPOLYTA, EGEUS, *and Train.*   *tivities*

   Dem. These things seem small and undistinguish-
      able,
Like far-off mountains turnéd into clouds.

   Her. Methinks, I see these things with *parted*^e eye,   ^e *divided*
When every thing seems double.

   Hel.   So methinks : 191
And I have found Demetrius, ¹*like a jewel,*
Mine own, and not mine own.

   Dem.   It seems to me
That yet we sleep, we dream.   Do not you think
The duke was here, and bid us follow him ?

   Her. Yea ; and my father.

   Hel.   And Hippolyta.

   Lys. And he did bid us follow to the temple.

   Dem. Why, then, we are awake : let's follow him ;
And by the way let us recount our dreams. [*Exeunt.*

   Bot. [*Waking.*] When my cue comes, call me, and
I will answer : my ²*next* is, ' Most fair Pyramus.'
Heigh-ho !   Peter Quince !   Flute, the bellows-
mender !   Snout, the tinker !   Starveling !   God's

---

   ¹ Perhaps a reminiscence of the parable of the lost treasure.   (*Cf.* Matt.
xiii. 44.)
   ² Bottom means ' my next cue '; but either he has not yet returned to the
full possession of his faculties and his memory, or else the play was changed
(as appears to have been the case) between the rehearsal and the performance.
(See V. i., l. 192.)

F

my life, stolen hence, and left me asleep! I have
had a most rare vision. I have had a dream,
past the wit of man to say what dream it was:
man is but an ass, if he go about to expound this
dream. [1]*Methought I was*—there is no man can
tell what. [1]*Methought I was*, and [1]*methought I
had,*—but man is but a *patched fool,*[a] if he will
offer to say what methought I had. The *eye*[b] of
man hath not heard, the *ear*[b] of man hath not
seen, man's *hand*[b] is not able to taste, his
tongue[b] to conceive, nor his *heart*[b] to report,
what my dream was. I will get Peter Quince
to write a ballad of this dream: it shall be
called Bottom's Dream, because it hath no
bottom; and I will sing it in the latter end of
a play, before the duke: peradventure, to make
it the more *gracious,*[c] I shall sing it at *her*[d]
death.   [*Exit.* 221

a *fool in parti-
coloured attire*

b *Bottom's
humorous
blunders*

c *beautiful*
d *i.e. Thisbe's*

SCENE II.—*Athens.* QUINCE'S *House.*

Enter QUINCE, FLUTE, SNOUT, *and* STARVELING.

Quin. Have you sent to Bottom's house? is he
come home yet?

Star. He cannot be heard of. Out of doubt, he
is *transported.*[e]

Flu. If he come not, then the play is marred. It
goes not forward, doth it?

Quin. It is not possible: you have not a man in
all Athens able to *discharge*[f] Pyramus, but he.

Flu. No; he hath simply the best wit of any
handicraft man in Athens.   10

Quin. Yea, and the best person too; and he is
a very paramour for a sweet voice.

Flu. You must say 'paragon[g]' a paramour is,
God bless us! *a thing of naught.*[h]

Enter SNUG.

Snug. Masters, the duke is coming from the

e *he means to
say 'trans-
lated,' i.e.
carried off (as
by the fairies)*
f *play the part
of. Cf. I. ii
93*

g *model of ex-
cellence*
h *a naughty,
wicked thing*

---

[1] Bottom is ashamed to tell it even to the winds, that he dreamt he was an
ass and had an ass's head on.

temple, and there *is*[a] two or three lords and ladies more married. If our sport had gone forward, we had all been made men.

Flu. O sweet *bully*[b] Bottom ! Thus hath he lost sixpence a day during his life ; he could not have 'scaped sixpence a day : *an*[c] the duke had not given him sixpence a day for playing Pyramus, I'll be hanged ; he would have deserved it : sixpence a day in Pyramus, or nothing.   24

Enter BOTTOM.

Bot. Where are these lads? where are these *hearts*[d] ?

Quin. Bottom ! O most *courageous*[e] day ! O most happy hour !

Bot. Masters, I *am*[f] to discourse wonders ; but ask me not what ; for, if I tell you, I am no true Athenian. I will tell you every thing, *right*[g] as it fell out.   32

Quin. Let us hear, sweet Bottom.

Bot. Not a word *of*[h] me. All that I will tell you is, that the duke hath dined. Get your apparel together, good strings to your beards, new ribbons to your *pumps*[i] : meet presently at the palace ; every man look o'er his part ; for the short and the long is, our play is *preferred.*[k] In any case, let Thisby have clean linen, and let not him that plays the lion pare his nails, for, they shall hang out for the lion's claws. And, most dear actors, eat no onions, nor garlic, for we are to utter sweet *breath,*[l] and I do not doubt, but to hear them say, it is a sweet comedy. No more words : away ! go, away !   [*Exeunt.* 46

a *are*

b *cf. III. i. 8*

c *if*

d *brave fellows*
e *perhaps he means 'glorious'*
f *have*

g *exactly*

h *from*

i *shoes*

k *offered for acceptance*

l *language, with a pun on the two meanings*

ACT V.

SCENE I. *Athens. The Palace of* THESEUS.

Enter THESEUS, HIPPOLYTA, PHILOSTRATE, *Lords, and Attendants.*

Hip. 'Tis strange, my Theseus, *that these lovers
speak of.[a]

The. More strange than true: I never *may*[b] believe

These *antique*[c] fables nor these *fairy toys*[d]:

Lovers and madmen have such *seething*[e] brains,

Such shaping fantasies, that *apprehend*[f]

More than cool reason ever *comprehends.*[g]

The lunatic, the lover and the poet,

Are of imagination *all compact*[h]:

One sees more devils than vast hell can hold;

That is the madman: the lover, all as frantic,   10

Sees *Helen's beauty*[i] in [1]*a brow of Egypt*:

[a] *that of which, etc.*
[b] *can*
[c] *quaint, old*
[d] *childish fairy tales*
[e] = *bubbling over (with imagination)*
[f] *conceive*
[g] *grasps*
[h] *altogether composed*
[i] *i.e. an ideal beauty*

---

* See page 109, on which this speech is paraphrased.
[1] A gipsy's swarthy features. (See III. ii., l. 258.)

The poet's eye, in *a fine frenzy*[a] rolling,
Doth glance from heaven to earth, from earth to
    heaven ;
And, as imagination *bodies forth*[b]
The forms of [1]*things unknown*, the poet's pen
Turns them to shapes, and gives to *airy nothing*[c]
A local habitation and a name.
Such tricks[d] hath strong imagination,
[2]*That, if it would but apprehend*[e] *some joy,*
It comprehends[f] *some bringer of that joy :*   20
Or in the night, imagining some fear,
How easy is a bush supposed a bear ?
   Hip. But all the story of the night told over,
And *all their minds transfigured so together,*[g]
More witnesseth[h] than fancy's images,
And grows to something of great *constancy*[i]*;*
But, howsoever, strange, and *admirable.*[k]
   The. Here come the lovers, full of joy and mirth.

     Enter LYSANDER, HERMIA, DEMETRIUS, *and*
             HELENA.

Joy, gentle friends ! joy, and fresh days of love,
Accompany your hearts !
   Lys.   More than to us   30
Wait in[l] your royal walks, your board, your bed !
   The. Come now ; what *masques,*[m] what dances
    shall we have ;
To wear away this long age of three hours
Between our [3]*after-supper* and bed-time ?
Where is our usual *manager of mirth*[n] ?
What revels are in hand ?   Is there no play,
To ease the anguish of a torturing hour ?
Call Philostrate.

Marginal glosses:

[a] *the splendid exaltation of inspiration*
[b] *invests with bodily form*
[c] *that which exists only in the imagination*
[d] *peculiar arts*
[e] *imagine*
[f] *imagines also*
[g] *such a change come over all of them at once*
[h] *testifies to something more*
[i] *consistency*
[k] *marvellous*
[l] *attend on*
[m] *dramatic performances*
[n] *master of the revels*

---

   [1] For example the fairies of this play, to which Shakespeare has given bodily
form and an existence almost real.
   [2] *I.e.* That it has the power of making an imaginary joy as real as though it
had an actual existence. 'Apprehend' and 'comprehend' have much the same
meaning here, viz. imagine.
   [3] This Mr. Wright (Cl. Pr. ed.) explains as 'rear-supper ; not the time after
supper, as it is usually explained, but a banquet so called which was taken after
the meal.'

Phil.   Here, mighty Theseus.

The. Say, what *abridgment*ᵃ have you for this
    evening ?

What masque ? what music ? How shall we beguile
The lazy time, if not with some delight ?   41

Phil. There is a *brief*ᵇ how many sports are ripe ;
Make choice of which your highness will see first.

                           [Giving a paper.

The. *[Reads.]* " The battle with the *Centaurs*,ᶜ to
    be sung

By an Athenian eunuch to the harp."
We'll none of that : that have I told my love,
In glory of my ¹*kinsman Hercules.*

    [Reads.] " The riot of the tipsy *Bacchanals*,ᵈ
Tearing the *Thracian singer*ᵉ in their rage."
That is an old device ; and it was play'd   50
When I from Thebes came last a conqueror.

    [Reads.] " ²*The thrice three Muses mourning for*
    the death

Of Learning, late deceased in beggary."
That is some satire, keen and *critical*,ᶠ
Not *sorting with*ᵍ a nuptial ceremony.

    [Reads.] " A tedious brief scene of young
    Pyramus

And his love Thisbe ; very tragical mirth."
Merry and tragical ! Tedious and brief !
That is, hot ice, and wondrous strange snow.
How shall we *find the concord of this discord*ʰ ?   60

  Phil. A play there is, my lord, some ten words
    long,

Which is as brief as I have known a play ;
But by ten words, my lord, it is too long,
Which makes it tedious ; for in all the play
There is not one word apt, one player *fitted*.ⁱ
And tragical, my noble lord, it is,

ᵃ *= something to shorten the time, hence, pastime*

ᵇ *summary*

ᶜ *see Clas. Names*

ᵈ *Bacchantes, Thracian women*
ᵉ *i.e. Orpheus*

ᶠ *severe*
ᵍ *suiting*

ʰ *reconcile these contradictions*

ⁱ *suited to his part*

---

¹ Theseus and Hercules were, according to tradition, associated in several
heroic exploits. Plutarch, in his life of Theseus, relates that they were cousins.

² These lines may allude to the death of the learned Robert Greene, who
died in great want in 1592. In this case they afford an indication of the date
of the play. (See Introduction, p. xi.)

For Pyramus therein doth kill himself
Which when I saw rehearsed, I must confess,
Made mine eyes water ; but more merry tears
The passion of loud laughter never shed.   70
  The. What are they that do play it?
  Phil. Hard-handed men, that work in Athens here,
Which never labour'd in their minds till now,
And now have toil'd their *unbreathed*[a] memories
With this same play against your nuptial.
  The. And we will hear it.
  Phil.   No, my noble lord ;
It is *not for you*[b] : I have heard it over,
And it is nothing, nothing in the world,
Unless you can find sport in their *intents*,[c]
Extremely stretch'd[d] and *conn'd*[e] with cruel pain, 80
To do you service.
  The.   I will hear that play :
For never anything can be amiss
When simpleness and duty tender it.
Go, bring them in : and take your places, ladies.
        [*Exit* PHILOSTRATE.
  Hip. I love not to see [1]*wretchedness o'er-charged,*
And duty in his service perishing.
  The. Why, gentle sweet, you shall see no such thing.
  Hip. He says, they can do nothing in this *kind.*[f]
  The. The kinder we, to give them thanks for nothing.
Our sport shall be to *take what they mistake*[g] :   90
And what poor duty cannot do, [2]*noble respect*
Takes it in might, not merit.
Where I have come, great *clerks*[h] have purposéd
To greet me with *premeditated welcomes*[i] ;
Where I have seen them shiver and look pale,
Make *periods*[k] in the midst of sentences,

a *unpractised*
b *fit for such as you*
c *attempts*
d *strained to the utmost*
e *learned*
f *way*
g *find the true meaning of their blundering representation*
h *scholars*
i *prepared speeches*
k *full stops*

[1] *I.e.* poor performers attempt what is beyond their power, and fail miserably whilst dutifully endeavouring to serve others.

[2] *I.e.* the courtesy of true nobility regards the intention (takes it in might, *i.e.* what it might be) and does not judge it on its (intrinsic) merits.

Throttle their *practised accent*[a] in their, fears,
And, in conclusion, dumbly have broke off,
Not paying me a welcome.   Trust me, sweet,
Out of this silence yet I pick'd a welcome ;   100
And in the modesty of *fearful*[b] duty
I read as much as from the rattling tongue
Of saucy and audacious eloquence.
Love, therefore, and tongue-tied simplicity,
In least[c] speak most, to my *capacity.*[d]

[a] studied speech

[b] timid

[c] i.e. when they say least
[d] judgment

Re-enter PHILOSTRATE.

Phil. So please your grace, the [1]*Prologue* is
address'd.[e]

The. Let him approach.   [*Flourish of Trumpets.*

[e] ready

Enter QUINCE *for the Prologue.*

Prol. If we offend, it is with our good will.
That you should think, we come not to offend,
But with good will.   To show our simple skill,   110
That is the true beginning of our end.
Consider then, we come but *in despite.*[f]
We do not come as *minding*[g] to content you,
Our true intent is.   All for your delight,
We are not here.   That you should here repent you,
The actors are at hand ; and, by their show,
You shall know all that you are *like*[h] to know.

[f] in defiance of opposition, i.e. to force ourselves upon you
[g] meaning
[h] likely

The. This fellow *doth not stand upon points.*[i]

Lys. He hath rid his prologue like a rough colt;
he knows not the stop.   A good moral, my lord : it
is not enough to speak, but to speak true.   121

[i] is not particular about stops

Hip. Indeed, he hath played on his prologue like
a child on a *recorder*[k] ; a sound, but not *in government.*[l]

[k] a flageolet

The. His speech was like a tangled chain ;
Nothing impaired,[m] but all disordered.   Who is next ?

[l] under any control
[m] i.e. possessing all the links

---

[1] The Prologue explains the action of the play, and apologises for imperfections in the performance.   His entrance was usually heralded by a flourish
of trumpets.   The humour of the prologue as spoken by Quince depends, not
merely on the fact that the punctuation is all incorrect, but that the mis-punctua-
tion gives precisely the opposite meaning to that intended.   For the true
punctuation see the Note on p. 84.

Enter PYRAMUS *and* THISBE, WALL, MOONSHINE, *and*
LION.

Prol. Gentles, perchance, you wonder at this
    show;
But wonder on, till truth make all things plain.
This man is Pyramus, if you would know;
    This beauteous lady Thisby is, certain.
This man, with lime and rough-cast, doth *present*ª   ª *represent*
    Wall, that vile Wall which did these lovers
        sunder;   132
And through Wall's chink, poor souls, they are
      content
    To whisper, at the which let no man wonder.
This man, with lanthorn, dog, and bush of thorn,
    Presenteth Moonshine; for, if you will know,
By moonshine did these lovers *think no scorn*ᵇ   ᵇ *not disdain*
    To meet at Ninus' tomb, there, there to woo.
This *grisly*ᶜ beast, which Lion *hight*ᵈ by name,   ᶜ *grim*
    The trusty Thisby, coming first by night,   140   ᵈ *called*
Did scare away, or rather did affright;
And, as she fled, her mantle she did *fall*,ᵉ   ᵉ *drop*
    Which Lion vile with bloody mouth did stain.
Anon comes Pyramus, sweet youth and tall,
    And finds his trusty Thisby's mantle slain:
Whereat with *b*lade,ᶠ with *b*loody *b*lameful *b*lade, ᶠ *Notice the ex-*
    He *b*ravely *b*roach'dᵍ his *b*oiling *b*loody *b*reast;   *cessive use of*
And Thisby tarrying in mulberry shade,   *alliteration*
    His *d*agger *d*rew, and *d*ied. For all the rest, ᵍ *tapped, opened*
Let Lion, Moonshine, Wall, and lovers twain, 150
At large discourse, while here they do remain.
    [*Exeunt* PROL., THISBE, LION, *and* MOONSHINE.

    The. I wonder, if the lion *be*ʰ to speak.   ʰ *has*

    Dem. No wonder, my lord: one lion may, when
many asses do.

    Wall. In this same interlude it doth befall,
That I, one Snout by name, present a wall;
And such a wall, as I would have you think,
That had in it a crannied hole, or chink,
Through which the lovers, Pyramus and Thisby,
Did whisper often very secretly.   160

This lime, this rough-cast, and this stone, doth
    show
That I am that same wall ; the truth is so ;
And this the cranny is, right and *sinister*,[a]
Through which the fearful lovers are to whisper.

    The. Would you desire lime and *hair*[b] to speak
better ?

    Dem. It is the wittiest partition that ever I
heard discourse, my lord.

    The. Pyramus draws near the wall · silence !

Enter PYRAMUS.

    Pyr. O *grim-look'd*[c] night ! O night with hue so
    black !   170
O night, which ever art, when day is not !
O night ! O night ! alack, alack, alack !
I fear my Thisby's promise is forgot !
And thou, O wall ! O sweet, O lovely wall,
    That stand'st between her father's ground and
    mine !
Thou wall, O wall ! O sweet and lovely wall,
    Show me thy chink, to *blink*[d] through with mine
    eyne.[e]   [WALL *holds up his fingers.*
Thanks, courteous wall : Jove shield thee well for
    this !
But what see I ?   No Thisby do I see.
O wicked wall, through whom I see no bliss ;   180
    Cursed by thy stones for thus deceiving me !

    The. The wall, methinks, *being sensible,*[f] should
curse again.

    Pyr. No, in truth, sir, he should not.   ' Deceiving
me,' is Thisby's cue : she is to enter now, and I am
to spy her through the wall.   You shall see, it will
fall *pat*[g] as I told you.   Yonder she comes.

Enter THISBE.

    This. O wall, full often hast thou heard my
    moans,
For parting my fair Pyramus and me !
My cherry lips have often kiss'd thy stones,   190
    Thy stones with lime and hair knit up in thee.

---

a *left. He holds
out his two
hands*
b *used in the
composition of
plaster*

c *gloomy-looking*

d *steal a look
through*
e *eyes*

f *possessing
sense or
feeling*

g *exactly*

Pyr. I *see*^a a voice : now will I to the chink,
To spy an I can *hear*^a my Thisby's face.
Thisby !

a cf. IV. i. 211

This. My love thou art, my love, I think.

Pyr. Think what thou wilt, I am thy lover's grace ;
And like *Limander*^b am I trusty still.

b *for Leander*

This. And I like *Helen,*^c till the Fates me kill.

c *for Hero*

Pyr. Not *Shafalus to Procrus*^d was so true.

d *for Cephalus to Procris*

This. As *Shafalus to Procrus,*^d I to you.   200

Pyr. O ! kiss me through the hole of this vile wall !

This. I kiss the wall's hole, not your lips at all.

Pyr. Wilt thou at Ninny's tomb meet me straightway ?

This. '*Tide life, 'tide death,*^e I come without delay.

e *i.e. whatever betide, or befall*

Wall. Thus have I, Wall, my part *discharged*^f so :
And, being done, thus Wall away doth go.

f *performed*

[*Exeunt* WALL, PYRAMUS *and* THISBE.

The. Now is the *mural*^g down between the two neighbours.

g *wall*

Dem. *No remedy,*^h my lord, when walls are so *wilful*ⁱ to hear without warning.   210

h *no help for it*

i *ready*

Hip. This is the silliest stuff that ever I heard.

The. The best in this kind are but *shadows*^k; and the worst are no worse, if imagination *amend them.*^l

k *imperfect representations*

l *i.e. 'pieces out their imperfections'*

Hip. It must be your imagination then, and not theirs.

The. If we imagine no worse of them than they of themselves, they may pass for excellent men.   Here come two noble beasts, in a man and a lion.

Enter LION *and* MOONSHINE.

Lion. You, ladies, you, whose gentle hearts do fear
The smallest *monstrous*^m mouse that creeps on floor,
May now perchance both quake and tremble here, 221
When lion rough in wildest rage doth roar.
Then know, that I, one Snug the joiner am,

m *a quibble on the two meanings ; (1) horrible, (2) huge*

A lion fell,[a] nor else no lion's dam :
For, if I should as lion come in strife
Into this place, *'t were pity on my life.*[b]

    The. A very gentle beast, and of a good con-
science.

    Dem. The very best at a beast, my lord, that e'er
I saw.   230

    Lys. This lion is a very fox for his [1]*valour*.

    The. True ; and a goose for his discretion.

    Dem. Not so, my lord ; for his valour cannot
carry his discretion, and the fox *carries*[c] the goose.

    The. His discretion, I am sure, cannot carry his
valour, for the goose carries not the fox. It is
well : leave it to his discretion, and let us listen to
the moon.

    Moon. This lant*horn* doth the *hornéd*[d] moon pre-
        sent.

    Dem. He should have worn the horns on his
head.   241

    The. He is *no crescent,*[e] and his horns are
invisible within the circumference.

    Moon. This lanthorn doth the hornéd moon
        present ;
Myself the man i'. the moon do seem to be.

    The. This is the *greatest error of all the rest.*[f]
The man should be put into the lanthorn : how is
it else the man i' the moon ?

    Dem. He dares not come there *for*[g] the candle ;
for, you see, it is already [2]*in snuff.*[h]   250

    Hip. I am aweary of this moon : would he
would change !

    The. It appears by his small light of *discretion,*[i]
that he is in the wane ; but yet, in courtesy, in all
reason, we must stay the time.

    Lys. Proceed, Moon.

    Moon. All that I have to say is, to tell you,
that the lanthorn is the moon ; I, the man in the

---

a sc. ' *Neither* '
  before ' *a*
  lion '
b *cf. III. i.* 43

c *carries off*

d *a pun on
  ' horn '*

e *not a waxing
  moon*

f *confusion of
  constructions
  (see p.* 103)

g *on account of*
h *offended, a pun
  on the two
  meanings*

i *wisdom*

---

  [1] The cunning of the fox is only equalled by its natural timidity.

  [2] *Cf.* Ben Johnson's *Poetaster* II. i. : " For I tell you true, I take it highly
in snuff, to learn how to entertain gentle-folks of you, at these years, I' faith."

moon ; this thorn-bush, my thorn-bush ; and this
dog, my dog.   260

Dem. Why, all these should be in the lanthorn ;
for all these are in the moon. But, silence ! here
comes Thisbe.

Enter THISBE.

This. This is old Ninny's tomb.   Where is my love ?

Lion. [*Roaring.*] Oh———— ! [THISBE *runs off*.

Dem. Well roared, Lion.

The. Well run, Thisbe.

Hip. Well shone, Moon.   Truly, the moon shines
with a good grace.

[*The Lion tears* THISBE's *mantle, and exit.*

The. Well *moused*,ᵃ Lion.   270

Dem. And then came Pyramus.

Lys. And so the lion vanished.

Enter PYRAMUS.

Pyr. Sweet moon, I thank thee for thy sunny
  beams ;
I thank thee, moon, for shining now so bright ;
For, by thy gracious, golden, glittering gleams,
 I trust to take of truest Thisby sight.
   But stay, O spite !
   But mark, poor knight,
 What dreadful dole is here !
   Eyes, do you see ?   280
   How can it be ?
O dainty duck ! O dear !
   Thy mantle good,
   What, stain'd with blood :
Approach, ye *Furies*ᵇ fell !
  O ¹*Fates*, come, come :
  ²*Cut thread and thrum;*
Quail,ᶜ crush, conclude, and quell !

---

a shaken (as a cat shakes a mouse)

b see Clas. Names

c kill

¹ Of the three Fates (Mœræ or Parcæ) Clotho (spinster) spun, Lachesis
(allotter) held, and Atropos (inevitable) cut, the thread of life.

² "An expression borrowed from weaving, the *thread* being the substance
of the warp ; the thrum, the small tuft beyond, where it is tied.   Hence,
metaphorically, the good and bad together" (Nare's "Glossary").   *Cf.* "All
moss hath here and there little stalks, besides the low *thrum*" (Bacon's *Natural
History*.)

The. This *passion*,[a] and the death of a dear
friend, would go near to make a man look sad. 290   a *violent emotion*

Hip. *Beshrew*[b] my heart, but I pity the man.   b *cf. II. ii.* 54

Pyr. O, wherefore, Nature, didst thou lions
frame,
Since lion vile hath here deflour'd my dear ?
Which is—no, no—which was the fairest dame,
That lived, that loved, that liked, that look'd *with*
       cheer.[c]   c *cheerily*
       Come, tears, *confound*[d] ;   d *destroy*
       Out, sword, and wound
The *pap*[e] of Pyramus :   e *breast*
       Ay, that left pap,
       Where heart doth *hop*[f] :   [*Stabs himself.*   f *beat*
Thus die I, thus, thus, thus !   301
       Now am I dead ;
       Now am I fled ;
My soul is in the sky :
       Tongue, lose thy light !
       Moon, take thy flight !   [*Exit Moonshine.*
    Now die, die, die, die, die.   [*Dies.*

Dem. [1]*No die, but an ace, for him; for he is but*
one.

Lys. Less than an ace, man, for he is dead ; he
is nothing.   311

The. With the help of a surgeon, he might yet
recover, and prove an ass.

Hip. How chance Moonshine is gone before
Thisbe comes back and finds her lover ?

The. She will find him by starlight. Here she
comes, and her *passion*[g] ends the play.   g *see l.* 289 *above*

Re-enter THISBE.

Hip. Methinks, she should not use a long one
for such a Pyramus ; I hope she will be brief.

Dem. *A mote*[h] will turn the balance, which   h *the smallest*
Pyramus, which Thisbe, is the better ; he for a   *particle (of*
man, God warrant us ; she for a woman, God   *difference)*
bless us.   323

---

[1] A pun on 'die.' The lowest point on a die (sing. of *dice*), *i.e.* the 'one,' is
called an ace. ' He is but one,' *i.e.* one *ace* (pronounced *ass*), another pun.

Lys. She hath spied him already with those sweet eyes.

Dem. And thus she *means*, *videlicet*[a] :—

This.   Asleep, my love ?
                What, dead, my dove ?
        O Pyramus, arise !
                Speak, speak ! Quite dumb ?   330
                Dead, dead ? A tomb
        Must cover thy sweet eyes,
                These lily lips,
                This cherry nose,
        These yellow cowslip cheeks,
                Are gone, are gone !
                Lovers, make moan !
        His eyes were green as leeks.
                O *Sisters Three*,[b]
                Come, come to me,   340
        With hands as pale as milk ;
                Lay them in gore,
                Since you have *shore*[c]
        With shears his thread of silk.
                Tongue, not a word :
                Come, trusty sword ;
        Come, blade, my breast *imbrue*[d] :
                                [Stabs herself.
                And farewell, friends ;
                Thus Thisby ends :
        Adieu, adieu, adieu.   *[Dies.* 350

The. Moonshine and Lion are left to bury the dead.

Dem. Ay, and Wall too.

Bot. No, I assure you : the wall is down, that parted their fathers. Will it please you to see the [1]*epilogue*, or to hear a *Bergomask*[e] dance between two of our company.

The. No epilogue, I pray you ; for your play needs no excuse. Never excuse ; for when the players are all dead, there need none to be blamed.

a *expresses her-self. Videlicet is used in the Classical sense = 'one may behold'*

b *The Fates, cf l. 286*

c *shorn*

d *drench (with blood)*

e *a rustic dance*

---

¹ Puck's speech at the end of this play is of the nature of an epilogue,— different though it be from what Bottom's epilogue would have been.

Marry, if he that *writ*[a] it had played Pyramus, and
hanged himself in Thisby's garter, it would have
been a fine tragedy : and so it is, truly ; and very
notably[b] discharged.   But come, your Bergomask :
let your epilogue alone.   [*A dance.*
The iron tongue of midnight hath *told*[c] twelve :   366
Lovers, to bed   'tis almost fairy time.
I fear we shall outsleep the coming morn,
As much as we this night have overwatch'd.
This *palpable-gross*[d] play hath well beguiled   370
The heavy gait of night.   Sweet friends, to bed.
A fortnight hold we this *solemnity*[e]
In nightly revels and new jollity.   [*Exeunt.*

a *wrote*

b *excellently*

c *struck*

d i.e. *the gross-
ness of which
is obvious to
all*

e *festivity*

Enter PUCK.

Puck. Now the hungry lion roars,
    And the wolf *behowls*[f] the moon ;
Whilst the heavy ploughman snores,
    All with weary task *fordone*.[g]
Now the *wasted*[h] brands do glow,
    Whilst the screech-owl, screeching loud,
Puts the wretch, that lies in woe,   380
    In remembrance of a shroud.
Now it is the time of night,
    That the graves, [1]*all gaping wide*,
Every one lets forth his *sprite*,[i]
    In the *church-way paths*[k] to glide :
And we fairies, that do run
    By the [2]*triple Hecate's* team,
From the presence of the sun,
    Following darkness like a dream,
Now are *frolic*[l] ; not a mouse   390
Shall disturb this hallow'd house :
I am sent with broom before,
To sweep the dust *behind*[m] the door.

f *howls at*

g *overcome*

h *spent*

i *spirit, ghost*

k *paths leading
to the church*

l *an adjective*

m sc. *that lies*

---

[1] *Cf. Hamlet* III. ii. :—
        " 'Tis now the very witching time of night,
            When churchyards yawn."

[2] Threefold, in allusion to her three-fold character—Luna in heaven
Diana on earth, and Hecate in the nether world.

Enter OBERON *and* TITANIA, *with their Train.*

Obe. Through the house give glimmering light,
    By the dead and drowsy fire ;
  Every elf and fairy sprite
    Hop as light as bird from brier :
  And this ditty, after me,
  Sing, and dance it trippingly.

Tita. First, *rehearse*ᵃ your song by rote,   400
  To each word a warbling note :
  Hand in hand, with fairy grace,
  Will we sing, and bless this place.
                     [Song and dance.

a *recite or repeat*

Obe. Now, until the break of day,
  Through this house each fairy stray.
  To the best bride-bed will we,
  Which by us shall blessèd be ;
  And the issue there create
  Ever shall be fortunate.
  So shall all the couples three   410
  Ever true in loving be ;
  And the *blots*ᵇ of Nature's hand
  Shall not in their issue stand ;
  Never mole, hare-lip, nor scar,
  Nor mark *prodigious*,ᶜ such as are
  Despisèd in nativity,
  Shall upon their children be.
  With this field-dew *consecrate*,ᵈ
  Every fairy take his *gait*,ᵉ
  And each several chamber bless,   420
  Through this palace, with sweet peace,
  And the owner of it blest
  Ever shall in safety rest.
  Trip away ; make no stay ;
  Meet me all by break of day.
        [Exeunt OBERON, TITANIA, *and Train.*

b *such as are enumerated in lines 414-5.*

c *portentous*

d *sacred, blessed*
e *way*

Puck. If we *shadows*ᶠ have offended,
  Think but this, and all is mended,
  That you have but slumber'd here,
  While these visions did appear.
  And this weak and idle theme,   430

f *spirits. cf. III. ii. 349*

I

No more yielding but[a] a [1]*dream,*
Gentles, do not reprehend :
If you pardon, we will mend.
And, as I'm an honest [2]*Puck,*
If we have *unearnéd luck*[b]
Now to 'scape *the serpent's tongue,*[c]
We will make amends ere long ;
Else the Puck a liar call :
So, good-night unto you all.
Give me your hands,[d] if we be friends,   440
And Robin shall *restore*[e] amends.   [*Exit.*

[a] *yielding nothing more than*

[b] *the undeserved good luck*
[c] *being hissed*

[d] *applaud me*
[e] *make*

[1] See Intro., p. xvii., on the title of the Play.
[2] Puck, pug and pouke are all general names for a fairy or goblin. (*Cf* 'The Puck' in l. 438 below.)

THE END.

SUPPLEMENTARY NOTES.

INTENDED PRINCIPALLY FOR SENIOR STUDENTS.

The play, as is apparent from the first few lines, is to be a story of love and marriage festivities. The poet, as usual, *seems* to plunge us at once *in medias res*. Really the first half of the first scene is of an Introductory character and enables us to understand the opening of the movement of the Action in the second half.

The scene is laid in Athens, but there is nothing in the play itself which suggests Athens, whilst innumerable allusions (to birds, flowers, customs, etc.), all point to the fact that Shakespeare had always in his mind English scenery and local customs with which he was familiar by association and experience.

2. **Four happy days.** The play contains several discrepancies, and this is one of them. We learn here that the marriage is to take place in four days. We shall see that it actually took place on the third day after the opening scene. The course of events is as follows. At line 164 of this scene the lovers arrange to meet "to-morrow night." They and the actors (cf. I. ii. 101), meet in the same wood on the same night. The action of Act II., and the greater part of Act III. takes place during the night of the second day (II. i. 18, 61, etc., III. i. 199, ii. 177, etc.), and the events of Act IV. Sc. i., happen in the early part of the third day, which we find (IV. i. 183-197), is also to be the wedding day of Theseus and Hippolyta. Act V. beholds the night of their solemnities, and the play ends almost immediately after " the iron tongue of midnight hath told twelve."

9. **The moon, like to a silver bow.** Here again there appears to be some inconsistency. The wedding is to take place at New Moon; but when the moon is new, that is when she is between the earth and the sun (or, in conjunction with the sun), she turns an unilluminated side to the earth (*i.e.* is invisible). In fact, " New Moon " is said to be nothing more nor less than a corruption of " no moon " (Elisha Noyce in *The Marvels of Nature*). And yet not only in this passage does the use of the expression " Silver bow " indicate a visible moon, but we read also in III. i. 55, that the moon " doth shine the night we play our play," *i.e.* on the night of the wedding. This, of course, might be set down to the ignorance of Quince and his fellow comedians, but we read also that on the same day " the wolf behowls the moon " (V. i. 375) at midnight, and that on the preceding day the moon " looks with a watery eye " (III. i. 199). These are difficulties which cannot be explained away.

It is interesting to note that the author of *The Burial of Sir John Moore* has fallen into precisely the same error. The poem tells us how the burial took place.

> By the struggling moonbeam's misty light.

The Nautical Almanac informs us that the moon was new on the 16th
January, 1809, and was therefore hardly a day old when the hero was
consigned to his grave. " But the moon in such a case," as Sir Robert
Ball states, " is practically invisible, and yields no appreciable moonbeams
at all, misty or otherwise. Indeed, if the funeral took place in the ' dead
of night,' as the poet tells us it did, the moon must have been far below
the horizon at the time."

16. **I woo'd thee with my sword.** Compare Chaucer's *Knight's Tale.*

> " What with his wisdom and his chevalrie,
> He conquered all the regne of Feminie,
> That whilom was ycleped Scythia ;
> And wedded the fresh quene Ipolita,
> And brought hire home with him to his contree
> With mochel glorie and grete solempnitee."

20. **Duke** M.E. *duk,* O.F. *duc,* is of course an anachronism when
applied to Theseus. In this Shakespeare has copied Chaucer, who
frequently speaks of " duk Theseus."

41. **The ancient privilege of Athens.** It is generally stated that
Shakespeare here anticipates the code of the great Athenian law-
giver, Solon, who enacted a law that parents should have absolute
power of life and death over their children. But as a matter of fact,
all members of a family were at the absolute disposal of the father of
the family, even before the legendary Theseus made Athens the seat
of a central government. The state of Athens grew from the house
or family upwards, and in the primitive Aryan states the master of
each household was its priest and king.

70. **Livery of a nun.** The terms ' nun,' ' cloister,' ' sister,' ' pilgrimage,'
belong properly to the age of Christianity, and are anachronisms
when applied to persons or things belonging to a pagan era. But
even in the pagan age the different gods and goddesses often had
their votaries. Diana, as a virgin goddess was especially venerated
by young maidens, whose patroness she remained till their marriage.
The Roman Diana possessed a very ancient shrine on Mount Algidus,
Tusculum (cf. line 89 of this scene).

74. **Thrice-blessed they.** This line and the next are often supposed to
convey a compliment to Elizabeth, the virgin queen.

136. **O cross !** On these lines Coleridge remarks: " I can never help
feeling how great an improvement it would be if the two former of
Hermia's exclamations were omitted ; the third and only appropriate
one would then become a beauty, and most natural."

167. **To do observance to a morn of May.** The following description, alluding to the mediaeval custom of commemorating the First
of May, is quoted by Drake: " On the Calends, or the 1st day of
May, commonly called *May-day,* the juvenile part of both sexes were
wont to rise a little after midnight, and walk to some neighbouring
wood, accompany'd with music, and the blowing of horns, where
they break down branches from the trees, and adorn them with

nosegays and *crowns of flowers*. When this is done, they return with their booty homewards, about the rising of the sun, and make their doors and windows to triumph in the flowery spoil. The after part of the day is chiefly spent in dancing round a tall pole, which is called a May Pole " (" Shakespeare and His Times," vol. I. 153). The expression " to do observance " occurs twice in Chaucer's *Knight's Tale*.

169. **Cupid, Venus, etc.** For the explanation of these and other classical allusions, see under Classical Names.

215. **Faint primrose beds.** The epithet 'faint' probably refers to the colour as we have explained it in the Marginal Notes. On the other hand it may refer to the odour of the flower, or it may be used proleptically, as Mr. Wright takes it ; primrose-beds " on which those rest who are faint and weary."

232. **Things base and vile.** A notable instance of the truth of this statement is that of Titania's becoming " enamour'd of an ass."

235. **Cupid painted blind.** Cupid (Greek, *Eros*), appears with wings in the art monuments of antiquity, but the notion of his blindness appears to be no more ancient than Chaucer. He was represented as a child by the later artists of the classical age because the mischievous pranks attributed to him by the poets were only adapted to the age of childhood.

ACT I. SCENE II.

We now make the acquaintance of the comic characters of the play. They have themselves of course no idea that they are comic. On the contrary, they are exceedingly serious in all they undertake. This unconsciousness of their absurdity in the "hard-handed men of Athens" adds very much to the humour of the situation. We see the same thing very finely exemplified in Don Quixote. The scene is in prose, as are most of the comic scenes in Shakespeare. The use of this medium here brings out the contrast between these homely characters and the more dignified and poetical characters of the other scenes.

11. **Lamentable comedy.** " The story of Pyramus and Thisbe was very familiar to an Elizabethan audience, not merely in translations of Ovid, but as having been told in prose and verse by numerous English writers of the sixteenth century " (Halliwell-Phillipps). We have already mentioned some of the forms in which it appeared (p. xii.). It is also related in the *Boke of the Cyté of Ladies* (1521), in the *Gorgeous Gallery of Gallant Inventions* (1578), and in *Silkewormes and their Flies* (1599).

17. **Nick Bottom.** Nick is a diminutive form of (St.) Nicholas. It was also a very old name for the devil, who, after the Reformation, was scoffingly converted into a saint in profane ridicule of the popish saint, the patron of scholars.

30. Play Ercles. The Clarendon Press edition refers to a passage in Sidney's *Arcadia*: "With the voyce of one that playeth Hercules in a play," and to Greene's *Groatsworth of Wit*: "The twelve labors of Hercules have I terribly thundred on the stage," and suggests that the verses recited by Bottom may be a quotation from such a play.

31. To tear a cat. To rant, and behave with violence. A bullying rogue in Middleton's *Roaring Girl*, takes the name of Tear-cat. In Day's *Isle of Gulls*, Induction, we read, "I had rather heare two good jests than a whole play of such *tear-cat* thunder-claps."
To make all split, a phrase expressing violence of action. Nares quotes from *Widow's Tears*: "To prepare my next encounter, but in such a way as shall *make all split.*"

43. The bellows-mender. Steevens says he was one who had the care of organs, regals, etc. Ben Jonson's Masque of *Pan's Anniversary* has the following passage: "Only one splay foot in the company, and he is a bellows-mender, allowed, who hath the looking to all of their lungs by patent."

54. Thisne, Thisne. This probably conveys Bottom's idea of uttering the word Thisbe in a "monstrous little voice." In the next line he appears to have already partially forgotten that he is personating a woman and reverts to his own pronunciation of Thisby.

97. French crown. This might mean three things:—(1) The crown of a Frenchman's head; (2) A piece of French money; (3) The baldness produced by a disease supposed to be French. Shakespeare puns on the word again in *Measure for Measure* and in *Henry V.*

99. Entreat, request, desire. Notice that the words are used in a descending not (as Bottom no doubt intended them) in an ascending scale of emphasis.

111. Hold or cut bow-strings. A metaphor from archery. To cut the bow-strings would of course render the bow useless and put the archer out of the game or contest.

ACT II. SCENE I.

In this scene further complications arise, and, as we shall see, these complications proceed not so much from the actions or characters of the persons themselves, as is usually the case in Shakespeare's plays, but from external causes from the fairies. So far we have Lysander and Demetrius both in love with Hermia, who favours the former in opposition to the will of her father. Helena loves Demetrius, to whom she was once betrothed, but who now looks upon her with scorn. Oberon, the powerful fairy king, determines to smooth "the course of true love" for Helena, and sends his fac-totum Puck on a mission to effect this purpose. We shall see later how Puck makes a mistake and further complicates the situation. From this scene also we learn something of the nature and attributes of the fairies (for a full account of which see Introduction xxi.),

nd we find, that like the "human mortals," they too have their jealousies **nd** their quarrels.

7. Sphere. Johnson gives as one of the meanings of *sphere*, **orb**, circuit of motion, and quotes from Milton—

> Half unsung, but narrower bound
> Within the visible diurnal *sphere*

9. Orbs. The fairies after their moon-light dances were supposed to leave behind either a scorched, or a deep green ringlet, the scorched or barren rings being left by bad fairies, the fresh-looking green ones by good fairies. These "fairy rings" are now generally explained as being caused by a certain kind of fungus that grows in a circle, and when decayed causes a rich and greener growth of grass to appear on the same spot.

16. Lob, a lubber, or clown. Dr. Johnson says, in his note on this passage *lob, lubber, looby, lobcock*, all denote both inactivity of body and dulness of mind. Neither of these qualities, however, can be said to characterise Puck.

23. Changeling, is here used for the human child stolen from the Indian king, not as it usually is, for the child substituted by the fairies It used to be customary in the Highlands of Scotland to watch children until the christening was over, under the idea that the power of the fairies, owing to the original corruption of human nature, was chiefly to be dreaded in the interval between birth and baptism. "The cause assigned for this evil propensity on the part of the fairies, was the dreadful obligation they were under, of sacrificing the tenth individual every, or every seventh year" (DRAKE). Shakespeare, however, has altogether eliminated the terrific aspect from his system of fairies.

48. Gossip's bowl. *Gossib*, now corrupted to *gossip*, formerly meant a sponsor in baptism. *Lit.* "related in god"; M.E. *god*, god; *sib*, related. From the intimacy often subsisting between such persons it came also to mean a familiar acquaintance, a crony. The ingredients of the "gossip's bowl" or "gossip's cup" were ale, nutmeg, sugar, toast and roasted crabs or apples.

55. "Tailor" cries. Halliwell thinks the expression is "one of contempt," equivalent to *thief*, and quotes from Pasquil's *Night Cap* (1612) :

> Thieving is now an occupation made,
> Though men the name of *tailor* doe it give.

The quartos and folios have *coffe* and *loffe* in this line and the next, thus showing the pronunciation which might be given to these words.

70. Steppe of India. It is sometimes thought that the *steppe* of the first Quarto was an error for *steepe* (the reading of the Second Quarto and the Folio), as it is doubtful whether the word steppe in the sense of a vast plain was known in Shakespeare's time.

99. **Nine men's morris.** This game of open air draughts was played by two men with twenty-four "counters" or stones which were arranged upon a diagram of three squares, one within the other, the figure being cut out on the turf. The players moved their pieces alternately, according to certain rules until the game was ended by one player having all his pieces taken or impounded. Der. F. *merelles* or *mereaux*, counters.

100. **Quaint mazes** were complicated labyrinths which differed from the mazes (formed by a series of hedges) with which we are familiar in that the track to be followed was marked out upon the green turf. The green grass would form the border of the track and was never to be overstepped by those who ran the figure.

104. **The moon.** The influence of the moon over diseases bodily and intellectual, its virtue in all magical rites, and its power over the weather and over many of the minor concerns of life, were almost universally accredited in the sixteenth century.

151. **Mermaid.** For the various explanations given of the "Oberon's vision," see the Introduction pp. xxv-xxvi.

206. **Spurn me.** Cf. *Julius Cæsar*, III. i. 45:

> If thou dost bend and pray and fawn for him,
> I spurn thee like a cur out of my way

218. **Opportunity.** Cf. the familiar adage "Opportunity makes the thief."

33. **The Griffin or Gryphon** was a fabled animal which was supposed to combine the qualities of the king of beasts and the king of birds. Its head, fore-legs, and wings were those of an eagle, while the rest of its body resembled that of a lion. In England a large kind of eagle was sometimes called a gripe or griffin, and it may be in this sense that Shakespeare here uses the word, as he evidently does in 2 *Henry IV.* III. i. where he speaks of "a clip-winged griffin and a moulten-raven."

253. **Musk**-roses. The name of musk-rose was given in Shakespeare's time to a wild rose of a white colour and does not here refer to the pink-coloured species which is cultivated in gardens.

ACT II. SCENE II.

The scene is changed to that part of the wood to which Oberon referred in lines 250-6 of the foregoing scene. This beautiful spot in fairy-land is to be the scene of most of the important incidents of the play. Here Titania, Hermia and Lysander fall asleep; here Lysander awakes and falls in love with Helena; and in the same neighbourhood the Athenian tradesmen will perform their play (Act III. Scene I.), and Titania will awake to fall in love with Bottom.

30. **Ounce,** *Felis uncia*, a native of some parts of Asia. "Early explorers," says Phipson, "seem to have been somewhat puzzled

by the different varieties of the leopard tribe, and this much-dreaded animal may have been the jaguar or puma."

104. **Nature shows art.** The Folios read "Nature here shews art,' which Malone altered to "Nature shews her art."

114. **Change a raven for a dove,** *i.e.* change Hermia, who was of a dark complexion, for Helena, who was fair and of a gentler disposition.

ACT III. SCENE I.

This scene, occurring in the middle of the play, shares with the preceding the crisis of the plot. There Lysander was made to fall in love with Helena, thus giving rise to the first complication. Here Titania falls in love with Bottom and thus the fairy part of the play becomes interwoven with the rustic part. The "green plot" of line 3 is in the same part of the wood as the "cradle of the fairy queen," which is "the bank whereon the wild thyme blows" of II. i. 250.

24. **Eight and six.** It will be seen that the prologue was eventually written in verses of 10 syllables (V. i. 108).

44. **Let him name his name.** Malone has suggested that Bottom may here allude to an incident which may have occurred in Shakespeare's time, and which is recorded in a collection entitled *Merry Passages and Jests:* "There was a spectacle presented to Queen Elizabeth upon the water, and among others Harry Goldingham was to represent Arion upon the Dolphin's back; but finding his voice to be very hoarse and unpleasant when he came to perform it, he tears off his disguise, and swears he was none of Arion, not he, but even honest Goldenham; which blunt discovery pleased the queen better than if he had gone through even in the right way :— yet he could order his voice to an instrument exceedingly well."

63. **Says the story.** Cf. Chaucer's *Legende of Thisbe and Babylon* :

> This wal, which that betwixt hem both ystode,
> Was cloven atwo, right fro the top adown,
> Of olde time, of his foundatioun,
> But yet this clift was so narrow and lite,
> It was nat seene, dere ynough a mite,
> But what is that, that love cannot espie?

108. **Sometime a horse I'll be.** The Protean versatility of Robin Goodfellow was traditional. Cf. *Robin Goodfellow, his Mad Pranks and Merry Jests* :

> "Thou hast the power to change thy shape
> To horse, to hog, to dog, to ape."

162. **Peaseblossom.** The names of the fairy queen's attendants are expressive of their delicacy and beauty.

170. **Glow-worm's eyes.** Monck Mason writes :—"Surely a poet is justified in calling the luminous part of the glow-worm the eye : it is a liberty we take in plain prose; for the point of greatest brightness in a furnace is commonly called the eye of it."

ACT III. SCENE II.

The first forty lines of this scene make plain to us by repetition incidents which we have already witnessed; 40 to 93 serve to connect the story of the lovers with that of the fairies; 94 to 121 prepare for the further complications which have arisen owing to Puck's mistaking Lysander for Demetrius; the double complication arising from this error is fully set forth between 122 and 346; from this point to the end of the scene the story of the lovers again mingles with that of the fairies and the unravelling of the plot begins.

36. **Latched.** We have explained this in the margin to mean 'caught or entrapped,' thus connecting it with A.S. *læccan*, to seize, catch hold of, and with the modern 'latch,' a catch or fastening. Mr. Skeat, however, derives the word from A.S. *leccan*, to moisten, and connects it with the modern 'leak.' Others connect it with 'lick' and the F. *lécher*; G. *lecken*. Puck's reply to Oberon's question, 'I *took* him sleeping' seems to point to the first explanation as being the correct one.

54. **So displease.** The meaning seems to be, cause a displeasing sensation among the inhabitants of the other side of the globe at noontide (when the appearance of the moon would be most unwelcome).

71. **Worm,** adder, serpent, snake are used by Shakespeare as different names for the same thing, the harmless English snake.

97. **That Costs.** The idea was prevalent in Shakespeare's time that each sigh consumed a part of the blood of the sigher. In II. *Henry VI.* the poet speaks of "blood-consuming sighs" and of "blood-drinking sighs." For the singular form see p. 101.

127. **Badge of faith.** This is said to be in allusion to the metal badges worn by the servants of the nobility, to denote the house or family to which they belonged.

213. **Two of the first.** Another explanation of this passage has been furnished by Mr. Monck Mason, who writes :—" Every branch of a family is called a house ; and none but the first house can bear the arms of the family without some distinction; two of the first, therefore, means two coats of the first house, which are properly due but to one."

274. **What news.** This expression of somewhat uncertain meaning is explained by Schmidt as equivalent to 'What is the matter?' Amongst other passages given to illustrate this use of the expression are *Othello* I. ii.

> The goodness of the night upon you, friends !
> What is the news ?

and *Merchant of Venice*, I. ii. 128, 'How now! what news?' He also refers to I. i. 21 of this play, 'What's the news with thee?' We must confess that we are not ourselves altogether satisfied with the explanation.

298. **Painted maypole. R.** Chambers' *Book of Days* contains several illustrations of the maypoles of ancient days. From the same source we take the following: " The fifth volume of Halliwell's folio edition of Shakespeare has a curious coloured frontispiece of a Maypole, painted in continuous vertical stripes of white, red, and blue, which stands in the centre of the village of Welford, in Gloucestershire, about five miles from Stratford-on-Avon. It may be an exact copy and legitimate successor of one standing there in the days when the bard himself visited the village. It is of great height, and is planted in the centre of a raised mound, to which there is an ascent by three stone steps : on this mound probably the dancers performed their gyrations."

381. **Night's swift dragons.** The chariot of the goddess Night is here represented as being drawn by a team of dragons or winged serpents, who were thought to be always awake, because they slept with their eyes open. Compare *Cymbeline* II. ii.

> Swift, swift, you dragons of the night.

In classical writers Night's chariot was drawn by horses.

385. **Crossways and floods.** The practice of burying suicides on a public highway, with a stake through the body was legal until the fourth year of the reign of George IV. Those who ' in floods have burial ' are those who commit suicide by drowning. The idea that the ghosts of those who did not receive proper burial were condemned to wander for a hundred years is classical (See *Vergil Æneid VI.* 329). Compare also *Hamlet* I. iv.

> I am thy father's spirit
> Doom'd for a certain term to walk the night,
> And for the day confined to fast in fires,
> Till the foul crimes done in my days of nature
> Are burnt and purged away.

391. **The morning's love.** The reference here is to the handsome hunter Cephalus, who was said to be a son of Hermes. Cephalus was carried off by Aurora, who was unable to shake the fidelity of his wife Procris. Procris had hidden herself among the bushes, in order to watch her husband, when Cephalus, taking her for a wild animal, unwittingly killed her. This story is indirectly referred to in V. i. 199.

ACT IV. SCENE I.

This act performs the function usually assigned to the Fifth Act in Shakespeare's comedies. Here the general unravelling of the various complications, which was begun in the last scene is completed. Titania and Bottom return to their own spheres of life ; Demetrius reverts to his first love, Lysander and Hermia are as they were wont to be ; Theseus and Hippolyta take their way to the temple of Hymen, and everything ends happily. The next Act, although lightly woven into the plot and though it brings together all the characters of the play, is nevertheless rather of the nature of an episode than an integral part of the play.

11. Red-hipped humble-bee. One species of ' humble bees '' (the *Bombus lapidarius*) has the lower half of the abdomen bright red. It is perhaps of this that Shakespeare is thinking in this passage.

13. Honey-bag. The honey-bag of a bee is its first stomach which " from being very small, is swelled when full to a considerable size."

27. Good ear in music. Weavers were generally supposed to be musical and given to singing, more especially to psalm-singing.

74. Diana's bud. This is referred to by Chaucer in *The Flower and the Leaf.*

> That is Diane, goddesse of chastite,
> And for because that she a maiden is,
> In her hond the braunch she beareth this,
> That *agnus castus* men call properly.

107. My hounds. The Theseus of Chaucer was a great hunter. Compare :—

> This mene I now by mighty Theseus,
> That for to hunten is so desirous,
> And namely at the grete hart in May,
> That in his bed ther daweth (dawneth) him no day,
> That he n'is clad, and ready for to ride
> With hunte and horne, and houndes him beside.

And the poet proceeds to describe a day's hunting in company

> With his Ipolita, the fayre quene.

Shakespeare appears to have had the poem in his memory when he composed this portion of the play.

118. Hercules and Cadmus. The name of Hercules is associated with that of Hippolyta in classical legend. For his ninth adventure the hero was commissioned by Eurystheus to demand the girdle of the queen of the Amazons. Plutarch relates that " some other hold opinion " that he accompanied Theseus in his expedition against the Amazons. Shakespeare's only apparent reason for mentioning Cadmus in this connection is that Cadmus was the mythical founder of Thebes, whilst Creon, a later king of the same city is an important personage (slain by Theseus) in Chaucer's *Knight's Tale.*

114. A Wood of Crete. It was in Crete that Theseus slew the Minotaur, an exploit which, says Chaucer, was stamped in gold upon the duke's penon.

115. Hounds of Sparta. Spartan and Cretan hounds are both celebrated in Ovid's *Metamorphoses.*

124. Match'd in mouth. Drake remarks in connection with this passage : " One great object at this period, in the construction of the kennel, was the modulation and harmony of the vocal powers of the dog. This was carried to a nicety and perfection little practised in the present day."

134. The rite of May. See the note on I. i. 167.

141. To couple now. "There was," says Chambers, "a prevalent notion amongst the common people, that this was the day on which the birds selected their mates," and, "It was supposed that the first unmarried person of the other sex whom one met on St. Valentine's morning in walking abroad was a destined wife, or a destined husband."

ACT IV. SCENE II.

This scene serves to connect the final scene of the play with what has preceded.

20. Sixpence a day. Shakespeare is here supposed to make an allusion, which would probably be understood at the time, to some actor who had been pensioned by Queen Elizabeth. Steevens tells us that Preston, the author of *Cambyses*, received from the Queen a pension of rather more than a shilling a day, as an acknowledgment of the pleasure she had derived from the performance of the play of *Dido*, at King's College, Cambridge, in 1564.

35. The Duke hath dined. Notice that Bottom, the practical man, has been busy during the interval that has elapsed since he awoke from his vision.

ACT V. SCENE I.

As already noticed, the incidents of this Act are of the nature of an episode, or, they bear pretty much the same relation to the rest of the play as an anti-masque did to the main masque. The Interlude, like the anti masques of Ben Jonson, is in some sense a parody of the principal theme of the play. As Gervinus says: "The play of the respectable citizens of Pyramus and Thisbe forms to the tragic-comic point of the plot a comic-tragic counterpart of two lovers, who, behind their parents' back 'think no scorn to woo by moonlight,' and through a mere accident come to a tragic end."

44. The battle with the Centaurs. This probably refers to the battle of the Lapithæ with the Centaurs in which Theseus fought on the side of the Lapithæ. Pirithous, the Thessalian king of the Lapithæ, invited the Centaurs to be present at his wedding with Hippodamia. In their drunkenness the Centaurs endeavoured to carry off the bride, and the contest that ensued ended in their complete defeat. Hercules, in some representations, figures as the opponent of the Centaurs, and Theseus in his modesty appears here (in lines 46-7) to attribute all the glory of the exploit to his kinsman.

49. The Thracian singer. Orpheus, not long after his unhappy visit to the lower world, whilst wandering over the Thracian mountains in despair at having for ever lost his beloved Eurydice, was torn in pieces by some women in the mad excitement of their nightly

Bacchanalian orgies. Ovid tells the story in his *Metamorphoses.* Cf. Milton's *Lycidas.*

> When by the rout that made the hideous roar
> His gory visage down the stream was sent,
> Down the swift Hebrus to the Lesbian shore.

98. Great clerks. Karl Elze is of opinion that the play of *A Midsummer Night's Dream* was composed to celebrate the marriage of the Earl of Essex with the widow of Sir Philip Sidney, and considers " Theseus and Hippolyta as the representatives of the bridal couple itself." He holds that these lines literally apply to Essex, and that in the expression " great clerks," there is a special reference to George Peel who dedicated his ' Eclogue Gratulatory ' to Essex upon his return from the Spanish campaign in 1589 (shortly before his marriage). It is more probable, however, that these lines contain an allusion to the addresses that were made to welcome Queen Elizabeth whenever she paid a visit to either Oxford or Cambridge.

108. Prologue. The correct punctuation of these lines would be as follows :

> If we offend, it is with our good will
> That you should think we come not to offend ;
> But with goodwill to show our simple skill ;
> That is the true beginning of our end.
> Consider then. We come ; but in despite
> We do not come. As minding to content you,
> Our true intent is all for your delight.
> We are not here that you should here repent you.
> The actors are at hand ; and by their show
> You shall know all that you are like to know.

128. This man is Pyramus. Golding's translation has—

> The name of him was Pyramus, and Thisbe call'd was she.

In Chaucer's poem on the same subject we read—

> This yonge man was cleped Piramus,
> Thisbe hight the maide (Naso saith thus).

No doubt Shakespeare had read the story both in Golding's Translation of Ovid's *Metamorphoses*, and in Chaucer's *Legende of Tisbe of Babylon.* The resemblances between Shakespeare's play and the Translation are, however, closer than those between the play and the Legend. In the Translation mention is made of " a fair high mulberry "; in the poem it is only " under a tree " that the lovers meet. In the Translation Thisbe " let her mantle fall "; in the poem the cloak is always called a " wimple." On the other hand, in Chaucer, the wall is the " cold wall," and " thou wicked wall," and there is a reference to " thy lime and eke thy stone "; in the Translation the " spiteful wall " is made " of brick." In both Golding and Chaucer the ' lion ' is a ' lioness.'

135. Lanthorn, dog, and bush of thorn. It is a very old popular notion that the Man in the Moon is the man referred to in the book of Numbers (xv. 32 *et seq.*) as having been detected by the children of Israel in the wilderness, in the act of gathering sticks on the Sabbath day, and whom the Lord directed to be stoned to death without the camp. So he appears in the moon with his burden of sticks upon his back, continually climbing up that shining height

with his little dog before him, but never getting a step higher
Chaucer refers to him—

> Bearing a bush of thorns on his backe,
> Which for his theft might clime so ne'r the heaven;

and Dante makes a reference to him in his *Inferno*, but with a
variation upon the popular English idea, in as far as he calls him
Cain.

> But now come on, for hastens to his home
> Cain with his thorns (*Inferno* xx. 124),

upon which Plumptre remarks, " The dark spots on the moon . . .
were in the Middle Age legends of Italy, the image of Cain holding
a burning bush, and condemned, as in *Gen.* iv. 12, to perpetual
wandering."

150. **Lion, Moonshine, Wall, and lovers twain.** In Act I. Scene II. we
learnt that Starveling was to " play Thisby's mother," Snout,
" Pyramus' father," Quince " Thisby's father." Quince has
evidently revised and re-cast the play since the first rehearsal.

197. **Limander.** For the story of Hero and Leander, see Classical Names,
and for that of Cephalus and Procris, see the note on III. ii. 391.

224. **A lion fell.** The text here seems to be corrupt. Snug wishes to tell
the audience that he is not really a lion, but the required negative
is missing in the quartos and folios. Some editors print " No lion
fell," others place a hyphen between lion and fell in which case
" I . . . . am a lion-fell " would mean " I am (only) a lion's skin."
Snug is here carrying out Bottom's suggestion of III. i. 36-46.

293. **Deflour'd properly means ravished.** The word is here misapplied by
Bottom, who may have intended to say ' devoured.'

356. **Bergomask.** A rustic dance framed in imitation of the people of
Bergamo (a province in the state of Venice), who are ridiculed as
being more clownish in their manners and dialect than any other
people in Italy. All the Italian buffoons imitate them.

358. **Epilogue.** Shakespeare uses an Epilogue in *The Tempest, As You
Like It, All's Well That Ends Well, II. Henry IV., Henry V.,
Henry VIII.,* and (in effect though not in name) in *A Midsummer
Night's Dream.*

374. **Now the hungry lions roar.** Of these verses Coleridge says: " Very
Anacreon in perfectness, proportion, grace, and spontaneity. So
far it is Greek ; but then add, O ! what wealth, what wild ranging,
and yet what compression and condensation of English fancy. In
truth there is nothing in Anacreon more perfect than these thirty
lines, or half so rich and imaginative. They form a speckless
diamond."

392. **Sent with broom before.** Not only in this passage does Shakespeare
dwell particularly on the attention of the fairies to cleanliness.
In the *Merry Wives of Windsor* (V. v.) and in *Romeo and Juliet*
(I. iv.) he refers to their love of cleanliness and hatred of " sluts
and sluttery."

406. **To the best bride-bed.** It was still customary in Shakespeare's time
to bless the bridal bed at night, in order to dissipate the supposed

illusions of the Devil. The ceremony is noticed by Chaucer in his *Merchant's Tale*, and is mentioned in the "Articles ordained by King Henry VII., for the regulation of his Household."

120. **If we shadows have offended.** We have already stated that this concluding speech bears the character of an Epilogue, and as such, was probably intended merely to secure the applause of the audience as the curtain descended. Elze, however, thinks that these lines were written with a more definite and particular purpose. He supposes the play to have been composed for the occasion of the marriage of the Earl of Essex (see the note on l. 93), and that the pardon is asked for because the Queen was averse to the marriage.

PART III. ELIZABETHAN ENGLISH.

On reading the works of Elizabethan authors we are apt at first sight to wonder at the many points of difference in grammar, syntax, and meaning which we observe when we compare them with the English of to-day. But, if we look into the matter closely, we shall not be surprised at what we find. The great "renascence" had just taken place. The literature of the ancient classics was being studied as it had never before been studied in England, and the zeal of the convert made itself manifest in our language. But old prejudices die hard, and must be combated, and as the struggle continues the result appears to be—chaos. Neither party will give way, so both reign and neither is supreme. But language is given to express thought, and out of the apparent chaos there arises a language clear in thought, but doubtful in expression. Such must the language be of all transitional periods, and the Elizabethan language was nothing if not transitional. Here English-Latin, there Latin-English, but always intelligible. The Englishman in a foreign country, possessing but a smattering of the foreign tongue, will express himself in a hybrid language, but he will make his meaning *clear*, though his grammar may be faulty, and his syntax inexact. So, too, the child,—and the new English was in its infancy. Hence we shall find that the Elizabethan English differs in many respects from the English of to-day, that it is trying to reconcile two conflicting systems, and that "syntax," or the orderly arrangement of words into sentences is hardly to be looked for. And we need not wonder at inflectional changes ; for language is a living organism, and we must expect a living thing to show some signs of change after a period of three hundred years.

We shall in this find the *raison d'être* of most of the so-called "grammatical difficulties" in Shakespeare. It may be added that in those days printed books were less common than now, and that, even to-day, the *spoken language* is frequently less "grammatical" than the *written book*. And we must not forget that Shakespeare was a dramatist even before he was a poet, and that he makes his men and women *speak* in their own character. Bottom will not use the same expressions as fall from the mouth of Titania, nor will any character under the influence of strong emotion use the same terms, or express himself with the same grammatical accuracy as he might use when not so moved.

K

SHAKESPEARIAN GRAMMAR ILLUSTRATED
FROM THE PLAY.

*It is almost superfluous to express my obligation to Dr. Abbott whose
Shakespearian Grammar has proved so great a boon to
modern editors.*

ADJECTIVES, USE OF.

Adjectives used as Adverbs.

Adverbs are by origin forms of declension, cases of substantives, *adjectives*, or pronouns. In Early English an adverb was commonly distinguished from the adjective from which it was derived by the addition of a suffix *e* (the dative ending). This suffix, in common with others, was gradually dropped, and the simple form of the adjective came thus to do duty for the adverb. We still use many adjectives adverbially, even when we have a corresponding adverb, *e.g.* quick. slow, nice, etc.

I. i. 3.	How *slow* this old moon wanes! = slowly.
I. i. 76.	*Earthlier* happy is the rose distill'd = in an earthly sense.
I. i. 134.	The course of true love never did run *smooth* = smoothly.
I. i. 149.	So *quick* bright things come to confusion = quickly.
I. ii. 24.	A lover that kills himself most *gallant* for love = gallantly.
I. ii. 51.	You may speak as *small* as you will = in as small a tone
II. i. 200.	Do I speak you *fair?* = kindly, gently.
II. ii. 74.	And here the maiden, sleeping *sound* = soundly; so also in III. ii. 451.
III. i. 2.	A *marvellous* convenient place = marvellously; so in IV. i. 451.
III. ii. 175.	Lest, to thy peril, thou aby it *dear* = pay dearly for it.
III. ii. 316.	And now, so you will let me *quiet* go = quietly.
III. ii. 405.	I will be with thee *straight* = straightway; so in IV. i. 61.
V. i. 10.	The lover, *all* as frantic, Sees Helen's beauty . . . = altogether, quite.
V. i. 22.	How *easy* is a bush supposed a bear = easily.
V. i. 53.	The death Of Learning, *late* deceased in beggary = lately.
V. i. 59.	Hot ice and *wondrous* strange snow = wonderfully.
V. i. 117.	You shall know all that you are *like* to know = likely.
V. i. 129.	This beauteous lady Thisbe is *certain* = certainly or for certain.
V. i. 370.	This *palpable* gross play = palpably.
V. i. 397.	Hop as *light* as bird from brier = lightly.

Adjectives used as Nouns.

I. i. 181. Call you me fair? that *fair* again unsay.
Demetrius loves your *fair :* O happy *fair.*

Shakespeare has here allowed himself to be carried away from grammatical correctness by an opportunity of indulging in a verbal quibble. It is worthy of notice that he frequently makes his characters perpetrate puns when under the influence of strong emotion. The first *fair* = ' word fair,' the second = ' fairness ' or ' beauty,' the third = ' fair one.'

II. i. 20. For Oberon is passing fell and *wrath* = wroth, but written 'wrath' in order to rhyme with ' hath.'

II. i. 118. We are their parents and *original* = originators.

II. i. 141. If you will patiently dance in our *round* = round dance. Cf. III. i. 106.

II. ii. 83. When thou wakest, it is thy *dear* = dear one, lover. Cf. 1 43, and III. ii. 158.

III. ii. 9. A crew of patches, rude *mechanicals.*

III. ii. 48. Plunge in the *deep* = depth (as it often does at the present time).

III. ii. 68. O, once tell *true*, tell *true*, even for my sake ! = true things, the truth.

V. i. 87. Why, gentle *sweet*, you shall see no such thing = sweet one.

V. i. 126. *Gentles*, perchance you wonder at this show = gentle folk ; and in

V. i. 207. Now is the *mural* down = wall. Pope's emendation of ' morall.'

Usual Forms or Significations.

Adjectives ending in *-ble* have in Elizabethan English both an active and a passive meaning. Thus:—

IV. i. 2. I thy *amiable* cheeks do coy = lovable. The word is now used only of persons.

IV. i. 125. A cry more *tuneable* was never holla'd to = tuneful.

Artificial has an active meaning in—

III. ii. 203. We, Hermia, like two *artificial* gods = exercising our power in the realms of art.

Afeard is used for ' afraid ' (*a-* is a corruption of the A.S. intensive *of*) in

III. i. 112. This is a knavery of them to make me *afeard.*

Only is used where we should now use ' alone,' in

IV. i. 171. The object and the pleasure of mine eye, Is *only* Helena. Or, we should transpose the word and say ' The only object,' etc

Double Comparatives.

The comparative ending sometimes received the addition of *more* in order to give greater emphasis. We still use the double Comparatives *nearer*, and (more rarely) *lesser.*

II. i. 209. What *worser* place can I beg in your love.

II. ii. 89. The more my prayer, the *lesser* is my grace

III. i. 20. For the *more better* assurance.

ADVERBS.

Formed from Nouns.

Adverbs are, in the earliest stage of a language as well as in the latest forms of declension, cases of *substantives*, adjectives or pronouns.

I. ii. 88.   You must *needs* play Pyramus. Needs = of necessity the -s being a Genitive Case ending. (Cf. *of force* in III. ii. 40). So it is in alway-*s*, sideway-*s*, on-*ce*, etc. and in:

III. ii. 376.   *Whiles* I in this affair do thee employ.

V. i. 59.   *Wondrous* strange snow. Wondrous is a corruption of wonder-*s*, retaining the genitive suffix *s*. In this way we must probably explain :

IV. i. 42.   Fairies be gone, and be all *ways* away. Here there appears to be a confusion of constructions. Cf. the expression in the Prayer-book, " *Anyways* afflicted or distressed."

III. ii. 425.   Thou runn'st before me, shifting *every place*. An adverb formed from an accusative case, now called the adverbial objective. Cf. no way, yesterday and

IV. i. 89.   Will to-morrow *midnight* solemnly dance

Formed from Pronouns.

The adverbs *where, whither, whence, when, how, why* are all formed from the relative pronoun (stem *who*), the adverbs *there, thither, thence, then, thus, the* are formed from the demonstrative *the*, the adverbs *here, hither, hence* from the demonstrative *he*. These adverbs are all still in common use. Illustrations will be found everywhere in the play. The use of *what* is peculiar in :

III. ii. 273.   *What* can you do me greater harm than hate, where it may be an adverb = how, or it may be merely a case of transposition = what greater harm, etc.

Double Negative.

This irregularity, like those of double comparatives and double superlatives, may be explained by the desire of emphasis which suggests repetition. In French the double negative ne . . . *pas*, ne . . . *point* has become the rule, not the exception, owing to a similar desire to strengthen the expression.

II. i. 202.   I do not, *nor* I cannot, love you. We should say " *and* I cannot."

II. ii. 23.   Worm *nor* snail, do *no* offence. We should use " *any* offence."

II. ii. 126.   I did never, no, *nor never* can. For " nor *ever* can."

III. i. 149.   *Not* so, *neither*. For " not so *either*."

III. ii. 135.   *Nor none*, in my mind. For " nor *any*."

IV. i. 126.   Was *never* holla'd to, *nor* cheer'd with horn In Crete, in Sparta, *nor* in Thessaly. For " *or* in."

V. i 224.   (Neither) A lion fell, *nor* else *no* lion's dam. For " *any* lion's."

Transposition of Adverbs.

The modern rule with respect to the position of adverbs is, that in general, they should be placed as near as possible to the word qualified. Elizabethan authors allowed themselves considerable licence in this respect.

L. i. 36. *With cunning* hast thou filched my daughter's heart. Here the adverbial phrase is placed first for the sake of emphasis. In such cases the pronoun (or subject) usually follows the verb as here. The order of the other words, however, is not influenced in—

I. i. 57. *Rather* your eyes must with his judgment look. Or in

I. i. 126. Of something *nearly* that concerns yourselves.

II. i. 37. *Bootless* make the breathless housewife churn. For "bootless churn."

III. ii. 354. *So far* am I glad it so did sort. For "I am so far glad.'

Sometime for sometimes.

According to modern usage *sometime* = formerly, *sometimes* = occasionally. Shakespeare seems to use either word indifferently.

II. i. 38. *Sometime* make the drink to bear no barm.

II. i. 53. *Sometime* for three-foot stool mistaketh me.

II. i. 254. There sleeps Titania *sometime* of the night = sometimes during.

III. ii. 362. Like to Lysander *sometime* frame thy tongue.

III. ii. 364. And *sometime* rail thou like Demetrius.

ARTICLES.

Omission of the Article.

In modern English there are many stock phrases (principally adverbial) in which no article is used, *e.g.* leave school, shake hands, at sea, at home, by day, in court, for love, over head and ears, etc. In Elizabethan English *a* (since it was then hardly distinguishable from the numeral "one") was more emphatic than with us, and was consequently more often omitted when no emphasis was required.

I. i. 184. More tuneable than lark to shepherd's ear.

II. i. 53. Sometime for three-foot stool mistaketh me

The definite article is omitted in :

II. i. 47. Neighing in likeness of a filly foal.

II. i. 49. In very likeness of a roasted crab.

II. i. 201. Do I not in plainest truth tell you.

III. ii. 84. For debt that bankrupt sleep doth sorrow owe.

III. ii. 104. Sink in apple of his eye.

Omitted in Archaic poetry.

A, an and *the* did not come into general use in our language as Articles until the Middle period of English. Hence poets who affected an ancient style, as for instance Spenser, frequently omitted them.

Shakespeare ridicules this practice in his parody of *Pyramus and Thisbe.*

V. i. 143.	Which *lion* vile *with bloody* mouth did slain.
V. i. 146.	Whereat *with blade*, with bloody blameful blade.
V. i. 148.	And Thisby tarrying in *mulberry shade*.
V. i. 222.	When *lion rough* in *wildest rage* doth roar.
V. i. 225.	For if I should *as lion* come in strife.

CONJUNCTIONS.

Omission of "that."

That is frequently omitted by Shakespeare before a subjunctive mood. This construction we should in Latin call a Quasi-dependent subjunctive or Oblique Jussive. Cf. *Omnia fecerit oportet* = He must have done everything (Cic.). *Cave putes* = Don't fancy.

II. i. 19.	Take heed the queen come not within his sight.
II. i. 268.	And look thou meet me ere the first cock crow.
III. ii. 95.	Helena of Athens look thou find. Notice also the inversion here.
III. ii. 98.	By some illusion see thou bring her here.
III. ii. 365.	And from each other look thou lead them thus. Here again note the inversion in the order of the words.

Against is used as a conjunction expressing time in—

III. ii. 99.	I'll charm his eyes against he do appear, *i.e.* against the time that he do appear. This use of against is not now allowed even colloquially.

An is a contraction of *and*, which in the Northern dialect of English meant "if."

I. ii. 52.	*An* I may hide my face, let me play Thisby too.
I. ii. 75.	*An* you should do it too terribly you would fright the duchess.
IV. ii. 21.	*An* the duke had not given him sixpence a day . . . I'll be hanged.
V. i. 193.	To spy *an* I can hear my Thisby's face.

An if is a reduplication = if if. This doubling of the conjunction is due to the same tendency which introduced the double comparative and the double negative. Cf. But *and* if that evil servant shall say (Matt. xxiv. 48).

II. ii. 153.	Alack! where are you? speak, *an if* you hear.
III. ii. 78.	*An if* I could, what should I get therefore?

An 'twere.

I. ii. 83.	I will roar you *an 'twere* any nightingale.

On this line Abbott says: "Some ellipsis is probably to be understood. 'I will roar you, and if it were a nightingale (I would still roar better),'" and compares the use of "ac," "atque" in Latin after "similis," "pariter," etc.

" **As** " with the Subjunctive is equivalent in Shakespeare to " as if."

II. i. 90. The winds . . . *as* in revenge = as if they were acting in revenge.

II. i. 111. An odorous chaplet . . . . is, *as* in mockery, set = as if it were done in mockery.

II. i. 135. Return again, *As* from a voyage = as if she were returning.

II. i. 160. Loosed his love-shaft . . . . *As* it should pierce a hundred thousand hearts = As if it should pierce.

III. ii. 260. Take on, *as* you would follow = Be furious, as you would be if you wished to follow.

" **As** " for " that " is used after " **so** " in :

III. ii. 354-5. And *so* far am I glad it so did sort.
As this their jangling I esteem a sport.

III. ii. 360-1. And lead these testy rivals *so* astray
As one come not within another's way.

Because, that and because that are used indifferently, and in the same sense.

II. i. 21. *Because that* she as her attendant hath
A lovely boy, stolen from an Indian king

In the same way " if that " is used for " if " in I. ii. 79

But is used for " that not " in

II. i. 238. Do not believe But I shall do thee mischief in the wood.

This use of " but " as a subordinative conjunction has arisen from the omission of the conjunction " that." If " that " were expressed, " but " would retain its original character as a preposition signifying " except," and the Noun-clause following it would be its object.

" **Since** " for " when " is used by Shakespeare after verbs denoting recollection.

II. i. 149. Thou rememberest *Since* once I sat upon a promontory.

" **That** " for " so that." *So* before *that* is very frequently omitted, the sense of the passage being always sufficiently clear without the adverb.

I. ii. 73. I will roar, *that* I will make the duke say, etc.

I. ii. 76. You would fright the duchess and the ladies *that* they would shriek.

II. i. 30. They do square, *that* all their elves . . . Creep into acorn cups.

II. i. 105. The moon . . . . washes all the air, *That* rheumatic diseases do abound.

III. i. 123. I will sing, *that* they shall hear I am not afraid.

III. ii. 40. *That* when he waked, of force she must be eyed.

III. ii. 417. I follow'd fast, but faster he did fly ;
That fallen am I in rough uneven way

NOUNS.

Abstract Nouns used in the Plural.

We do not often use abstract nouns in the plural; but Shakespeare often does to express (1) the *persons* possessing the quality, or (2) the *things* to which the action, state, or quality belongs.

I.   i. 48.   One that composed your *beauties*.
II. i. 13.   In those freckles live their *savours*.
III. ii. 292. She hath made compare between our *statures*.
III. ii. 388. For fear lest day should look their *shames* upon.
V.   i. 97.   Throttle their practised accent in their *fears*.

" The conversion of Abstract nouns to concrete is due to the fact that it is much easier to think of some person or thing, than to think of an abstract quality apart from any person or thing.   Hence we are naturally disposed to transfer the name of the quality to the name of the person or thing possessing the quality " (NESFIELD). In the following examples Shakespeare uses the Abstract term whilst thinking of the persons possessing the quality referred to.

Abstract for Concrete.

II. i. 235. When *cowardice* pursues and *valour* flies.
III. ii. 123. *Scorn* and *derision* never come in tears.
IV. i.   4.   And kiss thy fair large ears, my gentle *joy*.
V.   i. 83.   When *simpleness* and *duty* tender it.
V.   i. 103. The rattling tongue of saucy and audacious *eloquence*.

Irregular forms of Nouns.

I. i. 125. I must employ you in some business.
              Against our *nuptial*.
I. i. 242. For ere Demetrius look'd on Hermia's *eyne*.
II. ii. 99. Made me compare with Hermia's sphery *eyne*.
III. ii. 138. To what, my love, shall I compare thine *eyne*.

This old mode of forming the plural has survived in four words—*oxen, children, brethren, kine*.   NOTE.—The *n* in *swine* is not a plural ending

Nominative Absolute.

Most languages have an absolute use of a case.   In Latin it is the ablative, in Greek the genitive, and in Anglo-Saxon it was the dative. When the dative inflection was dropped, this looked like the nominative, and is now regarded as the nominative.   As in Latin, the participle is often omitted in this construction.

I.   i. 190. Were the world mine *Demetrius being bated*.
II. ii. 119. *I . . . . touching* now the point of human skill.
III. ii. 92. Then fate o'er-rules, that, *one man holding troth*, a million fail.
III. ii. 124. *Vows so born*, in their nativity all truth appears.
IV. i. 67.   That, *he awaking* when the other do.
              (They) may all to Athens back again repair.
V.   i. 21.   Or in the night, *imagining* some fear,
              How easy is a bush supposed a bear ?

When no noun or pronoun is expressed, as in the last example, the Participle is called an *Impersonal Absolute*.

Noun as Adjective.

Proper nouns are easily regarded as adjectives, and Shakespeare extends the use to common nouns. We still do this with the names of towns, and in many stock phrases such as a *cottage* garden, a *villa* residence, the *park* gates, where the two words form a kind of compound noun. Cf. " a *Birmingham* sword," " *Dresden* China." And in French any noun can be made into an adjective by prefixing *de, e.g.* vins *de France* = French wines.

I. i. 77.	Withering on the *virgin* thorn. Cf. also I. i. 80.
I. i. 173.	By that fire which burn'd the *Carthage* queen.
I. ii. 101.	Meet me in the *palace* wood.
II. i. 165.	In *maiden* meditation, fancy-free.
III. ii. 202.	All school-days' friendship, *childhood* innocence.
IV. i. 148.	I shall reply amazedly, half *sleep*, half waking.
V. i. 333.	These *lily* lips.
	This *cherry* nose,
	These yellow *cowslip* cheeks.

Noun as Verb.

We usually make short nouns and adjectives into verbs by the addition of *en*. But in Elizabethan English the tendency was to drop such suffixes. And at the present day also we often form verbs, without any suffix, from nouns and adjectives. Cf. to *train* to a place, to *bicycle,* to *black* boots.

I. i. 98.	All my right of her I do *estate* unto Demetrius.
I. i. 211.	Decking with liquid pearl the *bladed* grass.
II. i. 9.	To *dew* her orbs upon the green.
II. i. 68.	Playing on pipes of corn and *versing* love.
III. ii. 215.	Will you *rent* our ancient love asunder.
IV. i. 121.	So *flew'd*, so sanded = Having such *flews* or chaps.
V. i. 270.	Well *moused*, Lion.

So also *figure,* I. i. 237 ; *buskin'd,* II. i. 72 ; *throned,* II. i. 159 ; *eye.* III. ii. 20 and 40 ; *rounded,* IV. i. 52 ; *bodies,* V. i. 14.

PREPOSITIONS.

Prepositions frequently interchanged.

Perhaps what we are most struck with in Elizabethan English is the apparently loose use of prepositions. The reason of these apparent irregularities is that, owing chiefly to the influence of printing and a desire for uniformity, the functions of Prepositions have become narrowed. They are now used idiomatically, rather than with reference either to their origin or real meaning. Thus we say he died *of* fever, but always sick *with* fever, where *of* and *with* are both used in the sense of cause.

I. i. 226.	How happy some *o'er* other some = as compared with others.
I. ii. 9.	Say what the play treats *on* = of.
II. i. 255.	Lull'd in these flowers *with* dances and delight = by.
II. ii. 87.	Stay, *on* thy peril = at.

II. ii. 133. O that a lady *of* one man refused = by. So in 134 and 142.

III. i. 139. So is mine eye enthralled *to* thy shape = by.

III. ii. 27. Lost *with* their fears thus strong = through, or owing to.

III. ii. 33. *In* that moment = at.

III. ii. 59. Pierced through the heart *with* your stern cruelty = by.

III. ii. 142. Fann'd *with* the eastern wind = by.

IV. i. 132. I wonder *of* their being here together = at.

V. i. 31. More than to us wait in your royal walks = attend on.

Prepositions omitted. Prepositions are frequently omitted after verbs of motion and occasionally after other words. We still generally omit " to " after " give," but we could not write

I. i. 81. Unto his lordship, (to) whose unwished yoke
My soul consents not to give sovereignty.

III. ii. 160. Extort, a poor soul's patience, all to make you sport = for yourselves.

Prepositions transposed.

II. ii. 18. Come our lovely lady *nigh*.

III. ii. 387. For fear lest day should look their shames *upon*.

PRONOUNS.

Personal.

His for its. *Its* is a modern word, occurring rarely in Shakespeare, at the beginning of the 17th century, and frequently in Dryden at the end of it. It appears once in the Authorised Version of the Bible (*Levit.* xxv. 5) as it is now printed, but not at all in the original edition of 1611. *His* was formerly the genitive case of both *he* and *it*. Cf. If the salt have lost *his* savour.

II. i. 94. The ox hath therefore stretch'd *his* yoke in vain.

II. i. 96. The green corn hath rotted ere *his* youth attain'd a beard.

II. ii. 81. Let love forbid sleep *his* seat on thy eyelid.

III. ii. 87. If for *his* (sleep's) tender here I make some stay.

III. ii. 177. Dark night that from the eye *his* function takes.

III. ii. 370. To take from thence all error with *his* might, *i.e.* by *its* (the liquor's) power.

V. i. 86. I love not to see . . . . duty in *his* service perishing.

Personal Pronoun used Reflexively. *Me, thee, him*, etc., are often used in Elizabethan, and still more often in Early English, for *myself, thyself*, etc. *Self* was originally an adjective, as it still is in " self-same hour " and was declined with the preceding pronoun; thus we could say, *I self, mine self* (= of me self), etc. In later English " self " came to be used also as a noun and was qualified by the Possessive pronouns of the 1st and 2nd person. With the third person, however, it retains its function as an adjective : he hurt *him-self*.

II. i. 31. Creep into acorn cups and hide *them* there.

II. i. 228. I'll run from thee and hide *me* in the brakes.

II. ii. 37. We'll rest *us*, Hermia, if you think it good. Cf. **also**
III. ii. 420, 448.

III. i. 146. Will not make *them* friends.

III. ii. 161. All to make *you* sport = for yourselves.

IV. i. 1. Come, sit *thee* down, for "sit down," or set *thyself* down. This expression is still in use as a vulgarism.

IV. i. 151. And now I do bethink *me*, so it is.

V. i. 115. That you should here repent *you*.

In the last two examples we may notice the Elizabethan preference for transitive verbs, which caused many verbs which are now used intransitively to be used by Shakespeare reflexively.

Dative of Interest, Ethic Dative.

The *Ethic Dative* calls attention to a person, not the subject, interested in an action.

I. ii. 82-3. I will roar *you* as gently as any sucking dove; I will roar *you* an 'twere any nightingale. *You* = for you, or for your edification.

Closely corresponding with this use of the dative of the personal pronoun, the possessive case is also used colloquially to appropriate an object to a person addressed.

I. ii. 93. I will discharge it in either *your* straw-colour beard, *your* orange-tawny beard, *your* purple-in-grain beard, etc.

I. ii. 97. Some of *your* French crowns have no hair at all = those French crowns *that you talk of*.

III. i. 32. There is not a more fearful wild-fowl than *your* lion living, *i.e.*, the lion that *you are going to represent*.

III. ii. 18. And forth *my* mimic comes, *i.e.* the mimic *on whom I played my trick*.

IV. i. 32. I could munch *your* good dry oats. The *your* here shows the vulgarity of Bottom's speech as contrasted with that of Titania.

Relative Pronouns.

The Omission of the Relative is common in Shakespeare, especially where the antecedent clause is emphatic and evidently incomplete. Modern usage confines the omission mostly to the objective, but in Shakespeare either case is omitted. The *Nominative Case* is omitted in

II. ii. 73. This is he . . . . Despised the Athenian maid.

The *Objective Case* is frequently omitted. A few examples are:—

I. i. 177. In that same place thou hast appointed me.

II. ii. 79. All the power this charm doth owe.

II. ii. 140. Are hated most of those they did deceive.

III. ii. 227. Wherefore speaks he this to her he hates?

V. i. 1. 'Tis strange, my Theseus, that these lovers speak of.

" Who " with inanimate Antecedent is now rarely used except in prose.

III. ii. 368. This herb . . . *Whose* liquor hath this virtuous property

III. ii. 375. With league *whose* date till death shall never end.

"Which" for "who." In Shakespearian English *which* was commonly used relating to persons : Cf. Our Father *which* art in heaven.

I. ii.   5.   Here is the scroll of every man's name *which* is thought fit.
V. i. 73.   Hard-handed men . . . Which never labour'd in their minds.

The Which. The use of "the" before which may be compared with the French *le* quel.

V. i. 134.   At *the which* let no man wonder.

Other Irregularities.

I. i. 103.   And, *which* is more than all these boasts can be, I am beloved of beauteous Hermia.

Here the antecedent of which is "I am beloved," etc., which follows it. We should now say "*what* is more," etc.

V. i. 68.   *Which* when I saw rehearsed . . . Made mine eyes water.

Here *which* is really the subject of "made," but owing to the omission of the pronoun *it* apparently does duty also as the object of "rehearsed."

V. i. 321.   A mote will turn the balance, *which* Pyramus, *which* Thisbe, is the better.

Here *which* . . . *which* has been confused with *whether* . . . *or*, the confusion being due probably to the fact that "whether" was once a pronoun. Cf. *Whether* of them twain did the will of his father ?

VERBS.

Archaic Participial Forms.

Originally strong past participles ended in *-en*, but in Elizabethan English there was a great tendency to drop the suffix, both in the infinitive and in the participle, and so we get many shortened forms of the participle. When the shortened form was in danger of being confused with the infinitive, as in "mistaken," the past tense was often used for the participle.

I. i. 112.   With Demetrius thought to have *spoke* thereof. Also in I. i. 176.
I. i. 175.   By all the vows that ever men have *broke*. Cf. also V. i. 98.
II. ii. 36.   I have *forgot* our way. And in III. ii. 201 ; V. i. 173.
III. ii. 112.   And the youth *mistook* by me.
III. ii. 208.   As if our hands, our sides . . . . had been *incorporate*.
IV. i. 16.   To have you *over-flown* with a honey-bag.
V.   i. 119.   He hath *rid* his prologue like a rough colt.
V.   i. 139.   This grisly beast, which Lion *hight* by name. This verb, now almost obsolete, is the only passive verb found in English; *he hight* = he was named.
V.   i. 343.   Since you have *shore* with shears his thread of silk.
V   i. 408.   And the issue there *create*.
V   i. 418.   With this field-dew *consecrate*.

" Be " is used for " are " in

II. i. 10.   The cowslips tall her pensioners *be*.
II. i. 12.   Those *be* rubies, fairy favours.
III. ii. 115. Lord, what fools these mortals *be*.
IV. i. 87.   Rock the ground whereon these sleepers *be*.

In most cases *be* occurs at the end of a line and may have been used for the sake of rhyme or euphony. Dr. Abbott says " *Be* " is also used to refer to a number of persons, considered not individually, but as a kind or class, This *be* was in Tudor English *bin*, in A.S. *béo-th*, and is a form of the Present Indicative, *not* Subjunctive.

" Be " is used for " have " as an auxiliary of intransitive verbs. This is due to the fact that intransitive verbs express a *state* rather than an *action*. This use of " to be " is most common in the case of verbs of motion. The distinction is much the same as between " the flower has faded " and " the flower is faded."

III. i. 1.   *Are* we all *met*. And see III. ii. 11 ; IV. i. 178.
III. ii. 407. Thou runaway, thou coward, *art* thou *fled* ?
III. ii. 419. *Fallen am* I in dark uneven way.
IV. ii. 1.   *Is* he *come* home yet ?
V.   i. 303.   Now *am* I *fled*.
V.   i. 314.   How chance Moonshine *is gone*.

Gerundial Infinitive.

The Dative or Gerundial Infinitive is often used by Shakespeare for the Gerund. In Old-English the prep. " to " was prefixed to the gerund before it was prefixed to the infinitive, and hence arose the frequent use of the present infinitive form for the gerund.

II. i. 155.   Certain stars shot madly from their spheres,
               To hear the sea-maid's music.
               = at, or, on hearing.
II. i. 216.   You do impeach your modesty too much.
               To leave the city and *commit* . . . . . *To trust*, etc.
               = by leaving, and committing and entrusting.
II. i. 245.   Make a heaven of hell, *To die* upon the hand I love.
II. ii. 130.   You do me wrong . . . : In such disdainful manner
               me *to woo* = in wooing me. Notice also the inversion
               of the order of the words.
III. ii. 234. But miserable most *to love* unloved.

Intransitive Verbs used Transitively.

Verbs which are now intransitive are sometimes used transitively, perhaps because in Latin the impersonal verb was used with a personal object, *e.g.* they said, *me pudet* = it shames me, when we say " I am ashamed." We can still use a few intransitive verbs in a causal sense, *e.g.* He *ran* a thorn into his hand.

I. i. 4.   She *lingers* my desires.
I. i. 172.   That which knitteth souls and *prospers* loves = causes
               to prosper.

I.   i. 203.   Lysander and myself will *fly* this place. Cf. II. i. 247;
                II. ii. 97.
II. i. 236.   I will not *stay* thy questions. Cf. also V. i. 255.
III. ii. 424. *Abide* me if thou darest.
III. ii. 434. *Abate* thy hours: *shine* comforts from the east = cause
                to shine.
V.   i. 74.   Now have *toil'd* their unbreathed memories.
V.   i. 142.   As she fled, her mantle she did *fall* = cause to fall.

"May" for "Can," "Might" for "Could."

The original sense of *may* (A.S. *mæg* = I am able) and *might* is seen in

I.   i. 63.   The worst that *may* befall me in that case.
I.   i. 120.   Which by no means we *may* extenuate.
I.   i. 161.   There, gentle Hermia, *may* I marry thee.
I.   ii. 107. There we *may* rehearse more obscenely.
II. i. 162.   But I *might* see young Cupid's fiery shaft.
III. i. 72.   If that *may* be, then all is well.
IV. i. 153.   Our intent was to be gone from Athens where we *might*.

Omission of Verb.

With adverbs expressing motion the verbs which they should qualify
are often omitted.   The adverb thus becomes almost an interjection,
and in familiar speech to-day we often make the same omission,
especially when the mood would be imperative.

II. i. 58.   But room fairy ! = *Make* room.
II. i. 145.   Fairies, away ! Sc. *go*.
II. i. 147.   Thou shalt not from this grove. Sc. *go*.
II. ii. 2.   For the third part of a minute hence. Sc. *go*. Cf. II.
                ii. 7, 21, 25, 83, 85.
II. ii. 96.   Therefore (it is) no marvel though Demetrius, etc.
                Cf. III. ii. 282.
III. ii. 377. I'll to my queen, and beg her Indian boy.
III. ii. 435. That I may back to Athens by daylight. Sc. *go*.

Other examples will be found in IV. i. 23, 110, 187 ; V. i. 192, 345,
371, 401, 406.   It is to be observed that the verb omitted is generally
a verb of motion and most frequently the omission takes place after
will, *shall*, or other auxiliary

Plural Endings.

There were three forms of the plural in Early English—the Northern
in *es*, the Midland in *en*, the Southern in *eth*.

II. i. 57.   And then the whole quire hold their lips and laugh.
                And *waxen* in their mirth.

"Shall" and "Will," "Should" and "Would."

Shall and *should* are frequently used by Shakespeare where we should
now use *will* and *would*.

II. i. 264.   Thou *shalt* know the man. For *wilt* expressing
                futurity.

II. i. 269.   Your servant *shall* do so.

IV. i. 220.   I *shall* sing it at her death.   Perhaps containing a notion of compulsory necessity.

L. i. 186.   Were favour so (*i.e.* catching).
Yours *would* I catch, fair Hermia, ere I go
My ear *should* catch your voice, my eye your eye,
My tongue *should* catch your tongue's sweet melody.

Where *should* denotes contingent futurity.

III. ii. 122.   Why should you think that I *should* woo in scorn ?

Where *should* (says Dr. Abbott) denotes a statement not made by the speaker.

Singular Verb with Plural Subject.

This may be accounted for in several ways.

(1) The apparently singular form may be the Northern plural in *es* or *s*.

(2) The subject noun may be considered as singular in *thought*.

(3) When the verb precedes the subject, the writer has perhaps not quite settled what the subject is to be.   Cf. the use of *il y a* in French.

(4) By the presence near the verb of a singular noun or pronoun (not necessarily the subject or even part of a composite subject).

II. i. 92.   Contagious fogs, which . . . *hath* every pelting river made, etc.

Where the verb is in the singular apparently because the relative has no inflection to denote number.   The same reason (or No. 1 above) may account for :

III. ii. 97.   With sighs of blood that *costs* the flesh blood dear.

II. i. 190.   Where *is* Lysander and fair Hermia ?   See (3) above.

II. i. 251.   Where oxlips and the nodding violet *grows*.   See (4) above.

III. i. 47.   There *is* two hard things.   Cf. IV. ii. 16 and see (3) above.

III. ii. 440.   Two of both kinds *makes* up four.

The subject of *makes* is here, in thought, some such words as " a *collection* of."   See (2) above.

V. i. 24.   All the story . . . And all their minds . . . More *witnesseth*.

Which may be an example of the Southern plural in *eth*, or, more probably the verb here agrees with *the fact* of all their minds being, etc

V. i. 161.   This lime, this rough-cast, and this stone, *doth* show (2) or (4).

Subjunctive Mood.

The simple form of the Subjunctive (*i.e.* without any auxiliary) was much more commonly used in Shakespeare's time than it now is.

I. i. 225.   As you on him, Demetrius *dote* on you.   Optative use.

I. ii. 77.   That *were* enough to hang us all : when we should say *would be*.

I. ii. 91. What beard *were* I best to play it in ?

Which is probably an ungrammatical remnant of the older idiom (to) me (it) were best.

III. i. 42. It *were* pity of my life, and V. i. 226.

The simple Subjunctive is also used, where we should now probably use either the Indicative or Subjunctive auxiliary forms in II. ii. 51, 63, 64 and 65, 109 ; III. ii. 81, 108, 327, 412 ; IV. i. 207 ; ii. 5, 18 ; V. 440

MISCELLANEOUS IRREGULAR CONSTRUCTIONS.

I. i. 129. How chance the roses there do fade so fast ?

Here *chance* appears to be used as a verb, and the full expression would be " How may it chance that," etc. *Chance* may also be explained as an adverb = by chance.

I. ii. 229. He will not know what all but he do know.

The nominative after *but* appears to have arisen from a confusion between, *but* as an adversative conjunction of the Co-ordinative class and *but* as a preposition. The passage quoted is therefore a confusion between " He will not know what all know, but (= except) him," and " He will not know what all know, but he does not know."

II. i. 35.   Are you not he
That frights the maidens of the villagery
Skim milk, and sometime labour in the quern.

There is in this passage a confusion of constructions. *Frights* agrees with the relative *that* which takes the person of its antecedent *he*, and we should naturally expect *skims* and *labours*. But Shakespeare, forgetting perhaps that he has already written " he that frights," makes the two following verbs agree with *you*. The sentence would also be grammatically correct if *frights* were changed to *fright*. *Frights* is used for " affrights " or " frightens." *Villagery* is a Collective Noun.

II. i. 139. How long within this wood intend you stay ?

In early English there was no *to* before the simple infinitive. In the Elizabethan period, there was some difference of opinion as to which verbs did, and which did not, require the *to*. Consequently we often find it omitted where we should now insert it. Cf. also III. ii. 224-6 " made Demetrius . . . to call me goddess."

III. i. 92. He is to come again.

IV. ii. 27. I am to discourse wonders.

We should now say " He has to come " and " I have to discourse." In the above passages there appears to be an ellipsis, some word such as " bound " in the first, " ready " in the second, being left out.

III. i. 182. I shall desire you of more acquaintance.

Dr. Abbott explains that in this passage *of* means " concerning," " about," or " with respect to " and compares with " 'Twere pity of my life," III. i. 41.

III. ii. 8. While she was in her dull and sleeping hour.

Almost any relation between two nouns can be expressed in Eliza
bethan English by making one of them an adjective. In the above
" dull and sleeping hour " = hour of dullness and sleeping. *Sleeping* is
a gerund. Cf. " the lazy time," V. i. 40.

III. ii. 90. Of thy misprison must perforce ensue
Some true-love turn'd, and not a false turn'd true.

An example of ellipsis due to the Elizabethan desire of brevity. The
full expression would be " it must perforce ensue that some true-love
has turned false, and not a false love turned true." Turn is here a
verb of incomplete predication.

III. ii. 206. Both warbling of one song, both in one key.

The *of* here is redundant. This redundancy is probably due to a
confusion of constructions. Shakespeare might have written " a (= in)
warbling of " gerund, or " simply " warbling," present participle. He
has given us a combination of the two forms. So in I. i. 231, " So I,
admiring of his qualities."

IV. ii. 6. It goes not forward, doth it ?

Here the present indefinite tense is used to express a future action,
as " I go to town next week."

IV. ii. 9. He hath simply the best wit of any handicraft man in
Athens.

Another confusion of constructions, containing a combination of
" He hath the best wit of all men " and " He hath a better wit than
any man." The same confusion is apparent in V. i. 247, " This is the
greatest error of all the rest."

V. i. 398. And this ditty after me,
Sing and dance it trippingly.

It does not here refer to " ditty," but is used indefinitely as the object
of dance. See Abbott, § 226.

I

METRICAL CONSTRUCTION.

I am indebted to Dr. Abbott (Shakespearian Grammar) *for the arrange-ment and much of the subject-matter of this section on Prosody.*

The ordinary line in blank verse consists of five feet of two syllables each, the second syllable in each foot being accented.

> **V. i. 18.** Such tric'ks | hath stron'g | ima'g | ina' | tion
> That, i'f | it wou'ld | but app' | rehen'd | some jo'y :
> It com' | prehen'ds | some brin'g | er of' | that joy.

But as this line is too monotonous and formal for frequent use, the metre is varied, sometimes (1) by changing the position of the accent, sometimes (2) by introducing trisyllabic and monosyllabic feet.

The accent after a pause is frequently on the first syllable.

> **II. i. 163.** Qu'ench'd in | the chas'te | beams of' | the wa't | (e)ry mo'on.

This " pause accent " usually occurs at the beginning of a line. Sometimes it follows a full stop in the middle.

> **II. ii. 92.** How cam'e | her eye's | so brig'ht ? | No't with | salt tear's.

An extra syllable (rarely a monosyllable) is frequently added before a pause, especially at the end of a line.

> **V. i. 12.** The po' | et's ey'e, | i'n a | fine fre'n | zy ro'll(ing)
> Doth glan'ce | from hea'v(e)n | to ear'th | from ear'th | to hea'v(en).

Such extra syllables are called double (or feminine) endings, and afford a useful indication of the approximate date of the play. Speaking generally, if double endings are rare (*e.g.*, 4 per cent. in *Love's Labour's Lost*, 1588) we may infer that the play is of early date ; if they occur frequently, that the play belongs to Shakespeare's later period (*e.g.*, 33 per cent. in *The Tempest*, 1610). Feminine endings are comparatively rare in this play.

Unaccented monosyllables. Provided there be only one accented syllable, there may be more than two syllables in any foot. Although this departure from the normal line occurs with frequency in some of Shakespeare's later plays, this play affords no instance of a trisyllabic foot, that cannot be accounted for by the elision of one syllable in pronunciation.

Accented Monosyllables. Sometimes an unemphatic monosyllable (such as *and, at, for, from, if, in, of, or*) is allowed to stand in an emphatic place, and to receive an accent. When they occur at the end of a line, they are called " weak endings." These appear for the first time in considerable quantities in *Macbeth* (1605), and hardly appear at all in Shakespeare's earlier plays.

> **IV. i. 43.** So' doth | the woo'd | bine, *th'e* | sweet hon' | ey suc'k(le).
> **II. i. 85.** By pa' | ved fou'n | tain o'r | by rus'h | y bro'ok.

Other examples will be found in the lines quoted below.

Syllables omitted. Many syllables which we now pronounce might formerly be omitted in pronunciation.

I. i. 27. This man' | hath bewitc'h'd | the bo's | om of' | my ch'ild.
III. ii. 204. Hav'e with | our needles [*needls*] | crea' | ted bo'th | one flo'w(er).

Frequently two syllables coalesce, or are rapidly pronounced together.

I. i. 69. Whe'ther [*whe'r*], if | you yiel'd | n'ot to | your fa'th | er's cho'ice.
II. ii. 156. Either [*ei'r*] dea'th | or yo'u | I'll fin'd | imme' | diatel'y.

Lengthening of words. Many words are given an additional syllable in pronunciation.

II. i. 23. She ne'v | er ha'd | so swe'et | a chan'g | e lin'g.
V. i. 59. Tha't is | hot i'ce | and won'd | (e)ro'us | strange sno'w.

Thus the termination *ion* is frequently pronounced as two syllables at the end of a line (rarely in the middle).

I. i. 149. So quic'k | bright thing's | com'e to | confu's | io'n.
III. ii. 197. To ba'it | me wit'h | this fou'l | deri's | io'n.
III. ii. 372. When th'ey | next w'ake | all thi's | deri's | io'n.
Shall see'm | a drea'm | and frui't | less vi's | io'n.
IV. i. 111. An'd mar'k | the mu's | ica'l | confu's | io'n.
Of houn'ds | and ec'h | o i'n | conjun'ct | io'n.

Monosyllables are drawn out in pronunciation so as to serve as a foot or are pronounced as dissyllables.

II. i. 59. But ro' | om fa'i | ry, her'e | comes O'b | ero'n.
II. i. 250. I kno'w | a ban'k | *whe're* | the wil'd | thyme blo'ws.
III. ii. 201. For par't | ing u's, | ——O' | is a'll | forgo't.
III. ii. 439. Ye't but | thre'e. | Com'e one | more.
Tw'o of | bo'th kinds | ma'kes up | four.
He're she | co'mes, | cur'st and | sad.

The *ed* of past participles is frequently pronounced as a separate syllable, even where the *e* is usually mute. As such words are accented in the text, the student will readily find many examples in this play.

Alexandrines containing six pronounced accents are very rare in Shakespeare. Two occur in this play.

III. ii. 281. Ther'efore | be ou't | of hop'e, | of que's | tio'n | of dou'bt.
IV. i. 108. Uncou'p | le in' | the we'st | ern va'l | ley ; l'et | them go'.

Apparent Alexandrines are more frequent. These can usually be reduced to five-foot lines by the omission of unemphatic syllables.

I. i. 32. And stol'(e)n | th(e) impres's | ion o'f | her fan' | tas'y.
IV. i. 166. But b'y | some pow'(er) | it is' | my lov'e | to Her'm(ia).

Here we pass almost imperceptibly from the *Herm-* of this line to the *Melted* with which the next line begins.

Sometimes Apparent Alexandrines are really trimeter couplets, as in

III. i. 93. Most ra' | diant Py'r | amu's, | most li'l | y-whi'te | of hu'e.
III. i. 95. As tru'e | as tru' | est hors'e, | that ye't | would ne'v | er tir'e.

Short lines. Single lines are sometimes found with only four, three, or even two, accents.

    III. ii. 49. And ki'll | me t'oo.
    V. i. 92. Take's it | in mi'ght | not me'r (it).

        [Dr. Abbott thinks this line is not as Shakespeare wrote it].

    III. ii. 100. I go', | I go' ; | look ho'w | I g'o.

Proper names. The same name is not always pronounced in the same way in Shakespeare : thus Demetrius is sometimes a quadrisyllable, sometimes a trisyllable ; Helena and Hermia sometimes have the accent on the first syllable, sometimes on the second ; Theseus is sometimes dissyllabic, sometimes a trisyllable ; Egeus is always a trisyllable.

    I. i. 123. Deme' | tri'us and | Ege' | us go' | alo'ng.
    II. i. 77. Kno'wing | I kno'w | thy lov'e | to The' | seu's.
    II. ii. 52. For, I'y | ing s'o | Hermi' | (a), I d'o | not li'e.
    II. ii. 113. Not He'r | mia', | but He'l | ena' | I lo've.

    Notice that the accents have not all the same force. **In He'rmia and He'lena** in the above line the first syllable only is strongly accented.

Accent. Many words are accented otherwise than at present.

    I. i. 151. It stan'ds | as an' | *edic't* | in de's | tiny'.
    II. i. 106. That *rhe'u* | *mati'c* | disea's | es d'o | aboun'd.
    III. ii. 137. O He'l | en go'd | dess nym'ph | *perfec't* | divi'ne.
    III. ii. 237. Ay, d'o | *perse'v* | *er*, cou'nt | erfei't | sad lo'oks.
    III. ii. 388. They w'il | full'y | themselv'es | *exi'le* | from lig'ht.
    V. i. 3. These a'n | tique fa'b | les no'r | these fai'r | y toy's

Rhyme. Unlike most of Shakespeare's plays *A Midsummer Night's Dream* abounds in rhymed verse. About a third of the play is written in rhyming lines. This peculiarity is due to the masque-like character of this fairy comedy. The rhymes are of different kinds, that which occurs most frequently being the *heroic couplet.*

    II. ii. 113. Not Hermia, but Helena I love:
             Who will not change a raven for a dove?
             The will of man is by his reason sway'd,
             And reason says you are the worthier maid.

    Occasionally we have alternate rhyme.

    III. ii. 122. Why should you think that I should woo in scorn ?
             Scorn and derision never come in tears.
             Look, when I vow, I weep ; and vows so born,
             In their nativity all truth appears.

    The rhyme is also varied by (1) triplets, (2) feminine rhymes

    II. ii. 27. What thou seest, when thou dost wake
             Do it for thy true-love take.
             Love, and languish for his sake.

    II. ii. 117. Things growing are not ripe until their *season*,
             So I, being young, till now ripe not to *reason*.

    Rhyme occurs rarely in the more serious speeches.

VARIANTS AND PROPOSED EMENDATIONS. 107

The Fairy Speeches.

Most of the speech of the fairies consists of short rhyming lines in which the trochaic metre (*i.e.* an accented syllable followed by an unaccented syllable) preponderates.

II. i. 2. O'ver | hil'l, | o'ver | da'le.
Tho'rough | bu'sh | tho'rough | brie'r.
Ov'er | pa'rk, | o'ver | p'ale.
Tho'rough | floo'd, | tho'rough | fir'e.
I' do | wan'der | ev'ery | wher'e.

V. i. 374. No'w the | hun'gry | li'on | roars,
An'd the | wo'lf be | ho'wls the | moon ;
Whils't the | hea'vy | plou'ghman | snores
All' with | we'ary | ta'sk for | done.

Prose is used in the comic scenes, and where it is desired to lower the dramatic pitch. Thus the ordinary conversation of Bottom and his colleagues is in prose, except when they recite their crude verse. During the progress of the Interlude, Theseus and the courtiers speak in prose in order to set off the stilted verse of the tragic-comedy.

VARIANTS AND PROPOSED EMENDATIONS.

A few only of the more important are given. Other readings will be found in the Clarendon Press edition, to which I have occasionally referred.

I. i. 10. The quartos and folios have *Now-bent*; Rowe corrected to *New-bent*.
I. i. 27. The second folio omits *man*. Theobald suggests *witch'd*.
I. i. 187. This is Hanmer's correction for *Your words I catch*.
II. i. 7. Several editors have suggested *moony-sphere*.
II. i. 58. Dyce, to mend the metre, reads "But room *now* fairy !"
II. i. 62. The old copies have "*Fairy* skip hence !" Corrected by Theobald.
II. i. 110. The old copies have *chin* which Tyrwhitt corrected to *thin*.
II. i. 197. Lettsom suggested that we ought to read *though* for *for*.
II. i. 250. Pope altered *where* to *whereon* in order to improve the metre.
II. i. 252. Theobald and Collier conjectured *lush* (= luxuriant) instead of *luscious*.
II. i. 254. The order of this line and the next is reversed in the old copies.
Lettsom proposed *this bower*, and Collier *these bowers*, instead of *these flowers*.
II. ii. 77. Walker suggests *Near* instead of *Nearer* for the sake of the Metre; Theobald read *Near to*.
II. ii. 104. The folios have "Nature *her* shewes art"; Malone read "Nature shews *her* art."
III. i. 85. Pope suggested "So *doth* thy breath" for *hath*.
III. ii. 48. Coleridge proposed *knee-deep*.

III. ii. 144.   For *princess* Hanmer reads *pureness*, Collier *impress*, Lettsom *purest*.

III. ii. 213.   The quartos and folios read *life* for *like* which Theobald substituted.

IV. i. 36.   To mend the metre Hanmer suggested "fetch thee *thence*"; Walker "fetch thee *the* new nuts."

IV. i. 167.   Pope read "Is melted as the snow." The reading of the text is Capell's substitution for *Melted as the snow* of the folios.

V. i. 59.   Staunton suggested "*swarthy* snow"; Collier "*seething* snow": Elze "*sable* snow."

V. i. 168.   Farmer read "heard *in* discourse."

V. i. 207.   The reading of the folios is "Now is the *moral* down," and that of the quartos, "Now is the *Moon used*.' We have adopted Pope's emendation.

V. i. 218.   Theobald changed *man* of the folios to *moon*.

V. i. 224.   Rowe read "*No* lion fell." Other suggestions that have been made are "A lion fell" (= a lion's skin), and "*n'am* no lion fell" = am not (Gollancz).

HINTS ON PARAPHRASING.

1. Do not mistake the meaning of "to paraphrase." It is not to put into other words the *words* of a passage, but to put into *your own words* the *meaning* of that passage.

2. Read over the passage to be paraphrased several times, and be quite sure that you have seized the general sense before writing anything down.

3. Put nothing down that you do not know the meaning of yourself If *you* do not understand what you write, be sure no one else will.

4. If you use a dictionary (to be avoided as far as possible), make sure that you understand the meaning selected for any given word, and that it "fits in" with the rest of your rendering.

5. It is better to write nothing than to put down unintelligible rubbish.

6. In paraphrasing poetry or condensed prose (such as Bacon's) it is almost always necessary to amplify in order to bring out the full meaning of any given passage, *i.e.*, your version ought generally to be longer than the original.

7. Do not turn into the third person what is expressed in the text in the first person, and especially do not change from the one to the other without good reason.

8. Change the order of words or even sentences as much as you please so long as you preserve the meaning of the passage.

9. Maintain the spirit and general character of the composition as far as possible. If you know the context of the extract, that knowledge should help you to express yourself appropriately. If you do not know the context, imagine a setting for the extract; this will help you to make your meaning clear.

10. Do not use a greater number of words than is necessary to convey your meaning, and use the simplest words you can to express your thought.

EXAMPLES.

We would impress upon the junior student the fact that many paraphrases differing widely the one from the other may be equally good and equally acceptable to the Examiner. We have therefore, in the following examples given three versions of one passage shewing three different methods of treatment.

1. Paraphrase fifteen lines commencing " Therefore the moon, the governess of floods"   II. i. 104.

(*a*) Hence the moon, upon whose influence the tides depend, pale with anger at our dissensions has so charged with humidity the whole atmosphere that all diseases induced by cold and moisture are rife in the land ; and this same strife between us hath so disturbed the regular succession of the seasons that the white mantle of winter's frost now falls upon the blushing rose of summer, whilst the sprouting buds of summer flowers unseasonably come forth as if to mock the scattered hairs that silver the reverend head of father winter.   Spring and summer, prolific autumn and fierce winter, assume each an appearance not its own, and humanity, lost in wonderment, seeks in vain to know the season by its fruits.   Such are the ills our quarrel has brought about, such the calamities begotten by our discord.   We are responsible for them, we their originators.

(*b*) So, the pale moon, the ruler of the sea, grieved, fills the dripping air, and the poor mortal sighs with teasing rheums and aching limbs. The very seasons change, that even the lingering summer rose is whitened with unwonted hoar frost, and, as if for very mockery, winter is crowned with a wreath of tender buds checked ere they bloom : their accustomed dress spring, summer, fruitful autumn, fierce winter all alike do change, and nature, astonished at such strange confusion, knows not one season from another.   We need not to look beyond ourselves if we would account for this strange evil brood, bred from our own jealous wranglings and disputes.

(*c*) For that reason the angry influence of the moon fills the air with moisture causing rheumatic diseases : the seasons are disorganised : in the time of roses are cold frosts and the sweet scent of summer buds mocks the ice of winter.   All the seasons change their accustomed signs, and the bewildered world can no more distinguish them one from another. We, you and I, Titania, are the origin of all these evil changes.

2.   Paraphrase the first twenty lines of Act V.

Hip. These youths and maidens, bound with Love's sweet chain tell us marvellous things indeed.

The. Marvellous but deceptive. Such old-world stories and fantastic tales commend themselves not to me.   The minds of lovers and lunatics alike teem with wild and highly-coloured fancies ; they imagine more than can be grasped by beings of ordinary understanding.   Insanity, love and poetic genius are akin to one another insomuch as all proceed from the imagination.   The madman peoples his solitude with vast crowds of devils and demons of the pit.   The lover, no less wild in his fancies, beholds in a swarthy Egyptian maid, beauty such as that which brought about the Trojan war.   The poet gazing with ecstatic vision on all things in earth and heaven, imagines what the eye of mortal man has never seen, and with magic pen invests it with form and shape, names it and appoints its place of abode.   The poetic imagination hath such peculiar power that he who is possessed of it needs but to imagine a delight in order that for him it may have a real existence.

DRAMATIC IRONY.

Dramatic Irony has been defined as " a form of utterance that postulates a double audience, consisting of one party that hearing shall hear and shall not understand and another party that, when more is meant than meets the ear, is aware both of that more and of the outsiders' incomprehension."

Playgoers will have often observed situations on the stage where one actor or one set of actors is in possession of information which is lacking to the actor speaking, and they will have observed also that the dramatist sometimes produces a scene which is rendered particularly effective by reason of the fact that the audience knows (or sees) something which the actors on the stage cannot know. Here the surface meaning only is for the *dramatis personæ*, while the underlying meaning is for the spectators ; such effects are examples of dramatic irony.

Thus when Bottom appears on the stage wearing an ass's head and Snout exclaims, " O Bottom! thou art changed! what do I see ? " Bottom replies, " What do you see ? you see an ass-head of your own, do you ? " being quite unconscious that what he says is three parts true. Here Bottom's words have one meaning for himself, another for Snout and yet another for the audience. Snout sees and understands more than Bottom does while the spectators see all that Snout sees and understand still more.

Bottom's " translation " is the cause of several examples of dramatic irony the effect of which is produced chiefly by his own unconsciousness of the change that has been effected in his outward appearance.

PLAYS ON WORDS.

Plays in which puns and quibbles or verbal conceits and affectations abound belong usually to Shakespeare's early period of composition. They are, unless characteristic of the person using them, offences against good taste which the poet himself discarded in his later plays, notwithstanding that they were the fashion of the day and were common to all the dramatic writers of the time. In this play the puns in which Theseus and the courtiers freely indulge in the Fifth Act tend to degrade these characters to the level of the clowns whom they criticise.

I. i. 181-2.	On the different meanings of *fair*.
I. ii. 95, 97.	On three meanings of *crown*.
II. i. 193.	On two meanings of *wood*.
II. i. 197.	On two meanings of *iron*.
II. ii. 52, 55.	On two meanings of *lie*.
III. i. 116.	On two meanings of *ass*.
III. i. 131, 136.	On two meanings of *cuckoo*.
III. i. 140.	On *force* and *perforce*.
III. ii. 184-6.	On different meanings of *love*.
III. i. 188.	On *oes* and *eyes* (O's and I's).
III. ii. 270.	On two meanings of *bond*.
IV. ii. 44.	On two meanings of *breath*.
V. i. 118.	On two meanings of *points*.

V. i. 120.	On two meanings of *stop*.
V. i. 152-3.	On two meanings of *wonder*.
V. i. 229.	On *best* and *beast*.
V. i. 234-6.	On different meanings of *carry*.
V. i. 239.	On lant*horn* and *horned*.
V. i. 250.	On two meanings of *snuff*.
V. i. 252.	On two meanings of *change*.
V. i. 308-9.	On *die* (a verb and a noun).
V. i. 310, 313.	On *ace* (pronounced " ass ") and *ass*.

Other conceits, such as unnatural, far-fetched imagery, rhetorical speech-making, elaborate and extravagant compliments, excessive use of alliteration will be found in Helena's speech in III. ii. 128-133, Demetrius' speech III. ii. 137-144, and (purposely used in the manner of a burlesque) in the whole of the play of Pyramus and Thisbe.

ANACHRONISMS.

An Anachronism is an error in computing time by which customs, circumstances, or events are misplaced with regard to each other. Thus Vergil committed an anachronism in his Æneid in making Æneas and Dido contemporary : " For it is certain," says Dryden, " that the hero lived almost two hundred years before the building of Carthage." Shakespeare was never scrupulously accurate with regard to insignificant details which are valuable in a play only in proportion as they assist the demands of art, or produce an effect on the imagination. In *A Midsummer Night's Dream*, a servile attention to accuracy of historic detail must be looked for even less than in a more ordinary play, for in dreams " bright visitants wander through gardens of unearthly flowers, and a primitive creature re-arises in bloody gambol there, on whom time has shed its centuries in vain." Hence we must not be surprised to find that in this play whole scenes are anachronistic, as well as innumerable allusions. Without attempting therefore to enumerate all the several anachronisms we will endeavour briefly to classify them.

References to the Classics. The Tartar's bow (III. ii. 101), Helen of Troy (V. i. 11) belong to an age subsequent to the period of the play. Dido and Æneas (I. i. 173-4) could not have been contemporary, and the same may be said of Hercules and Cadmus (IV. i. 113). See also the note on I. i. 41.

References to Christianity. All such references are, of course, anachronisms in a play dealing with a pre-historic period. A few of them are : the allusions to *nun, cloister, sister, hymns, pilgrimage* (I. i. 70-5), *paradise, heaven, hell* (I. i. 205-7), the christian names *Nick* (for Nicholas), *Peter, Francis, Tom, Robin* and the Saint's day, *St. Valentine* (IV. i. 140).

Reference to Contemporary Customs. In matters relating to the stage Shakespeare refers to customs, and uses terms of recent origin in his own day, *e.g. interlude, abridgement* and *masque* (V. i.) the parts of *a lover, a tyrant, Ercles, a wandering knight* (I. ii.). So, too, in the case of references to May day (I. i. 167), *may-pole* (III. ii. 298), the *rite of May* (IV. i. 134), the games, *nine men's morris, mazes* (II. i. 99, 100), as well as to *knights* (II. ii. 144) and *heraldry* (III. ii. 213), *duke* and *duchess*, as applied to Theseus and Hippolyta.

Allusions to Animals and Flowers. We do not know, of course, that ousels, throstles, wrens, finches, sparrows, etc., were not natives of Athens in the pre-historic age, nor that cowslips, pansies, violets, woodbine, etc., did not flourish in the woods around the ancient city, but we do know that Shakespeare has faithfully observed and beautifully described the Warwickshire life and scenery with which he was familiar, and that the whole of the setting for the fairy scenes appears to be particularly English and not at all pre-historic.

The Fairy World. The origins of Fairies and Elves and their development from earliest times are discussed in the Notes on pages 113-114. From these pages it will be evident that Shakespeare has by no means endeavoured to pourtray a race of beings such as might be supposed to have existed (even in the imagination) in the age of Theseus and Hippolyta.

ON MASQUES AND ANTI-MASQUES.

It is often said of *A Midsummer Night's Dream* that it is more of a masque than of a regular drama. In order that this statement may be properly understood we will give a general account of masques before proceeding to point out the resemblance between our play and this species of entertainment.

Masques were first introduced from Italy into England in the year 1512-3. In that year "the king with eleven others were disguised after the manner of Italy, called a Mask, a thing not seen afore in England." They were costly *disguisings* or pageants devised for some special occasion and performed by distinguished amateurs, usually princes or members of the court. The Italian masque grew out of the carnival, and the performance of masques in England was at first associated with such festivals as Christmas Day, Twelfth Day, and May Day. The masque admitted of dialogue, singing and dancing, and its essence was pomp and glory. Movable scenery of the most costly and splendid kind was lavished on it, and the most celebrated artists and musicians of the day were employed to embellish it. Masques were presented at the Court of Elizabeth, but it was in the reign of James the First that they attained their highest degree of excellence in the hands of Ben Jonson, whose principal entertainments were produced between 1605 and 1630. In order to diversify the performance Ben Jonson frequently introduced amusements of another kind called *Anti-masques*. These were usually parodies, or in some sense illustrations of the main masque, and were performed partly by servants, partly by actors hired for the purpose, whilst the masque itself was performed only by princely amateurs. Of this kind of entertainment Lord Bacon says : " Let anti-masques not be long ; they have been commonly of fools, satyrs, baboons, wild men, antics, beasts, spirits, witches, Æthiopes, pigmies, turquets (Turks), nymphs, rustics, cupids, statues moving, and the like." These Anti-masques, to which the Interlude in *A Midsummer Night's Dream* in some measure corresponds, were probably borrowed from the old interludes with which the people had been long familiar, and although fantastic and extravagant were often made the medium of useful satire. " Double masques," says Lord Bacon, " one of men, another of ladies, addeth state and variety."

SHAKESPEARE'S FAIRY WORLD.

In speaking of Shakespeare's Fairy Kingdom we shall consider first the origins of fairy lore, and after touching upon some of the characteristics of the fairies and elves of the different earlier systems, shall then endeavour to show how Shakespeare's influence has had the effect of almost entirely changing the popular conception of this delightful order of mythological personages.

The Origin of Fairies. Andrew Lang writes : " Fairies are doubtless much older than their name, as old as the belief in spirits of woods, hills, lonely places, and the nether world. The familiar names, *fées, fades,* are apparently connected with *Fatum,* the thing spoken, and with *Fata,* the Fates who speak it, and the god *Fatuus* or Faunus, and his sister or wife *Fatua*." These fairies, or fays, seem to have been originally regarded as spiritual maidens of the forests and elements, and when Christianity reached Gaul these minor goddesses survived the official heathen religion. They lived on in the hearts of peasants, and "the secret shame-faced worship lasted deep into the middle ages," and they appear, principally as enchantresses, in the early romances of Spain, Italy and France. These fays are not often represented as diminutive in stature, and have little to distinguish them from human beings, except their supernatural power. They preside at the birth of man and influence his destiny, taking individuals under their special protection. They take lovers from among men, and are often described as of delicate and surpassing beauty. To this class belong the fairies of Spenser.

The Origin of Elves. Whilst tradition was developing a fairy kingdom in the southern countries of Europe, and in Gaul, popular superstition was independently at work in the northern Scandinavian kingdoms, and it is to the elves (Icel. *alfr,* Dan. *alf,* Gk. *alp*), and dwarfs or duergars (Icel. *dvergr*), of the northern mythology that we must go for the origin of those little creatures that dance in the woods and meadows.

These elves were divided into two classes, the Bright or Beneficent, and the Swart or Malignant. They are said to have animated the clay below the earth like maggots, and one of the leading features of their character with relation to man is a desire for fair human children, to obtain which they used to practise many tricks. They are often represented as animated by a spirit of malicious mockery towards men, which is not, however, altogether malignant. Gervase of Tilbury, Chaucer and Lydgate, all refer in their works to fairies of the northern or Gothic system.

Blending of two Systems. The traditions which connected the inhabitants of faerie with the mythologies of Greece and Rome, and the superstitions which owe their origin to northern mythology were, owing to various agencies, gradually blended together. And although the northern system was the first to take root in England, and occupied much the larger place in popular tradition, yet it seems to have been considerably modified, even before Shakespeare's time, by the addition of some of the features of the more classical system of the romances. The original character of the swart elves of Scandinavia continued for a long time in the popular Scottish traditions.

Huon of Bordeaux and the History of Oberon. *Huon de Bordeaux* is the name given to one of those famous French romances of which the mythical history of Charlemagne forms the central design, and which spread throughout Europe during the middle ages. It was compiled in prose in 1454, from a poem which dates back to the 12th century, and was translated into English about 1540. It is of importance to us because in it Oberon, " the dwarf of the fayry," plays the best part of the narrative. Huon is one of the paladins or knights of Charlemagne, who goes through many wonderful and perilous adventures, assisted by the pretty dwarf, King Oberon, who always makes his appearance when the hero's needs are greatest.

But even before *Huon de Bordeaux,* Oberon had already made his appearance in epic literature of Teutonic origin. He had appeared in the *Heldenbuch* (" Book of Heroes "), as Elberich (= elf-king), a dwarf king, who played very much the same part as Oberon in the French romance, and in the *Niebelungen Lied* (" Song of the Race of Niebelungen "), where he is the guardian of the treasure that was won by Siegfried.

Shakespeare's Influence on our Conceptions of Fairies. When *A Midsummer Night's Dream* was written, nearly the whole of Fairy Mythology seems to have been modified and added to by Shakespeare. As Drake says : " The Fairies of Shakespeare have been truly denominated the *favourite children of his romantic fancy,* and, perhaps, in no part of his works has he exhibited a more creative and visionary pencil, or a finer tone of enthusiasm, than in bodying forth " these airy nothings," and in giving them in brighter and ever-durable tints, once more

" A local habitation and a name."

Of his unlimited sway over this delightful world of ideal forms, no stronger proof can be given than that he imparted an entirely new cast of character to the beings whom he has evoked from its bosom, purposely omitting the darker shades of their character, and, whilst throwing round them a flood of light, playful, yet exquisitely soft and tender, endowing them with the moral attributes of purity and benevolence. In fact, he not only dismisses altogether the *fairies of a malignant nature*, but clothes the milder yet mixed tribe of his predecessors with a more fascinating sportiveness, and with a much larger share of unalloyed goodness."

Characteristics of Shakespeare's Fairies.

1. They have a Court, a King and a Queen. Their court is situated somewhere in the farthest steppe of India (II. i. 70). "The King and Queen of Faiery, who in Chaucer are identified with the Pluto and Proserpine of hell, are under the appellations of Oberon and Titania, drawn by Shakespeare in a very amiable and pleasing light." Although they quarrel with one another yet they are represented as being usually employed in alleviating the distresses of the worthy and unfortunate. The queen has her pensioners (body-guard) (II. i. 10), the king his clown or jester ('thou lob of spirits') (II. i. 16 and 45), and his train of knights (II. i. 25).

2. They have influence over the physical powers of nature. They can "overcast the night" (III. ii. 357) and cover "the starry welkin" with black fog (III. ii. 359). When they quarrel all nature is disturbed, the seasons alter and the moon

> " *Pale in her anger, washes all the air*
> *That rheumatic diseases do abound* "   (II. i. 105).

3. They delight in conferring blessings. Oberon desired and ultimately was able to make smooth the course of love for Helena. With Titania he blesses the house of Theseus " to all prosperity " (IV. i. 91) and makes the issue of the Duke and Duchess " ever fortunate " (V. i. 409). Oberon averts a duel between Lysander and Demetrius (III. ii. 360) and uses his power in such a manner that in the end " all things shall be peace " (III. ii. 379). Even when Titania steals a baby she does it, not in accordance with tradition, from malignant motives, but from an impulse of humanity and compassion (II. i. 137).

4. They are diminutive in size. Shakespeare has made them diminutive as the Scandinavian elves, but in his descriptions of them he has painted them with many picturesque and fanciful touches that are all his own. They can " creep into acorn cups " (II. i. 31), wear robes of the snake's ' enamelled skin ' (II. i. 256) and coats of the ' wings of rere-mice ' (II. ii. 4) ; the pensioners of the queen are " the cowslips tall " (II. i. 10), her lacquies Peaseblossom, Cobweb, Moth and Mustardseed (III. i. 162) ; her lamps the green lustre of the glow-worm (III. i. 170) and her servants ' fan the moonbeams ' with wings of ' painted butterflies ' (III. i. 172).

5. They move with extreme rapidity. They 'wander everywhere, swifter than the moon's sphere' (II. i. 7). Puck can 'put a girdle round about the earth in forty minutes' (II. i. 176), or go 'swifter then the wind' (III. ii. 94), or 'than arrow from the Tartar's bow' (III. ii. 101). Titania sends her servants away 'for the third part of a minute' (II. ii. 2) with numerous duties to perform, and she herself and her lord can compass the globe 'swifter than the wandering moon' (IV. i. 99).

6. They occupy and amuse themselves in many various ways. They dance in circles on the green (II. i. 9, 141 ; II. ii. 1), they 'seek dew-drops' and 'hang a pearl in every cowslip's ear' (II. i. 15); they can 'fetch jewels from the deep' (III. i. 158) and shake the earth (III. ii. 25) or 'rock the ground' (IV. i. 87). They fall in love with mortals (II. i. 69, 72 ; III. i. 156) and Oberon 'with the morning's love has oft made sport' (III. ii. 391). They 'kill cankers' in flowers, war with rere-mice or keep back the clamorous owl (II. ii. 3-6).

7. They are invisible by mortals (II. i. 187) and can see what is denied to the sight of inferior beings (II. i. 156), and they are immortal (II. i. 136), and purged of all 'mortal grossness' (III. i. 160). Such are the characteristics of the fairy world over which Oberon and Titania were king and queen. Puck, however, being a spirit 'of another sort,' with special attributes of his own, will be further considered when we come to deal with the characters of the play.

"That which Shakespeare received in the rough form of fragmentary popular belief, he developed in his playful creation into a beautiful and regulated world. He here in a measure deserves the merit which Herodotus ascribes to Homer ; as the Greek poet has created the great abode of the gods and its Olympic inhabitants, so Shakespeare has given form and place to the fairy kingdom, and with the natural creative power of genius, he has breathed soul into his merry little citizens, which imparts a living centre to their nature and their office, their behaviour and their doings. He has given embodied form to the invisible and life to the dead, and has thus striven for the poet's greatest glory . . . . If it were Shakespeare's object, expressly to remove from the fairies that dark ghost-like character (Act III. Sc. 2), in which they appeared in Scandinavian and Scottish fable, if it were his desire to pourtray them as kindly beings in a merry, harmless relation to mortals, if he wished in their essential office as bringers of dreams, to fashion them in their nature as personified dreams, he carried out this object in wonderful harmony both as regards their actions and their condition. The kingdom of the fairy beings is placed in the aromatic flower-scented Indies, in the land where mortals live in a half-dreamy state. From hence they come, "following darkness," as Puck says, "like a dream." . . . They are represented, these little gods, as natural souls, without the higher human capacities of mind, lords of a kingdom, not of reason and morality, but of imagination and ideas conveyed by the senses ; and thus they are uniformly the vehicle of the fancy, which produces the delusions of love and dreams . . . . The sense of the beautiful is the one thing which elevates the fairies not only above the beasts, but also above the low mortal, when he is devoid of all fancy and uninfluenced by beauty. . . . The only pain which agitates these beings, is jealousy, the desire of possessing the beautiful sooner than others ; they shun the distorting quarrel ; their steadfast aim and longing is for undisturbed enjoyment " (GERVINUS).

" The *Midsummer Night's Dream* is, I believe, altogether original in one of the most beautiful conceptions that ever visited the mind of a poet, the fairy machinery. A few before him had dealt in a vulgar and clumsy manner with popular superstitions ; but the sportive, beneficent, invisible population of the air and earth, long since established in the creed of childhood and of those simple as children, had never for a moment been blended with ' human mortals ' among the personages of the drama. . . . It is unnecessary to observe that the fairies of Spenser, as he has dealt with them, are wholly of a different nature " (HALLAM).

" In further explication of this peculiar people, it is to be noted that there is nothing of reflection or conscience or even of a spiritualized intelligence in their proper life ; they have all the attributes of the merely natural and sensitive soul, but no attributes of the properly rational and moral soul. They worship the clean, the neat, the pretty and the pleasant, whatever goes to make up the idea of purely sensuous beauty : this is a sort of religion with them ; whatever of conscience they have adheres to this : so that herein they not unfitly represent the wholesome old notion which places cleanliness next to godliness. Everything that is trim, dainty, elegant, graceful, agreeable, and sweet to the senses, they delight in : flowers, fragrances, dewdrops, and moonbeams, honey-bees, butterflies, and nightingales, dancing, play, and song,—these are their joy ; out of these they weave their highest delectation ; amid these they ' fleet the time carelessly,' without memory or forecast, and with no thought or aim beyond the passing pleasure of the moment " (HUDSON).

PART IV. **APPENDIX I.**

PROBABLE DATE OF THE PLAY.

The evidence whereby the date of the composition of any play of Shakespeare's is determined is of two kinds : External and Internal.

External Evidence, usually the more definite, includes—

(1) The form in which the play first appeared, *i.e.* Quarto or Folio.
(2) Records in the Registers of the Stationers' Company.
(3) Allusions in contemporary publications of known date.

The only external evidence which we need consider in connection with *A Midsummer Night's Dream* is the fact that it is mentioned in a list of Shakespeare's plays published in 1598 by the learned Francis Meres in his *Palladis Tamia, Wit's Treasury, a Comparative Discourse of our English Poets, with the Greeke, Latine and Italian Poets*. This is really the only positive evidence that we possess of the date of the composition of the play. We know that it must have been written earlier than 1598. But if there is no positive proof of the exact date at which the play was written, there are many conjectures. These depend entirely upon

Internal Evidence, which is to be sought for in a variety of ways, and includes

(1) Treatment of subject, train of thought, general character of the play.
(2) Considerations of style—*e.g.* proportion of end-stopt to run-on-lines, number of rhyming lines, profusion or otherwise of imagery, number of classical allusions, puns, conceits, etc.

An examination of *A Midsummer Night's Dream* by the aid of these tests leads to the conclusion that the play was

composed between the years of 1593 and 1596.

For this somewhat indefinite and unsatisfactory result we will now give the following reasons, all based upon internal evidence :—

The Treatment of the Subject is such that we should not feel justified in assigning to the play a date earlier than 1593. As Knight has well observed, " Of all the dramas of Shakespeare, there is none more entirely harmonious than *A Midsummer Night's Dream*. All the incidents, all the characters, are in perfect subordination to the will of the poet . . . . . the exquisite beauty of Shakespeare's conception is, that under the supernatural influence, " the human mortals " move precisely according to their respective natures and habits," and he goes on to point out that " in all the higher attributes of poetry " it " far exceeds " the comedies of *The Two Gentlemen of Verona, Love's Labour Lost,* and the *Comedy of Errors,* all of which plays are generally acknowledged to have been composed before 1593. And yet, looking at the play from this same point of view of treatment of the subject, we cannot admit that it was composed later than 1596, for the bracing freshness, the unclouded cheerfulness, the lack of strict characterisation, and the constant preponderance of the lyrical over the dramatic, together with the absence of deep reflection or moral lesson, all point to a youthful period.

Considerations of Style. To these we are unable to attach the same importance in the case of *A Midsummer Night's Dream* as we may in the case of Shakespeare's more regular dramas. This play is more or less of the nature of a Masque, and is treated as such ; consequently the number of rhyming lines and the number of classical allusions afford no evidence as to the date, because these peculiarities were at all times characteristic of masques. Still, the number of lines ending with a pause (end-stopt), the harmonious balance and regular swing of the verses, the "language picturesque, descriptive, and florid with conceits (fanciful thoughts and affected expressions), the too apparent alliterations, the doggerel passages which extend over the passionate scenes," are all characteristic of the poet's earlier methods.

References to contemporary events. Here we begin to tread upon the most dangerous ground. The play contains two passages which are supposed by many editors to afford a clue to the date of its composition. First comes the passage in Act II. Scene i, ll. 89-118 descriptive of the tempestuous and unnatural weather supposed to have been caused by the dissensions of Titania and Oberon. This passage has been thought to have been suggested to the poet by the disastrous season of 1593 and 1594, during which there were "thunders and lightnings neither seasonable for the time, and withall most terrible, with such effects brought forth, that the childe unborne shall speake of it." This weather may, indeed, have inspired the poet in the composition of the passage referred to, in which case we might definitely fix the date as 1594 ; but, on the other hand, there is no reason why the description should not have proceeded from the poet's imagination, and should refer to no particular year.

The second passage by which the minds of editors have been considerably exercised, and from which many very different conclusions have been drawn, is that in Act V. Scene i. 52-3, where we read of

> " The thrice three Muses mourning for the death
>   Of Learning, late deceased in beggary."

This has been taken to refer to (1) the death of Robert Greene, in extreme poverty, in 1592 ; (2) the publication of Spenser's *The Tears of the Muses* in 1591, and (3) the death of Spenser in 1599. If the passage refers to the death of Spenser it must have been added by the poet, subsequent to the first production of the play. The arguments in favour of the supposition that it refers to the death of Robert

K

Greene are given in the note on the passage. Taking all things into consideration we are disposed to agree with Mr. Wright, the editor of the Clarendon Press Series, who says : " On the whole, I am inclined to think that Spenser's poem may have suggested to Shakespeare a title for the piece submitted to Theseus and that we need not press for any closer parallel between them."

We will conclude our consideration of this question by stating that although commentators have assigned to the play every date between 1590 and 1596, and although the majority of editors (amongst others Malone, Scottowe, Knight, Gervinus) are in favour of the year 1594, yet we do not feel that the arguments justify our coming to any more definite conclusion than that the play was written at some time during the period 1593-1596, probably nearer the earlier than the later date.

Other Plays of about the same date

are *Romeo and Juliet* 1591—3, *Richard II.* 1593—4, *Richard III.* 1594, *King John* 1595. Of these plays the two first mentioned are those which in character and style most resemble *A Midsummer Night's Dream. Romeo and Juliet* treats of the same subject, the subject of love, whilst both this play and *Richard II.* are remarkable for an interfusion of the lyrical with the dramatic. The three plays resemble one another in style, and are all plays of emotion rather than of character.

SOURCES AND AUTHORITIES CONSULTED.

A Midsummer Night's Dream is one of the most original of Shakespeare's plays ; for although numerous authorities are quoted as having provided the poet with suggestions for various parts of the drama, yet the actual assistance which he can be shewn to have derived from any or all of these sources hardly amounts to more than the names of some of the characters.

The following list contains the names of the works which are usually supposed to have been known to Shakespeare at the time of the composition of *A Midsummer Night's Dream :—*

Chaucer's ' The Knight's Tale ' probably furnished the poet with the names of Theseus, Hippolyta and Philostrate. From this tale Shakespeare may have copied the anachronism of calling Theseus, *Duke* of Athens, for the opening lines tell that

" Whilom, as olde stories tellen us
Ther was a duk that highte Theseus,
Of Athenes he was lord and governour."

A few slight verbal resemblances (indicated in the Supplementary Notes) point to Shakespeare's knowledge of the earlier work, but we cannot discover any evidence that he made much use of his knowledge in the invention of his plot or in the composition of the play.

Chaucer's ' Legend of Thisbe of Babylon ' tells the story of Pyramus and Thisbe, and may have been read by Shakespeare. The poem refers to the grave of King Ninus, but contains none of the classical names with which Bottom and his colleagues take such liberties.

North's 'Plutarch's Lives,' from which Shakespeare borrowed so much for other plays, probably supplied him with the names Egeus, Ægle, Perigenia, Ariadne and Antiopa, all of which, in one form or other, occur in Plutarch's " Life of Theseus."

Golding's 'Translation of Ovid's Metamorphoses ' appeared in 1567, and was frequently reprinted. In this, as well as in Chaucer's *Legend*, Shakespeare may have read the story of Pyramus and Thisbe. If, as seems probable, Shakespeare read *Ovid* in the original, he may have borrowed from the Latin poet the name Titania.

A new sonnet of Pyramus and Thisbie appears in Clement Robinson's *A Handbook of Pleasant Delites*, 1584, and tells the same tragic tale. Here, as in Shakespeare's version, Pyramus is styled a " knight," and both the Muses and the Fates are alluded to.

Huon de Bordeaux was translated into English by Lord Berners in 1534, and may have furnished the name Oberon. Oberon or Auberon is the French form of the German Alberich. The same name occurs in Spenser's *Faerie Queene* and in

" The Scottish Historie of James IV., Entermixed with a pleasant comedie presented by Oboram, King of Fayeries," by Robert Greene. This play was not printed until 1598, but must have been written some years earlier, inasmuch as its author died in 1592.

John Lyly's plays treated of mythological or pastoral subjects, and were somewhat of the nature of masques. His influence, as Sidney Lee has pointed out, is perceptible in *A Midsummer Night's Dream*, in the raillery in which both mortal and immortal indulge.

Reginald Scot's Discovery of Witchcraft, 1584, describes many of the characteristics of Puck, or as he is there called, Robin Goodfellow.

The origin and history of the fairies are more fully discussed on another page. It is enough to state here that they were not borrowed from any classical sources, but are for the most part beings of Shakespeare's creation, developed from popular traditions with which the English people are familiar.

In the case of the Athenian Swains, Bottom and his fellow actors, there is no doubt but that Shakespeare drew upon his own observation for these inimitable characters. They are no real Athenians, but purely English tradesmen, such as Shakespeare may have met in Stratford or London, or such as may have exhibited their crude performance at the " *Ludos Coventriæ* " at Coventry.

APPENDIX II.

COMTEMPORARY OR HISTORICAL ALLUSIONS.

1. **To Queen Elizabeth.** The 'fair vestal throned by the west' of II. i. 159 and the 'imperial votaress' of line 164 of the same scene no doubt refer to Queen Elizabeth whom 'Cupid's fiery shaft' was powerless to wound. These allusions and the compliment which appears to be paid the virgin queen in the lines :

> "*Thrice blessed they that master so their blood,*
> *To undergo such maiden pilgrimage.*"
>
> (I. i. 74),

lend an air of probability to the conjecture that the play was written to celebrate some wedding which was graced by the presence of the Queen.

2. **To Mary Queen of Scots.** The allegory contained in II. i. 149-169 has received various ingenious explanations. In one of them the mermaid is said to refer to Mary, Queen of Scots, the dolphin to the Dauphin of France, the 'rude sea' is Scotland which was in a state of disorder until the arrival of its queen in 1561, and the 'certain stars' which 'shot madly from their spheres' are the English nobles who fell in her cause.

3. **To the Earl of Leicester.** Another explanation of Oberon's vision supposes the allegory to refer to the festivities which took place when the Earl of Leicester entertained Elizabeth at Kenilworth in 1575. According to this explanation Cupid stands for the Earl of Leicester, whose love shafts were 'quench'd in the chaste beams of the watery moon' which represents Queen Elizabeth ; the earth stands for Lady Douglas, Countess of Sheffield, to whom the Earl was supposed to be privately married ; and 'the little western flower' is Lettice Knollys, Countess of Essex, the mother of the Earl of Essex, who afterwards also married the Earl of Leicester ; the dolphin uttering 'dulcet and harmonious breath' refers to the image of a dolphin which figured in the pageant at Kenilworth and within which "a consort of musicke was secretly placed," and the stars are the fireworks with which the entertainment was enlivened.

4. **To Spenser.** As we have already stated (on p. 118.) there appears to be an allusion to Spenser's *The Tears of the Muses* in the lines :

> "*The thrice three Muses mourning for the death*
> *Of Learning, late deceased in beggary*"
>
> (V. i. 52-3).

5. **To Robert Greene.** The same lines have sometimes been thought to refer to the death of the poet and dramatist Robert Greene, which took place in 1592.

6. **To the Winter of 1593-4.** Titania's speech in II. i. 82-118 is often supposed to describe the severity of the weather of this period of which there are contemporary accounts in Stowe's *Annals*, in Dr. King's

Lectures upon Jonas, delivered in 1594, in Thomas Churchyard's *Charity*, and in the journal of Dr. Simon Forman, the Astrologer.

7. **To the Earl of Essex.** One theory (which places the date earlier than we can think possible) supposes the play to have been composed in honour of the marriage of the Earl of Essex (Theseus, in the play) with the widow of Sir Philip Sidney (Hippolyta). "Like Theseus, Essex courted many an ' Ægle and Perigenia ' and then left them," and Sidney's wife is said to have " delighted in the chase and in the barking of hounds, like the Amazon queen." Other references to this theory will be found in the notes on V. i. 93 and 426.

"A MIDSUMMER NIGHT'S DREAM" AND "THE TEMPEST."—A CONTRAST.

The contrast between *A Midsummer Night's Dream* and *The Tempest* is of particular interest to the student of Shakespeare, because it enables him to perceive some of the striking differences between the poet's earlier and later methods. Both plays are irregular in form, and have in them something of the nature of a masque. In both the influence of Ovid is seen, and in both fairies play a very prominent part. But here the resemblance ends.

The Tempest displays quite a different mood in the poet. In the earlier play all is bright and fresh, full of fascinating poetry without any very deep thought running through it. In the later play we can see Shakespeare, as Dr. Dowden expresses it, " tenderly bending over the joys and sorrows of youth." In the earlier play the poet writes from the point of view of one who enters zealously into the feelings of youth, taking life not too seriously, smiling at the perplexities and entanglements caused by the mischievous sprite Puck, and enjoying the absurdities of the unimaginative Athenian swains ; but in *The Tempest* he has a more serious purpose in view than merely to amuse or delight. He has a lesson to enforce. He teaches mankind the lessons of duty. In *A Midsummer Night's Dream* Oberon's madcap minister Puck plays his pranks simply for the fun of the thing, and laughs at the pain or embarrassment he causes. Ariel, on the other hand, in *The Tempest* is " a minister of retribution, who is touched with the sense of pity at the woes he inflicts." Puck is the familiar Robin Goodfellow of tradition, with an extra strain of poetry infused into his composition ; Ariel is the pure creation of the poet. In *A Midsummer Night's Dream* the fairies are half irresponsible actors in whose hands ' human mortals ' are mere puppets, but in *The Tempest* the fairies themselves are the ministers of the powerful human will of their superior, Prospero.

" The characteristic attributes of the fairy people are, perhaps, most availably represented in Puck ; who is apt to remind one of Ariel, though the two have little in common, save that both are preternatural, and therefore live no longer in the faith of reason. Puck is no such sweet-mannered, tender-hearted, music-breathing spirit, as Prospero's delicate prime minister ; there are no such fine interweavings of a sensitive moral soul in his nature, he has no such soft touches of compassion and pious awe of goodness, as link the dainty Ariel in so smoothly with our best sympathies " (HUDSON).

APPENDIX III.

SHAKESPEARE'S TREATMENT OF CLASSICAL SUBJECTS.

To the most superficial student of the play it must be evident, even upon a first perusal, that Shakespeare in *A Midsummer Night's Dream* has not attempted to treat his subject in a scholarly or learned fashion. He herein presents a strong contrast to his contemporaries the "University Wits"—Marlowe, Greene, Peele, Lodge, Nash, and Kid—who were all of academic education, and had even a decided contempt for "the only Shakescene," and the "upstart crow beautified with our feathers" whose university was the world and whose model was human nature. He presents also a very strong contrast to Ben Jonson, who in his Masques (produced at a later period than our play) also treats of mythological subjects and, in one case at least, introduced an Oberon and a fairy world (Oberon, The Fairy Prince, A Masque of Prince Henry's). But whereas Jonson has sought above all things for correctness and consistency, and has found it necessary even to accompany his masques with copious notes, Shakespeare, on the contrary, has treated the subject from the point of view of the practical playwright and has devised a play for a popular audience. His scene is placed in Athens but his characters are English to the backbone. He combines the loves of Theseus and Hippolyta with the Gothic mythology of fairies and attributes to Grecian characters of a pre-historic period customs and superstitions of his own time. He introduces classical names and alludes to classical stories because his audience were familiar with these names and legends; but he did not aim at classical accuracy or consistency. He wrote to be understood, and to give pleasure, and it mattered not to him when he made Hermia swear "by that fire which burn'd the Carthage queen," that Dido was born many hundreds of years after the period at which Hermia is supposed to have lived; nor did he hesitate for a moment to mingle with his pagan and classical mythology terms and customs relating to the Christianity of the middle ages.

"Those legends from old priesthood were received,
And he then writ, as people then believed."

He knew that, as Coleridge says, "Greek manners in English should be a still grosser improbability than a Greek name transferred to English manners."

"This sort of anachronism, common to all modern writers before and during the age of Shakespeare, seems to have arisen in part from a comparative dearth of classical learning, which left men to contemplate the heroes of antiquity under the forms into which their own mind and manners had been cast. Thus their delineations became informed with the genius of romance; the condensed grace of ancient character giving way to the enlargement of chivalrous magnanimity and honour, with its 'high-erected thoughts seated in the heart of courtesy.' Such in Shakespeare's case appears to have been the no less beautiful than natural result of the small learning, so often smiled and sometimes barked at, by those more skilled in the ancient languages than in the mother-tongue of nature" (HUDSON).

CLASSICAL NAMES WITH THEIR CONTEXT.

The references to the play are to the first line of each quotation.

Acheron ('Stream of Anguish'), in classical mythology one of the rivers of the lower world. In late classical writers the name is used in a general sense to designate the whole of the lower world, and may have been so used by Shakespeare in the following lines, though, in other plays he seems to regard it as a pit or lake.

Oberon bids Puck to 'overcast' the night.

> The starry welkin cover thou anon
> With drooping fog as black as Acheron.   III. ii. 359.

Ægle ('Brightness'). A maiden whom Theseus loved, and for whom he forsook Ariadne. Shakespeare obtained the name from North's *Plutarch's Lives*, where we read in the life of Theseus—

> Ægles the Nymph was lou'd of Theseus,
> Which was the daughter of Panopeus?

Oberon, in the play thus reproaches Titania

> Didst thou not lead him through the glimmering night
> From Perigenia, whom he ravished?
> And make him with fair Ægle break his faith,
> With Ariadne and Antiopa.   II. i. 79.

Amazons (*Ammas* 'Mother'), originally nymphs, attendant as huntresses on Artemis, dwelling on the southern shore of the Black Sea. They were also reputed to be the daughters of the Theban deities Ares and Harmonia. They fought, as bold horsewomen, with Bellerophon, Hercules, Theseus, and Achilles. On the occasion of an inroad made by them into Attica, Theseus won the love of their queen Hippolyte, whom he had conquered. The occasion of their wedding forms the framework of this play.

Titania accuses Oberon of excessive devotion to

> the bouncing Amazon,
> Your buskin'd mistress and your warrior love.   II. i. 71.

Antiopa. Plutarch, in his life of Theseus, relates that "to honour his valiantness, Hercules gave him Antiopa the Amazon. But the more part of the other Historiographers . . . do write, that Theseus went thither alone, after Hercules' voyage, and that he took this

Amazon prisoner, which is likeliest to be true." For
the context see under Ægle.

Antipodes. Gk. *anti*, opposite; and *podes*, feet. Those
who live on the opposite side of the globe, and
whose feet are directly opposite to those of the
speaker.

> Hermia rebuking Demetrius, who protests that he loves her,
> says—
>
>   I'll believe as soon
> This whole earth may be bored and that the moon
> May through the centre creep and so displease
> Her brother's noontide with the Antipodes.   III. ii. 55.

Apollo. A Grecian god, son of Zeus and Leto (L. *Latona*)
and twin-brother of Artemis. He was born at Delos,
the second great seat of his worship. In art he is
represented as the ideal figure of a fully grown slender
youth, beardless, with long curling hair.

> For the story (related by Ovid, *Mett.* i.) alluded to by Helena
> during her pursuit of Demetrius, see the footnote on the passage
>
> Run when you will, the story snall be changed:
> Apollo flies, and Daphne holds the chase.   II. i. 231.

Ariadne, the daughter of Minos, king of Crete, who, after
having marched against Athens, exacted from the
vanquished Athenians a tribute of seven youths and
seven maidens, to be devoured every nine years by the
minotaur. Theseus undertook to do battle with the
monster, and Ariadne, falling passionately in love with
the hero, rendered him every possible assistance in his
undertaking. Theseus, after escaping every danger by
her means, took her away from Crete in order to marry
her. He deserted her, however, whilst asleep on the
island of Nascos, and Plutarch relates that "some say
that Ariadne hung herself for sorrow, when she saw
that Theseus had cast her off." For the context see
under Ægle.

Athens. The capital of Attica, and the supposed scene of
the events of the play. The city is said to have owed
its origin to Theseus, who united the twelve inde-
pendent states or townships of Attica into one state
and made Attica their capital. It has been pointed
out in the notes (p. 73), that in his allusions to Athens

and the Athenians, Shakespeare has paid little attention to classical topography or customs. See also p. 74 on "the ancient privilege of Athens" (I. i.).

Aurora, Eos or Dawn, the sister of Helios and Selene, and goddess of light. She represents the brightness of the break of day.

> Puck warns Oberon that his work must be done with haste, for—
>
> Yonder shines Aurora's harbinger,
> At whose approach, ghosts, wandering here and there,
> Troop home to churchyards.   III. ii. 382.
>
> The "morning's love," in III. ii. 391, refers to Cephalus, who was carried off by Aurora.

Bacchanals, or Bacchantes ('shouters'), worshippers of Bacchus, the god of wine. Bacchus, or Dionysus in Thrace, was worshipped at night time by these women, who, under the influence of wine, wandered about the mountain woodlands in passionate excitement with torches in their hands. See also under Orpheus.

> The title of one of the entertainments offered to Theseus was—
>
> The riot of the tipsy Bacchanals,
> Tearing the Thracian singer in their rage.   V. i. 48

Bergomask. The name of a dance of clowns, so called from the Italian district of Bergamo in Northern Italy. The inhabitants were regarded as being particularly rustic.

> Bottom asks the duke if it pleases him—
>
> to see the epilogue, or to hear a Bergomask dance between two of our company (V. i. 356).

Cadmus was a son of the Phœnician king Agenor, and brother of Europa. He does not appear in mythology to have been connected in any way with Hercules. He was on his way to Crete to seek his sister Europa, who had been carried thither by Zeus, when, on arriving at Bœotia, he founded Thebes.

> Hippolyta relates to Theseus—
>
> I was with Hercules and Cadmus once,
> When in a wood of Crete, they bay'd the bear
> With hounds of Sparta.   IV. i. 113.

Carthage. A city of Northern Africa, near the site of the modern Tunis. For allusion see under Dido.

Centaurs. In Homer's account the Centaurs are an old
Thessalian mountain tribe of giant strength and savage
ferocity. Their battle with the Lapithæ took place on
the occasion of the marriage of Pirithous and Hippodamia. They attempted to carry off the bride, but
were completely defeated by the bridegroom aided by
Theseus. On another occasion Hercules, while in
pursuit of the Erymanthian boar, was attacked by
the Centaurs of Arcadia. He drove them back with
arrows and firebrands, and completely vanquished them
after a terrible fight.

> Probably the battle with the Lapithæ is alluded to in the title
> which Theseus reads—
>
>> The battle with the Centaurs, to be sung
>> By an Athenian eunuch to the harp.   **V. i. 44**
>
> for this is told by Ovid in his *Metamorphoses.*

Cephalus, a handsome hunter, said to be a son of Hermes.
He was carried off by Aurora, who was unable to
shake his fidelity for his wife Procris. Procris, in
her jealousy of Aurora, hid herself among some bushes
in order to watch her husband, when he, taking her for
a wild animal, unwittingly killed her. He is referred
to as "the morning's love" in III. ii. 391.

> Pyramus and Thisbe avow their fidelity to one another:
>
>> *Pyr.* Not Shafalus to Procrus was so true.
>> *This.* As Shafalus to Procrus, I to you.   **V. i. 199**

Corin. A traditional name for a lover in pastoral poetry.
The Corin of *As You Like It* is a shepherd, who in his
youth was "as true a lover as ever sighed upon a
midnight pillow."

> Titania accuses Oberon of sitting all day "in the shape of
> Corin,"
>
>> Playing on pipes of corn and versing love
>> To amorous Phillida.   **II. i. 68.**

Crete, one of the largest islands in the Mediterranean Sea,
nearly equi-distant from Europe, Asia, and Africa.
Minos, the reputed son of Europa, was the first king of
Crete, and it was in Crete that Hercules performed
his seventh labour, the capture of the Cretan bull or
Minotaur.

> For context, see under CADMUS.

Cupid, the Greek *Eros*, the son of Venus and Mars, was represented in art as a winged boy, or a tender youth, bearing a bow and arrows as his attribute, the pain of love excited by him being regarded as a wound. With golden arrows he inspired happy love, with blunt leaden shafts an unlucky passion.

Hermes swears to be true to Lysander—

> By Cupid's strongest bow ;
> By his best arrow with the golden head.   I. i. 169.

Oberon relates to Puck his vision of " Cupid all arm'd," whose " fiery shaft," failing to pierce the " imperial votaress "—

> fell upon a little western flower,
> Before milk-white, now purple with love's wound.   II. i. 158, etc.

The pansy, or heart's-ease, is referred to as Cupid's flower, (III. ii. 102), (IV. i. 74) ; Cupid, or Love (I. i. 236, 238), or " the boy Love " (I. i. 241), is said by Helena to be " painted blind " (I. i. 235), and to be " perjured everywhere ; " and Puck, pitying the condition of Helena, says :

> Cupid is a knavish lad
> Thus to make poor females mad.   III. ii. 442.

Diana, identified with the Greek Artemis, was originally a goddess of the moon. She was a daughter of Zeus and Latona, and twin-sister of Apollo. As a virgin goddess she was especially venerated by young maidens, whose patroness she remained till their marriage, and to whom she afforded an example of chastity.

Theseus tells Hermia that the penalty for refusing to wed Demetrius will be either to die—

> Or on Diana's altar to protest
> For aye, austerity and single life.   I. i. 89.

The plant which had the power to counteract the effect of Cupid's flower is called " Dian's bud " in IV. i. 74.

Dido, the reputed founder of Carthage. Vergil makes her a contemporary of Æneas, with whom she falls in love on his arrival in Africa. When Æneas left her to seek the home in Italy which the gods had promised him, Dido in despair destroyed herself on a funeral pile.

Hermia swears to Lysander—

> By that fire which burn'd the Carthage queen,
> When the false Troyan under sail was seen.   I. i. 173.

Daphne, daughter of Tellus (the Earth), and a river god. She was extremely beautiful, and was loved by Apollo.

When he pursued her she prayed for aid to her father, who changed her into a laurel tree.

Helena, in love with Demetrius, who flies from her, says:

Run when you will, the story shall be changed:
Apollo flies, and Daphne holds the chase.   II. i. 231.

Egypt, a country in the N.E. of Africa. The word Gipsy is corrupted from Egyptian, for when gipsies appeared in Europe they declared that they were driven from Egypt by the Turks. Their original home was India.

Theseus declares that the lover is " as frantic " as the madman, in that he—

Sees Helen's beauty in a brow of Egypt.   V. i. 11.

Ercles. See under HERCULES.

Ethiope, Ethiopian, a native of Ethiopia (a country of Africa, which included the modern Abyssinia), and as such, supposed to be black.

Lysander, when under the influence of Cupid's flower, addresses Hermia—

Away, you Ethiope.   III. ii. 258.

Fates. The goddesses of Fate—Parcæ or Moirae—decided the destiny of man. They were three in number— *Klotho,* the spinner of life's thread ; *Lachesis,* the giver of life's portion ; and *Atropos,* the unswerving, inexorable one, who sends death.

Bottom recites tragic verses, in which he speaks of—

The foolish Fates.   I. ii. 39.

and in the Interlude, on seeing the body of Thisbe, invokes them thus :

Approach, ye Furies fell !
O Fates, come, come:
Cut thread and thrum ;
Quail, crush, conclude and quell.   V. i. 285.

Thisbe promises to remain true to Pyramus—

till the Fates me kill.   V. i. 198.

and appeals to them after the death of Pyramus—

O Sisters Three,
Come, come to me.   V. i. 339.

Furies, the daughters of the Night, were avenging goddesses, who punished crime. Like the Fates, they were three in number, and their names were Tisiphone, Alecto and Megæra. For context see above under FATES.

Hecate (far-striking) was originally a moon goddess. The daughter of the Titan Perseus and Asteria. She presided over all nocturnal horrors, haunted tombs and cross-roads, and sent nightly phantoms from the lower world.

Puck, after the dance that concluded the Interlude, sang:

> And we fairies, that do run
> By the triple Hecate's team,
> From the presence of the sun.　　　　　V. i. 386

Helen, daughter of Tyndareus, king of Sparta, married Menelaus, who became king of Sparta after the death of Tyndareus. While Menelaus was absent in Crete, she was carried off by Paris to Troy. This led to the Trojan war related in the *Iliad* of Homer. Her beauty was proverbial.

Theseus asserts that the imaginative lover "sees Helen's beauty" in the features of a gipsy (**V. i. 11**). Thisbe compares herself to *Helen*, meaning *Hero*, *q.v.*

Hercules, the personification of strength and conquest, was a legendary hero, especially honoured among the Bœotians, Dorians, and Thessalians. Zeus was his father, and Thebes his home. Amongst the famous "twelve labours" imposed upon him by Eurystheus were the slaying of the Erymanthian boar, the conquest of the Centaurs, the taming of the Cretan bull, and the fight with the Amazons. In the *Mysteries* of the Middle Ages he is represented on the stage as a typical tyrant.

Bottom, whose "chief humour is for a tyrant," declares that he "could play Ercles rarely" (I. ii. 30), and to prove his assertion, quotes verses in "Ercles' vein" (I. ii. 41). Theseus says that he has told Hippolyta of the battle with the Centaurs—

> In glory of my kinsman Hercules.　　　　　V. i. 47.

Hero, a Greek priestess of Sestos, for love of whom Leander, a youth of Abydos, swam every night across the Hellespont, guided by a torch from her tower. When he was at length drowned in the attempt, Hero threw herself from the tower on the corpse of her lover and perished.

> Pyramus, in the Interlude, says to Thisby, "I am thy lover's grace "—
>> And like Limander am I trusty still.
> to which Thisbe replies:
>> And I like Helen, till the Fates me kill.   V. 1. 196.
> Here Limander and Helen are the actors' blunders for Leander and Hero.

Hiems, the Roman personification of winter.

India formerly stood for the whole of the S.E. part of Asia and the islands of the Indian Archipelago. The fairies of the play seem to have been all natives of India.

> Titania, with her train of fairies, meets Oberon in the wood, and asks—
>> Why art thou here,
>> Come from the farthest steppe of India.   II. 1. 69
> The changeling, the cause of the quarrel between the king and queen, was—
>> A lovely boy, stolen from an Indian king.   II i. 22
> Titania has often gossiped "in the spiced Indian air" (II. i. 125). Oberon, before releasing Titania from the spell begs from her "her Indian boy" (III. ii. 377).

Limander, Bottom's mistake for *Leander.* See under HERO.

Muses, The, daughters of Zeus and Mnesnosyne. They were nine in number, and were created to perpetuate in song the mighty deeds of the gods. Their names indicate their several functions: *Clio* (Glorifier), *Melpomene* (Songster), *Terpsichore* (Dance-gladdened), *Polyhymnia* (She of many hymns), *Thalia* (Joy), *Urania* (Heavenly), *Euterpe* (Delighter), *Erato* (Charming), *Calliope* (Sweet-voiced). Spenser in his *Tears of Muses* (1591) laments "the neglect and contempt of learning."

> The title of one of the entertainments offered for Theseus' acceptance is—
>> The thrice three Muses mourning for the death
>> Of Learning, late deceased in beggary.   V t. 59

Neptune, the son of Cronos and Rhea, and the representative of water in general.

> Titania has often sat " on Neptune's yellow sands " (II. i. 127).
> Oberon describes the sun rising over the sea—
>> Even till the eastern gate, all fiery-red,
>> Opening on Neptune with fair blessed beams,
>> Turns into yellow gold his salt green streams.   III. ii. 393.

Ninus, the reputed founder of Nineveh, about B.C. 2182. His wife Semiramis built the city of Babylon, and erected a magnificent tomb for her husband.

> " Ninus' tomb " is the appointed meeting-place of Pyramus and Thisbe (III. i. 97, 98, V. i. 138, 203).

Orpheus, a mythic bard of Thrace, whose songs of lamentation were so piteous as to move the very rocks and trees from their places. He released his wife Eurydice from the Lower World, but afterwards lost her. Whilst wandering in his despair over Thracian mountains, he was torn in pieces by some women in the mad excitement of their nightly Bacchanalian orgies.

> For the allusion in the play, see under BACCHANALS.

Perigenia, in North's *Plutarch* Perigouna, was the daughter of one Sinnis, whom Theseus slew in the Straits of Peloponnesus.

> She is referred to in II. i. 79 as one of the early lovers of Theseus.

Phœbe, identified with Selene and Luna, and often confounded with Artemis or Diana. As a deity Phœbe embodies the moon, and is a sister of Sol (Helios) the sun.

> Lysander persuades Hermia to fly with him from Athens—
>> To-morrow night when Phœbe doth behold
>> Her silver visage in the watery glass.   I. ii. 209.

Phœbus or *Apollo,* the purest and highest representative of light, was identified with the Sun among late classical writers. The chariot of the Sun, in which he passes daily from Oceanus in the east to the west, where he sets, was drawn by four fiery horses. See also under Apollo.

> Bottom's specimen of tragic verse contains the lines—
>> And Phibbus' car
>> Shall shine from far.   I. ii. 56.

Phillida.   A traditional name for a shepherdess in pastoral poetry.

> For allusion, see under CORIN.

Philomel, the Greek name for a nightingale. Philomela, in Ovid, was with her sister Procne, pursued by Tereus with an axe, and on being overtaken, prayed to the gods to be changed into a bird.

> The refrain in the Fairies' song commences—
> > Philomel with melody
> > Sing in our sweet lullaby.   II. ii. 13.

Procris.   See under CEPHALUS.

Shafalus.   See under CEPHALUS.

Sparta, also called Lacedœmon, the chief city of Peloponnesus, in Greece.   For the allusion, see under CADMUS.

Tartar, a vague term usually applied to certain roving tribes which inhabited the steppes of Central Asia.

> Puck, describing to Oberon the rapidity of his movements, says :
> > I go, I go ; look how I go,
> > Swifter than arrow from the Tartar's bow.   III. ii. 100.
> Lysander, under the influence of the spell, addresses Hermia as "tawny Tartar" (III. ii. 265).

Taurus, a mountain chain in Asiatic Turkey, stretching from the Euphrates to the Ægean Sea.

> Demetrius draws a comparison between the whiteness of Helen's hand and—
> > That pure congealed white, high Taurus' snow.   III. ii. 141

Thebes, a city of ancient Greece, the principal city of Bœotia, said to have been founded by Cadmus in 1500 B.C. Chaucer's *Knight's Tale* tells how Theseus slew Creon, king of Thebes, and destroyed the city.

> Theseus speaks of the play that was acted—
> > When I from Thebes came last a conqueror.   V. 1. 51.

Thessaly, the north-eastern division of Greece.   The early kings of Thessaly are said to have been descendants of

Hercules. The country is mountainous, and its earliest inhabitants were Œolians.

Theseus speaks of his hounds " crook-knee'd, and dew-lapp'd like Thessalian bulls," whose note was as musical as any ever heard—

In Crete, in Sparta, or in Thessaly   IV. i. 127.

Thrace, a name applied at an early period among the Greeks to a region lying north of Macedonia.

For the allusion to the " Thracian Singer," see under ORPHEUS.

Troy, an ancient city in the Troad, a territory in the N.W. of Asia Minor, rendered famous by Homer's epic of the *Iliad* and Vergil's *Æneid*.

For the allusion to Æneas, " the false Troyan," see under DIDO.

Valentine, a saint of the Roman calendar, said to have been martyred in 306 A.D. The custom of choosing valentines on his day (February 14th) has been accidentally associated with his name. A similar custom prevailed in the Roman Lupercalia, to which the modern practice has been traced. See also the notes on pp. 54 and 83.

Theseus, finding the lovers asleep in the wood, addressed them thus—

Good morrow, friends. St. Valentine is past;
Begin these wood-birds but to couple now.   IV. i. 140.

Venus, identified with the Greek Aphrodite, was the daughter of Jupiter, and goddess of beauty and love. She is painted by the poets as the most beautiful of all the goddesses, and is endowed with a celebrated love-begetting magic girdle. Amongst her attributes are the dove, the sparrow, the myrtle, the rose, and the apple.

Hermia swears to Lysander—

By the simplicity of Venus' doves,
By that which knitteth souls and prospers loves.   I. i. 171

L

APPENDIX IV.

GLOSSARY OF UNCOMMON WORDS WITH THEIR CONTEXT.

The Editor's indebtedness to Professor Skeat's Etymological Dictionary and to Schmidt's Shakespeare Lexicon is such as to call for special acknowledgment.

Abbreviations.—A.S. = Anglo-Saxon; M.E. = Middle English; O.F. = Old French. M.F. = Middle French; F. = French; G = German; Gk. = Greek; L. = Latin; Icel. = Icelandic; Port. = Portuguese; Arab. = Arabic.

Adv. = adverb; der. = derived; dimin. = diminutive; lit. = literally; orig. = originally; p.p. = past participle.

Abridgement, used in the sense of pastime, something to shorten the time. Subst. formed from "abridge." O.F. *abreger,* L. *abbreviare,* to shorten. "Abbreviate" is a doublet of abridge.

> Say, what abridgement have you for this evening? V. i. 39.

Aby, to stand the consequences of, pay for. M.E. *abyen,* to pay for; A.S. *abycgen;* connected with buy. Sometimes written and confused with "abide," to await, with which it has no etymological connection.

> Lest to thy peril, thou aby it dear. III. ii. 175.
> Thou shalt aby it. III. ii. 337.

Adamant. (1) Any hard stone; (2) a magnet, lode stone. From Gk. ἀδάμας = unconquerable, through O.F. *adamant.* The words "diamond" and "tame" are both allied to it.

> You draw me, you hard-hearted adamant. II. i. 196.

Admirable, to be wondered at. This is the original meaning of the word. L. *admirabilis* from *admirari,* to wonder at.

> But, howsoever, strange and admirable. V. i. 27.

An, if. Formerly also and, with the same meaning. A.S. *and.* For illustrations see p. 92.

Apricocks, a form of "apricot," derived from Port. *albricoque.* Arab. *al barquq,* where *al* is the def. art. The modern form "apricot" is from F. *abricot.*

> Feed him with apricocks, and dewberries. III. i. 166.

Aunt, old woman. M.E. *aunte.* O.F. *ante* (Mod. F. *t-ante*). L. *amita,* a father's sister.

> The wisest *aunt,* telling the saddest tale.   **II. i. 52.**

Used also in its ordinary sense in I. i. 157.

Bay, to chase, to drive to bay. Short for *abay.* F. *aboyer,* to yelp, bay.

> They bay'd the bear with hounds of Sparta.   **IV. i. 114.**

Barm, yeast. A.S. *beorma,* cognate with Low G. *barm.*

> And sometime make the drink to bear no barm.   **II. i. 38.**

Bergomask, a dance of clowns. Ital. *bergomasco,* from the name of the town *Bergamo.*

> But come, your Bergomask : let your epilogue alone.   **V. i. 365.**

Beshrew, a mild form of imprecation ; *be,* intensive prefix ; and M.E. *shrewe,* wicked, bad. A.S. *scrēawa,* a shrew-mouse, fabled to have a very venomous bite.

> Now much beshrew my manners and my pride.   **II. ii. 54.**
> Beshrew my heart, but I pity the man.   **V. i. 291.**

Beteem, supply, afford ; *be,* intensive prefix ; and *teem,* an old word, probably connected with G. *ziemen,* to be fit ; and Dutch *tamen,* to be seemly.

> Belike for want of rain, which I could well
> Beteem them from the tempest of mine eyes.   **I. i. 131.**

Bootless, unavailingly, uselessly. A.S. *bōt,* profit (*better* and *best* are from the same base), and the E. suffix, *less* ; A.S. *léas,* loose, or free from.

> And bootless make the breathless housewife churn. **II. i. 37.**
> Bootless speed, when cowardice pursues, and valour flies !
>   **II. i. 234.**

Bottle, a bundle of hay. O.F. *botel,* a small bundle, dimin. of *botte,* a bundle, as of hay.

> Methinks, I have a great desire to a bottle of hay. **IV. i. 32.**

Broach, to stab, pierce. M.E. *setten on broche* = to set a-broach, tap liquor. F. *mettre en broche,* to tap, by piercing, a barrel. F. *brocher,* to pierce.

> He bravely broach'd his boiling bloody breast.   **V. i. 147.**

Bully, comrade. The oldest sense is "dear one, lover."
M. Dutch *boel*, of a lover (of either sex).

> What sayest thou bully Bottom?   III. i. 8.

Buskin, a high-heeled boot, worn by hunters and huntresses.
Origin doubtful; either from Dutch *broosken*, buskin;
or from M.F. *brousequin*, now *brodequin*.

> Your buskin'd mistress and your warrior love.   II. i. 72.

Canker, a worm that eats into blossoms. Der. through F.
from L. *cancrum*, acc. of *cancer*, a crab.

> Some to kill cankers in the musk-rose buds.   II. ii. 3.
> O me! you juggler! you canker-blossom.   III. ii. 284.

Cavalery, cavalier, used by Bottom for Sp. *cavallero*, or
cavaliero, L. *caballarium*, from *caballus*, a horse.

> Nothing, good mounsieur, but to help Cavalery Cobweb to
> scratch.   IV. i. 22.

Changeling, usually=a child substituted by the fairies for
the one stolen by them; in this play the stolen
child. F. *change*, Late L. *cambium*, L. *cambīre*, to
exchange, and -*ling*, an E. double dimin. suffix, -*el*,
-*ing*.

> She never had so sweet a changeling.   II. i. 23.
> I do but beg a little changeling boy.   II. i. 121.
> I did then ask of her her changeling child.   IV. i. 60.

Cheer. M.E. *chere*, the face. O.F. *chere*. L. *cara*, face, used
in two senses in the play—

    (1) spirits, cheerfulness.

> Come, my Hippolyta: what cheer, my love?   I. i. 122.
> That lived, that loved, that liked, that look'd with cheer.
>   V. i. 295.

    (2) countenance, face.

> All fancy-sick she is and pale of cheer   III. ii. 96.

Childing, productive, fruitful, fertile; Der. of child. A.S.
cild, and suffix -*ing*.

> The childing autumn, angry winter.   II. i. 112.

Coil, confusion, disturbance, trouble. Orig. a colloquial or slang expression, probably connected wiith " coil," to twist. O.F. *coillir*, L. *colligere*, to collect.

> You mistress, all this coil is long of you.   III. ii. 341.

Collied, coal-black, dark. An adjective from " coal." A.S. *col*, coal.

> Brief as the lightning in the collied night.   I. i. 145.

Con, learn by heart. A.S. *cunnan*, to know. Cf. the Scotch " ken."

> I desire you to con them by to-morrow night.   I. ii. 100.
> Extremely stretch'd and conn'd with cruel pain. V. i. 80.

Conceit, used in the plu. = presents fancifully devised. Formed as if from the p.p. of O.F. *concevoir*, by analogy with " deceit."

> With bracelets of thy hair, rings, gawds, conceits. I. i. 33.

Continents, banks. L. *continentem* p.p. of *continēre*, to hold together. L. *con-* (*cum*), together; and *tenēre*, to hold.

> They have overborne their continents.   II. i. 98.

Coy, caress, fondle. O.F. *coi*, older form *quei*. L. *quietum*, still; hence " to coy " is really to make still or quiet.

> While I thy amiable cheeks do coy.   IV. i. 2.

Cry, pack of hounds, so called from their " cry " or " note." F. *crier*; L. *quirītare*, to shriek; *lit.* " to implore the aid of the *Quirites* or Roman citizens."

> A cry more tuneable was never holla'd to.   IV. i. 125.

Dewlap, the loose flesh that hangs from the throat of a cow or (in this play) of a woman. So called because it laps or licks up the dew. A.S. *dēaw*, dew; and *lapian*, to lap; allied to L. *lambere*, to lap with the tongue.

> And on her wither'd dewlap pour the ale.   II. i. 51
> Crook-knee'd and dew-lapp'd like Thessalian bulls.
>   IV. i. 123.

Distemperature, strife (either of the fairies or of the elements). L. *dis*, with a sinister or bad sense;

temperare, to mingle in due proportion; and L. suffix
-ura.

> And thorough this distemperature we see
> The seasons alter. II. i. 107.

Dole, sorrow, grief. O.F. *dol;* L. *dolium, dolēre*, to grieve.

> But mark, poor knight, what dreadful dole is here. V. i. 278.

Dowager, a widow with a jointure. O.F. *douagere;* L.
dotare, to endow. Allied to *donum*, a gift; *dare*, to
give.

> Like to a step-dame, or a dowager. I. i. 5.
> I have a widow aunt, a dowager. I. i. 157.

Elf, a diminutive supernatural being. Icel. *alfr;* Dan. *alf;*
also G. *alp*, a nightmare.

> Our queen and all her elves come here anon. II. i. 17.
> To make my small elves coats. II. ii. 5.
> Nod to him elves and do him courtesies. III. i. 174.
> Every elf and fairy sprite. V. i. 396.

Extenuate, diminish the force of, lessen. From p.p. of L.
extenuare, to thin, reduce, palliate. L. *ex*, out, very;
tenuis, thin.

> Which by no means we may extenuate. I. i. 120.

Fell, angry, fierce. O.F. *fel*, cruel. Late L. *fello, felo* a
malefactor, felon.

> For Oberon is passing fell and wrath. II. i. 20.
> A lion fell. V. i. 224.

Filch, to steal (usually applied to things of small value).
Etym. unknown; possibly related to M.E. *felen*, to
conceal.

> With cunning hast thou filch'd my daughter's heart. I. i. 36.

Flew'd, a verb, coined from " flews," the overhanging chaps
of a dog.

> My hounds are bred out of the Spartan kind,
> So flew'd, so sanded. IV. i. 121.

Flout, to mock, jeer at. Prob. from M.E. *flouten*, to play the
flute. Similarly, M. Dutch *fluyten*, to play the flute,
once meant " to mock."

> But you must flout my insufficiency. II. ii. 128.
> Why will you suffer her to flout me thus? III. ii. 329.

Fond, foolish, foolishly doting on. M.E. *fond* or *fonn-ed*, p.p.
of *fonnen*, to act as a fool. Allied to A.S. *fœmne*, a
virgin.

> Effect it with some care that he may prove
> More fond on her than she upon her love.   II. i. 266
> O, I am out of breath in this fond chase.   II. ii. 88.
> Shall we their fond pageant see.   III. ii. 114.
> You see how simple and how fond I am.   III. ii. 318.

Fordone, tired out, done up. A.S. *for-* intensive prefix and
dōn to do, orig. to put or place.

> All with weary task fordone.   V. i. 376.

Gawd or gaud, an ornament, toy, trinket. L. *gaudium*,
gladness, joy ; hence, an ornament.

> And stolen the impression of her fantasy,
> With bracelets of thy hair, rings, gawds, conceits. I. i. 32.

Gleek, to jest, scoff ; probably connected with "gleek," a
game at cards. O.F. *glic*, a game at cards.

> Nay, I can gleek upon occasion.   III. i. 146.

Gossip, a crony ; formerly a sponsor in baptism. M.E.
gossib, also *godsib*, lit., "related in god." O.Northumb.
sibbo, pl. relatives. See page 77.

> And sometime lurk I in a gossip's bowl.   II. i. 48.

Henchman, a page, servant. Formerly *hengestman, henseman,
henshman*, for *hengest-man*, *i.e.* a groom. From A.S.
hengest, a horse.

> I do but beg a little changeling boy
> To be my henchman.   II. i. 122.

Imbrue, to moisten, drench. M.F. *embruer*, to imbrue. F.
em (L. *in*, in), and *bruer*. O.F. *bevrer*. L. *biberare*,
from *bibere*, to drink.

> Come, blade, my breast imbrue.   V. i. 347.

Interlude, originally an entertainment in the intervals of a
banquet or festival. L. *inter* between, and *ludus*, a
game ; *ludere*, to play.

> To play in our interlude before the duke and the duchess on
> his wedding-day at night.   I. ii. 6.
> in this same interlude   V. i. 154.

Juvenal, youth. L. *juvenalis,* from *juvenis,* a youth.

> Most brisky juvenal, and eke most lovely Jew. III. i. 95.

Knack, trifle, toy. Of imitative origin, like **knap.** Orig. meant " snap "; next, " snap with the finger "; then, " a jester's trick "; hence joke, trifle. The word " knock " is allied to it.

> Knacks, trifles, nosegays, sweetmeats. I. i. 34.

Lakin, a contracted form of " ladykin." *Lady* was specially used to mean the Virgin Mary; hence *lady-bird, lady's slipper,* etc. A.S. *hlæfdige* = loaf-kneeder, and dimin. suffix -*kin.*

> By'r lakin a parlous fear. III. i. 18.

Lanthorn, lantern. F. *lanterne,* through L. from Gk. λαμπτήρ, a light, torch. The spelling *lanthorn* is due to the fact that *horn* was used for the sides of lanterns.

> One must come in with a bush of thorns and a lanthorn.
> III. i. 60.
> This lanthorn doth the horned moon present. V. i. 239.

Latch = (1) to catch, from A.S. *læccan,* to seize, catch hold of; (2) to moisten, A.S. *leccan,* to moisten (giving prov. E. *letch,* a vessel for making lye). Professor Skeat holds that *latch* in this play means " to moisten," being a causal form of *leak,* but I think Puck's reply, " I took him sleeping," points to the former meaning and derivation.

> But hast thou yet latch'd the Athenian's eyes. III. ii. 36.

Leviathan, a whale. Late L. *leviathan;* Heb. *livyáthán,* an aquatic animal, dragon, serpent; named from its twisting itself in curves.

> Ere the leviathan can swim a league. II. i. 175.

Lode-star or **Load-star,** the polar star. Lit. the " way-star," star that leads or guides. A.S. *lád,* a way, a course. Similarly " lode-stone " or magnet is a stone that leads or draws.

> Your eyes are lode-stars I. i. 183.

Mermaid, a sea-maiden; an animal with a woman's head and a fish's tail. A.S. *mere*, a lake; allied to L. *mare*, a sea; and A.S. *mœgden*, maiden.

> Heard a mermaid on a dolphin's back. II. i. 150.

Mew, to pen up or cage. M.E. *mewe, mue*, a cage where hawks were kept when moulting. O.F. *mue*, a moulting; F. *muer*, to change, moult; L. *mutare*, to change. N.B.—The pl. *mews* now means a range of stabling, because the royal stables were rebuilt (1534) in a place where the royal falcons had been kept.

> For aye to be in shady cloister mew'd. I. i. 71.

Mimic, actor player. L. *mīmicus*, farcical. Gk. μῖμος, an imitator, actor, mime.

> Anon his Thisbe must be answered.
> And forth my mimic comes. III. ii. 18.

Minimus, most diminutive creature. L. *minimus*, superlative adjective — smallest, least.

> Get you gone, you dwarf,
> You minimus of hindering knot-grass made. III. ii. 330.

Misgraffed, misgrafted. Prefix *mis*, bad. L. *minus* and *graff*. O.F. *graffe*, a sort of pencil, also a slip for grafting, because it resembled a pointed pencil in shape. L. *graphium*, a style to write with.

> Or else misgraffed in respect of years. I. i. 137

Misprise, to mistake. O.F. *mesprendre*. See next word.

> You spend your passion on a misprised mood. III. ii. 74

Misprision, a mistake, neglect. M.F. *mesprison*, error. O.F *mes-*, badly. Late L. *prensionem*, a seizing; from L. *prehendere*, to take.

> Of thy misprision must perforce ensue
> Some true-love turn'd, and not a false turn'd true. III. ii. 90.

Murrion, cattle-disease. O.F. *morine*, a carcase of a beast; from *morir*, to die. L. *mori*. Used as an adjective in

> And crows are fatted with the murrion flock. III. i. 98.

Neaf or **Neif**, the fist. M.E. *neue* (*u* = *v*). Icel. *knefi*, fist.

> Give me your neaf Mounsieur Mustardseed. IV. i. 19.

Neeze or **Neese**, to sneeze. M.E. *nesen*; not in A.S. Connected with G. *niesen*.

> And waxen in their mirth and neeze and swear
> A merrier hour was never wasted there. II. i. 57.

Nole, head. Also spelt "Noll," "Noule," "Nowl." A.S. *knoll*, the crown of the head.

> An ass's nole I fixed on his head. III. ii. 17.

Ounce, a kind of lynx. F. *once*; M.F. *lonce*. Ital. *lonza*, which was treated as if = *l'onza*. Late L. type *lyncea*, from L. *lynx*, a lynx.

> Be it ounce, or cat, or bear. II. ii. 29.

Ousel, a kind of thrush. M.E. *osel*. A.S. *ōsle*.

> The ousel-cock, so black of hue. III. i. 125.

Parlous, short for "perilous." M.F. *peril*. L. *periculum*, danger; lit. = a trial. L. *periri*, to try; and suffix. *-ous* = full of.

> By'r lakin, a parlous fear. III. i. 13.

Pelting, paltry, petty. Probably connected with "paltry." Swed. *paltor*, rags; Lowland Sc., *paltrie* = trash; and Norfolk *paltry* = rubbish, refuse.

> Contagious fogs, which, falling in the land,
> Hath every pelting river made so proud. II. i. 91.

Prefer, to offer or present (for approval). O.F. *preferer*; L. *præferre*, to set in front. L. *præ*, before; *ferre*, to bear, set.

> Our play is preferred. IV. ii. 38.

Preposterously, contrarily, perversely. L. *præposter-us*, inverted, hind side before; with adj. suffix. *-ous*, and advl. suffix. *ly*. L. *præ*, before; *posterus*, later, coming after; from *post*, after.

> And those things do best please me.
> That befall preposterously III. ii. 121.

Prodigious, portentous, unnatural. L. *prodigium*, a token portent.

> Nor mark prodigious, such as are
> Despised in nativity.   V. i. 415.

Puppet, a small figure, marionette, doll. M.E. *popet;* M.E. *poupette,* a little baby, puppet ; dimin. of L. *pupa,* a girl ; allied to *puer,* a boy.

> You counterfeit, you puppet, you.   III. ii. 290.

Purple-in-grain, red with the dye of cochineal insect. F. *pourpre.* L. *purpura,* the purple-fish; and O.F. *graine.* L. *granum,* seed. Cf. Sp. *grana,* the cochineal dye ; and It. *grana,* the redness upon the surface of some work. The L. *purpureus* included very different shades of colour, as red, reddish, violet, brownish, etc., and in Shakespeare, *purple* often = red.

> I will discharge it in either your straw-colour beard, your
> orange-tawny beard, your purple-in-grain beard. I. ii. 93.

Quail, to crush, overpower. A.S. *cwelan,* to die.

> Quail, crush, conclude, and quell.   V. i. 287.

Quell, to kill. A.S. *cwellan,* to kill; causal of *cwelan,* above.

> Quail, crush, conclude, and quell.   V. i. 287.

Quern, a handmill for grinding grain ; also spelt "kern." A.S. *cweorn.*

> Skim milk, and sometimes labour in the quern. II. i. 36.

Recorder, a kind of small flute. "The figures of recorders, and flutes and pipes are straight; but the recorder hath a less bore, and a greater above and below. . . . In a recorder, the three uppermost holes yield one tone, which is a note lower than the tone of the first three" (BACON). From the M.E. verb *record,* to sing. L. *recordare,* to recall to mind.

> He hath played on his prologue like a child on a recorder.
>   V. i. 122.

Reremouse, a bat. A.S. *hreremūs,* a bat; from the flapping of its wings. A.S. *hrēran,* to agitate.

> Some, war with rere-mice for their leathern wings. II. ii. 4.

Roundel, a round dance. O.F. *rondel,* a poem containing a line which recurs or comes *round* again. (The E. *roundel* is commonly used in this sense.)

> Come, now a roundel and a fairy song.   II. ii. 1.

Scrip, a piece of writing. M.F. *escript,* a writing. L. *scriptum,* pp. of *scribere,* to write. Not in any way connected with *scrip* = a small bag.

> You were best to call them generally, man by man, according to the scrip.   I. ii. 2.

Sheen, brightness, splendour. A.S. *scéne,* fair, showy; allied to *scéawian,* to show, see.

> By fountain clear or spangled starlight sheen.   II. i. 29.

Shrewd, malicious, peevish. From the M.E. *shrewe,* malicious; A.S. *scréawa,* a shrew-mouse, fabled to have a very venomous bite.

> Or else you are that shrewd and knavish sprite
> Call'd Robin Goodfellow.   II. i. 33.

Sinister, on the left, evil. L. *sinister,* on the left hand, inauspicious.

> And this the cranny is, right and sinister.   V. i. 163.

Spleen, sudden impulse; commonly of anger. L. *splēn.* Gk. σπλήν, the spleen, formerly supposed to be the seat of melancholy, anger, or vexation.

> That, in a spleen, unfolds both heaven and earth.   I. i. 146.

Streak, to anoint in lines or stripes. M.E. *streke,* more commonly *strike.* A.S. *strica*; from *strican,* to stroke, rub. Allied to " strike " and " stroke."

> And with the juice of this I'll streak her eyes.   II. i. 258.

Thrum, the tufted end of a weaver's thread. Connected with Icel. *thrömr,* the edge (as of a web). *Cf.* G. *trumm,* ends of thread, thrum.

> O Fates, come, come:
> Cut thread and thrum.   V. i. 226.

Toy, a trifle. Du. *tuig,* tools, stuff, trash; whence *speel-tuig,* playthings, toys; lit. " stuff to play with."

> These antique fables nor these fairy toys.   V. i. 18.

Translate, to transform. F. *translater*. L. *translatus*, transferred used as pp. of *transferre*.

> The rest I'll give to be to you translated.   I. i. 191.
> Bless thee, Bottom! bless thee! thou art translated.
>   III. i. 118.

Vaward, another spelling of *vanward* or *vanguard*, the front part (generally of an army). O.F. *avant-warde*; later, *avant-garde*.

> We have the vaward of the day.   IV. i. 106.

Votaress, a female, devoted, as by a vow, to any particular service or state of life. Der. from L. *votum*, p.p. of *vovēre*, to vow.

> Her mother was a votaress of my order.   II. i. 125.
> And the imperial votaress passed on,
> In maiden meditation fancy-free.   II. i. 164.

Weed, a garment. A.S. *wǣd*, a garment; *lit.* something woven.

> Weed wide enough to wrap a fairy in.   II. i. 257.
> Weeds of Athens he doth wear.   II. ii. 71.

Wood, mad, furious. A.S. *wōd*, mad, raging. Perhaps allied to L. *vates*, a prophet; and to the name *Woden*, seen in "Wednesday."

> Thou told'st me they were stolen into this wood:
> And here am I, and wood within this wood.   II. i. 192.

APPENDIX V.

EXAMINATION PAPERS.

*" The greatest weakness in these papers results from answering, **not** the question asked by the examiners, but some other propounded by the inclination of the examinee." In other words ' stick to the point.'*

ACT I. SCENE I.

1. Describe the relation in which the following characters stand towards one another at the opening of the action of the play : Hermia, Helena, Lysander, Demetrius.

2. Explain the following with reference to the context :

   (i) Earthlier happy is the rose distilled.
   (ii) The course of true love never did run smooth.
   (iii) Sickness is catching : O, were favour so.

3. Who were the Amazons ? In what way are they connected with this play ?

4. Give an account of the conversation between Hermia and Lysander when they are left alone.

5. Give the substance of Helena's soliloquy on love.

ACT I. SCENE II.

1. What is the meaning of the word *interlude* ? Name the characters of the interlude in *Midsummer Night's Dream.*

2. Describe the different characteristics of the six artisans collected in Quince's house.

3. Give the meaning of the following expressions, and show the connection in which they severally occur in the play : *to the rest ; here is a play fitted ; I will draw a bill of properties ; hold, or cut bowstrings.*

4. Give briefly your opinion of Bottom's character as shewn in this scene.   Quote examples of his verbal errors.

5. " Meet me in the palace wood, a mile without the town, by moonlight."

   (i) To whom were these words addressed and by whom ?
   (ii) What reason is given for meeting in the wood ?
   (iii) In what connection has this wood been previously mentioned ?

ACT I. AND GENERAL

1. What arrangements made in this Act promise to lead to confusion in later scenes ?

2. Explain what is meant by saying that the lyrical in this play preponderates over the dramatic.

3. Write out, being careful of the division of lines, the passage from
   " Call you me fair ? " *to* " Sway the motion of Demetrius' heart."

4. At what period of Shakespeare's career was *A Midsummer Night's Dream*
   composed ? What other plays belong to the same period ?

5. Give the context of the following passages and explain them :

   (*a*) Were the world mine, Demetrius being bated,
   The rest I'd give to be to you translated
   (*b*) And therefore is wing'd Cupid painted blind.

ACT II.   SCENE I.

1. Give an account of the scene in which Oberon quarrels with Titania.

2. Describe, with quotations, Robin Goodfellow's customary activities.

3. Write out in your own words, bringing out the meaning clearly and
   concisely

   from " These are the forgeries of jealousy "
   to " Hath rotted ere his youth attain'd a beard "

4. Quote from the play passages illustrating the rapidity of Puck's move-
   ments.

5. Describe the first meeting between Helena and Demetrius.   Where did
   it take place and in whose hearing ?

ACT II.   SCENE II.

1. Give some account of the occupations of the fairies.

2. Describe the scene between Lysander and Hermia when the former woke
   from his sleep in the wood.

3. By whom, to whom, and under what circumstances were the following
   lines spoken ?

   (i) With half that wish the wisher's eyes be press'd.
   (ii) And run through fire I will for thy sweet sake.
   (iii) Methought a serpent eat my heart away,
   And you sat smiling at his cruel prey.

4. What aspects of Hermia's character are brought out in this scene ?

5. What blunder is made in connection with the love-juice and with what
   immediate result ?

ACT II. AND GENERAL.

1. " The play comprises four different histories of most dissimilar ingredients."   Explain this fully.

2. What characteristics distinguish this play from any other of Shakespeare's with which you may be familiar ?

3. Quote ten lines beginning, " I know a bank . . ."

4. Answer briefly the questions below each of the following quotations :

> (a) " And in the shape of Corin sat all day,
> Playing on pipes of corn and versing love
> To amorous Phillida."

> (i) Who speaks these words and on what occasion ?
> (ii) What reproach are the words intended to convey ?
> (iii) Explain Corin, pipes of corn, Phillida.

> (b) " Yet mark'd I where the bolt of Cupid fell :
> It fell upon a little western flower,
> Before milk-white, now purple with love's wound."

> (i) At whom was the bolt directed ?
> (ii) What strange occurrences marked the time when the bolt
> was aimed ?
> (iii) What were the properties of the flower ?

> (c) " And touching now the point of human skill
> Reason becomes the marshal to my will
> And leads me to your eyes."

> (i) Who speaks these words and on what occasion ?
> (ii) Explain the first two lines.
> (iii) Was it true that ' reason ' had become the speaker's guide ?

5. Give an account of what is known as " Oberon's Vision." What explanations have been offered of the allegory contained in it ?

ACT III. SCENE I.

1. Show that Bottom performs all the duties which should properly have fallen to the share of Quince.

2. Describe the effect of Bottom's transformation upon his fellows.

3. How do the rustic players propose to deal with the scenery and properties required for their play ?

4. Describe the circumstances under which the following passages were spoken, and explain them where explanation is needed.

> (i) There is not a more fearful wild-fowl than your lion living.
> (ii) What hempen home-spuns have we swaggering here ?
> (iii) Mine ear is much enamour'd of thy note.
> (iv) I pray you, commend me to Mistress Squash, your mother, and to Master Peascod, your father.

5. Write out, with due attention to the division of the lines, the passage beginning " Be kind and courteous to this gentleman " *and ending,* " do him courtesies."

ACT III. SCENE II.

1. Give some account of the simultaneous wooing of Helena by Lysander and Demetrius.

2. Describe the close intimacy which formerly existed between Helena and Hermia.

3. Contrast the personal appearances of Hermia and Helena.

4. Explain the following extracts and give the context in each case :

    (i) All fancy-sick she is and pale of cheer.
    (ii) Dark night, that from the eye his function takes,
        The ear more quick of apprehension makes.
    (iii) How low am I, thou painted maypole ? speak.

5. Contrast, with illustrative quotations, the language of the fairy world with that used by mortals.

ACT III. AND GENERAL.

1. What are the chief characteristics of Shakespeare's fairies ? Give quotations.

2. Describe the quarrel between Helena and Hermia, stating briefly the circumstances that originated it and the measures adopted to end it.

3. What steps are taken to prevent a fight between Demetrius and Lysander ?

4. How is Puck's proverbial love of mischief shown in the play ? Show that it is tempered with some kindly qualities.

5. Give the context of the following passages, adding explanations where necessary :

    (a) This falls out better than I could devise.
        But hast thou yet latch'd the Athenian's eyes ?
    (b) Then fate o'er-rules, that one man holding troth,
        A million fail, confounding oath on oath
    (c)   Get you gone, you dwarf ;
        You minimus, of hindering knot-grass made :
        You bead, you acorn.

ACT IV. SCENE I.

1. Where, and under what circumstances did Oberon first begin to pity Titania ?

2. Describe Bottom's demeanour amongst the fairies.

3. Give an account of the awakening to their senses of the two pairs of Athenian lovers.

4. Paraphrase the fifteen lines beginning, "Her dotage now I do begin to pity."

5.   "Enough, enough, my lord ; you have enough :
        I beg the law, the law, upon his head."

    (i) Who says this and to whom ?
    (ii) What is the law to which he refers and whose the head ?
    (iii) What explanations follow this request, and with what result ?

ACT IV. SCENE II.

1. Give in your own words the substance of the second scene, and shew how it serves to connect the preceding scene with what follows.

2. How do you suppose Bottom to have been occupied in the interval between these two scenes ?

3. Quote various persons' opinions of Bottom. To which do you incline ? Give reasons.

4. What are Bottom's final instructions to the players before the performance in the palace ?

5. Why does Bottom always use prose when speaking in his own person ?

ACT IV. AND GENERAL.

1. Who was in love with whom at the beginning of the play and who at the end ? How was the transition effected ?

2. What part is played in this Act by Theseus and Hippolyta ?

3. What contemporary or historical allusions are contained in this play ? Which of them may be supposed to throw light on the question of the date ?

4. If you were producing this play what sort of persons would you choose to play the parts of the Fairies, and what instructions would you give them ?

5. Show how in this Act the various complications of the play are unravelled.

ACT V. SCENE I.

1. Enumerate the various forms of entertainment offered by Philostrate for the Duke's acceptance, with his comments on each.

2. Give, and enlarge upon, Shakespeare's views (as expressed by Theseus) on dramatists and dramatic performances.

3. Explain the following with reference to their context :

    (i) Out of this silence yet I pick'd a welcome.
    (ii) This is the silliest stuff that ever I heard.
    (iii) I am sent with broom before,
         To sweep the dust behind the door.

4. Explain the allusions contained in the following :

    (i) Sees Helen's beauty in a brow of Egypt.
    (ii) The riot of the tipsy Bacchanals.
    (iii) As Shafalus to Procris I to you.
    (iv) O Sisters Three.

5. Quote 16 lines beginning, " The lunatic, the lover and the poet."

GENERAL QUESTIONS.

1. Show how the Fairies serve as a link connecting the other dissimilar actors in this Comedy.

2. What points of resemblance and of contrast do you observe between this play and *The Tempest* ?

3. Sketch, with quotations, the character of Bottom. What, in your opinion, should be the outward appearance of the actor who plays this part ?

4. "The reading of this play is like wandering in a grove by moonlight." Discuss this statement, paying attention to the imagery in the play.

5. Answer briefly the questions below each of the following quotations :

    (a) " Love looks not with the eyes, but with the mind,
        And therefore is wing'd Cupid painted blind :
        Nor hath Love's mind of any judgment taste."

      (i) Who speaks these words and what occasioned them ?
      (ii) Give the meaning of the passage and the substance of the continuation.
      (iii) Mention any other allusions to Cupid in the play.

    (b) " Well, we will have such a prologue, and it shall be written in eight and six."

Who proposed this prologue and for what purpose ?
Who spoke the words quoted and what did he mean ?
Quote one or two lines of the prologue as actually spoken.

    (c) " For, meeting her of late behind the wood
        Seeking sweet favours for this hateful fool,
        I did upbraid her, and fall out with her."

      (i) By whom and to whom were these words spoken ?
      (ii) Describe very briefly the two persons alluded to.
      (iii) What followed the upbraiding referred to and what took place at the end of the speech in which these words occur ?

6. Describe the character and attributes of Puck. What part does he take in the play ?

7. What are the principal characteristics of the versification of this play ?

8. Quote twelve consecutive lines of one of the Fairies' songs.

9. Justify from the incidents of the play the title *A Midsummer Night's Dream.*

10. Show how the course of events in the play is influenced by magic.

11. Describe the fairy world as Shakespeare envisages it. What part in this is played by the love-juice ?

12. Show that the misadventures of lovers form an essential part of the double plot of the play.

13. It has been said that the moon is the most important influence in *A Midsummer Night's Dream.* Explain or comment upon this.

14. What part does Titania take in the play ? Illustrate your answer with quotations.

15. If you were given the choice of acting the part of Helena or Hermia (*or* Theseus or Bottom), which would you choose and why ? How would you treat the part ?

16. Show how Shakespeare varies his verse according to the character of the speaker or the nature of the theme.

17. "That which is perhaps most remarkable about this play is the harmonious blending in it of widely different elements." Comment on this statement.

18. Explain the following with reference to their context :

    (i) " Or on Diana's altar to protest.
        For aye, austerity and single life."
    (ii)   " Are not you he
        That frights the maidens of the villagery ;
        Skim milk, and sometimes labour in the quern ? "
    (iii) " That pure congealed white, high Taurus' snow,
        Fann'd with the eastern wind, turns to a crow,
        When thou hold'st up thy hand."

19. Show that the atmosphere and background of the play is English rather than Athenian.

20. Explain the terms Masque, Anti-masque, Bergomask, Interlude, Dramatic Irony.